1987

University of St. Francis
GEN 940.5472 H669

SO-AJB-493

3 0301 00094257 9

THE POLICIES OF GENOCIDE

THE
POLICIES OF
GENOCIDE

*Jews and Soviet Prisoners
of War in Nazi Germany*

Edited by

Gerhard Hirschfeld

With an Introduction by

Wolfgang J. Mommsen

THE GERMAN HISTORICAL INSTITUTE

ALLEN & UNWIN

London   Boston   Sydney

LIBRARY
College of St. Francis
JOLIET, ILLINOIS

© German Historical Institute, 1986
This book is copyright under the Berne Convention.
No reproduction without permission. All rights reserved.

**Allen & Unwin (Publishers) Ltd,
40 Museum Street, London WC1A 1LU, UK**

Allen & Unwin (Publishers) Ltd,
Park Lane, Hemel Hempstead, Herts HP2 4TE, UK

Allen & Unwin, Inc.,
8 Winchester Place, Winchester, Mass. 01890, USA

Allen & Unwin (Australia) Ltd,
8 Napier Street, North Sydney, NSW 2060, Australia

First published in 1986

British Library Cataloguing in Publication Data

The Policies of genocide: Jews and Soviet prisoners of war
in Nazi Germany.
1. World War, 1939–1945 – Prisoners and prisons, German
I. Hirschfeld, Gerhard
940.53'15'03924 D805.G3
ISBN 0–04–943045–9
ISBN 0–04–943046–7 Pbk

Library of Congress Cataloging-in-Publication Data

Main entry under title:
    The Policies of genocide.
    Bibliography: p.
Includes index.
1. Holocaust, Jewish (1939–1945) – Addresses, essays,
lectures. 2. World War, 1939–1945 – Prisoners and
prisons, German – Addresses, essays, lectures. 3. Prisoners
of war – Soviet Union – Addresses, essays, lectures.
4. Prisoners of war – Germany – Addresses, essays,
lectures. 5. Germany. Heer – History – World War,
1939–1945 – Addresses, essays, lectures.
I. Hirschfeld, Gerhard, 1946–
D810.J4P618 1986 940.54'72'43 85–31567
ISBN 0–04–943045–9 (alk. paper)

Set in 10 on 11 point Bembo by Computape (Pickering) Ltd
and printed in Great Britain by Billing and Son Ltd, London and
Worcester

940.5472
H669

Contents

123,335

Notes on Contributors

Jürgen Förster, D. Phil., is with the Militärgeschichtliches Forschungsamt in Freiburg/Breisgau. He has published widely on the history of the Second World War (for example, *Stalingrad. Risse im Bündnis 1942/43*, 1975) and is one of the authors of *Der Angriff auf die Sowjetunion* (1983), vol. 4 of *Das Deutsche Reich und der Zweite Weltkrieg*.

Gerhard Hirschfeld, D. Phil., is a Fellow of the German Historical Institute in London. He is the author of *Fremdherrschaft und Kollaboration. Die Niederlande unter deutscher Besatzung 1940–1945* (1984) and has edited (among others) *Exile in Great Britain. Refugees from Hitler's Germany* (1984).

Lothar Kettenacker, D. Phil., is a Fellow and Deputy Director of the German Historical Institute in London. He has published (among others) *Nationalsozialistische Volkstumspolitik im Elsaß* (1973) and is editor (with Gerhard Hirschfeld) of *The 'Führer-State': Myth and Reality* (1981). A study on British planning for post-war Germany 1939–1945 will appear shortly.

Hans Mommsen, D. Phil., is Professor of Modern History at the Ruhr-University Bochum. His numerous publications on the history of the Third Reich include *Beamtentum im Dritten Reich* (1966) and *The German Resistance to Hitler* (1970). A major study about *Das Ende des 'deutschen Wegs', 1918–1945*, vol. 8 of *Propyläen Geschichte Deutschlands*, is forthcoming.

Falk Pingel, D. Phil., former lecturer at the University of Bielefeld, is now with the Georg-Eckert-Institut für internationale Schulbuchforschung in Brunswick. His publications include *Häftlinge unter SS-Herrschaft. Widerstand, Selbstbehauptung und Vernichtung im Konzentrationslager* (1978).

Christian Streit, D. Phil., is a teacher at a Grammar School in Mannheim. He is the author of the much-acclaimed book *Keine Kameraden. Die Wehrmacht und die sowjetischen Kriegsgefangenen, 1941–1945* (1978).

Introduction

WOLFGANG J. MOMMSEN

Over the past few years the German Historical Institute in London has arranged a series of seminars devoted to the policies of genocide and the conduct of the war in Eastern Europe after 1941, including the desperate plight of Russian prisoners of war in German hands. The following essays derive from papers given on these occasions. They deal with one of the darkest chapters of German history – the systematic killing of 5½ million Jews and the death of more than 3 million Soviet prisoners of war in German captivity. Even now, forty years after these frightful events were made public to the world, it is extremely difficult to understand how atrocities of such magnitude could ever have occurred, even given a totalitarian regime such as the National Socialist dictatorship and the extreme conditions of the Second World War.

It is still difficult to discuss these issues with the objectivity and impartiality of scholarly research. But approaching these events with intellectual honesty is the only way to confront them and to help prevent anything similar ever happening again. Contrary to some currents of public opinion in the Federal Republic of Germany and elsewhere, which would sometimes prefer to pass over them in silence, we believe that the facts must be faced squarely. On the other hand, it is necessary to go beyond moral indignation and investigate the objective causes that made human beings, who were otherwise quite ordinary, not to say civilized, actively take part in these policies. Historians must, therefore, not only look into the ideological and political issues, but also take into account the social, socio-psychological and institutional factors that made this genocide possible.

A passionate debate on these issues has been conducted in the Federal Republic during the last few years. The essays collected here provide an insight into the controversy that has emerged. They also illustrate the substantial advances that have been made in empirical research. Particular attention is paid to the role of the German Army in Eastern Europe. Up until now, most Germans have tended to believe that the *Wehrmacht* (the armed forces) had by and large avoided complicity in the policies of genocide. It has gradually emerged that, while the infamous mobile execution units, the *Einsatzgruppen*, spearheaded the racial warfare in East Central Europe, the German Army allowed itself to become increasingly implicated in the sinister activities of the *Einsatzgruppen*. An important factor in this was that the military leadership in general accepted the National Socialist propaganda regarding the Soviet people, and especially its radical anti-semitic message that the Jews were largely responsible for communism. The *Wehrmacht* therefore put up little, if any, resistance to the idea that the war against Soviet Russia should be conducted as a racial war with the virtual annihilation of the enemy, or at least of its leadership cadres, as a 'legitimate' objective. For some, these findings are painful indeed.

Furthermore, it emerges that direct links existed between the mass execution of Soviet prisoners of war and the systematic killing of Jews, which was perfected with the establishment of 'death factories' in Auschwitz, Belzec, Sobibor, Treblinka, Chelmno and Majdanek. Without in the least condoning these dreadful events, it appears correct to say that the Final Solution could only have been implemented to such an extreme extent under the inhuman and barbarous conditions in the occupied areas of Poland and Russia where human lives had become cheap and death was an everyday occurrence.

It is unlikely that a decision will ever be reached about whether the Holocaust was the ultimate stage of a neatly thought out plan deeply embedded in National Socialist ideology, or whether the machinery of the National Socialist system of rule also played an important role, if only because it weakened or neutralized the moral responsibility of all the parties concerned with these frightful policies. The decision-making process within the National Socialist leadership is still largely unknown territory, despite energetic attempts to reconstruct command structures in relation to the Final Solution. Neither have the motives of the rank and file who operated the huge machinery that implemented the policy of genocide with a high degree of precision been sufficiently researched. It seems that these men acted on the basis of a totally perverted sort of morality, which defined as duty what was in fact plain murder, or at least abetting murder. Even less is known about the situation of the inmates of the concentration camps who, if they wanted to escape complete resignation to their fate, were forced to embark upon a combination of collaboration and resistance; the latter could not be conducted without a certain element of the former.

In view of the fluid state of research, these essays do not so much provide definite answers as pose new questions. In no way are they supposed to cover the events commonly associated with the term Holocaust in their entirety, even though a chronology has been added that lists the major turning-points in the history of the Holocaust. We hope, though, that the essays will stimulate the debate and encourage further research. For some years German historians were understandably reluctant to concentrate on the depressing events that culminated in the annihilation of millions of Jews and Russian prisoners of war; as these essays show, this is no longer the case. Even so, it is not easy to research these issues; it requires as much moral fortitude as diligence and balanced judgement to do so. But one way to prevent a genocide of these dimensions from ever occurring again is to write its history with the rational tools of scholarship and an awareness of the historian's moral responsibility towards the public.

1

The German Army
and the
Policies of Genocide

CHRISTIAN STREIT

The genesis of the decision to exterminate the European Jews still to a large extent lies in the dark, in spite of historians' efforts.[1] For a long time it was thought that a direct order to exterminate all the Jews had been given by Hitler. As any such order would have been very similar to the liquidation orders on record, such as the Commissar Order for example, it was assumed that it had been given in the spring of 1941.[2] This assumption was based partly on statements by those responsible who pleaded a *Führer* order[3] and partly on the postulate that, in the totalitarian National Socialist state, Hitler himself *must* have given the order for the extermination of all Jews. This postulate was temptingly plausible because of the seemingly 'logical' development of Hitler's radical anti-semitism, from the gradual deprivation of rights to the extermination of all Jews.

On the other hand, in his study of National Socialist policy towards the Jews, published in 1972, Uwe Dietrich Adam denied that there had been such an order from Hitler before September 1941.[4] In 1977 Martin Broszat argued that 'the physical liquidation of the Jews was set in motion, not by a single decision, but far more by degrees'. In the same article he convincingly refutes David Irving's thesis that the extermination of the Jews had been set in motion by Himmler and Heydrich without Hitler's knowledge.[5]

I am not in a position to answer the question of how the decision to exterminate the Jews originated, but I believe that I can contribute further material to corroborate the theses of Adam and Broszat.

The goal of removing the Jews from all areas of the world under German control already existed in general terms at the beginning of 1941, although the way in which this objective was to be realized

1

was not clear. The development to be outlined here makes it necessary to assume that at this point the 'territorial final solution' – the so-called Madagascar Plan – was uppermost in the thoughts of the National Socialist leaders and that the total annihilation of the European Jews had not yet been seriously considered.

By the autumn of 1941, however, a situation had been created in which the elimination of *all* Jews within the German sphere of influence was made possible. This was due not only to the intellectual disposition of the power elite in the German Reich, but also to technical and infrastructural developments. An important factor also seems to have been that the circle of collaborators as well as the circle of victims was extended only gradually.

The turning-point in this development was the war against the Soviet Union, which in the planning phase had been conceptualized as an ideological war of annihilation, without, however, implying the extermination of the Jews. In this context the orders that had been worked out by the political and military leadership of the Reich for the treatment of Soviet prisoners of war and the civilian population played a vital role. These orders and their execution by the majority of the *Wehrmacht* in the East contributed – in my opinion decisively – to the development of a situation in which the Final Solution (*Endlösung*) became possible.[6]

The first reference on record to the later extermination policy was a statement made by Goering on 26 February 1941 to the head of the Economics and Armaments Office (*Wehrwirtschafts- und Rüstungsamt*) in the High Command of the *Wehrmacht* (OKW), General Thomas. In the occupation of the Soviet Union, Goering said, the point was first of all to do away with the Bolshevik leaders quickly.[7] A few days later, in a directive to the *Wehrmachtführungsstab* (operation staff of the OKW) Hitler demanded that, as a condition for the establishment of states dependent on Germany instead of Russia, the Jewish–Bolshevik intelligentsia should be eliminated as former oppressors of the people. This was such a difficult task, · Hitler's directive said, 'that it could not be demanded from the regular army'. The head of the *Wehrmachtführungsstab*, General Jodl, specified:

> Whether it is necessary to engage agents of the *Reichsführer*-SS already there as well, alongside the Secret Police, must be checked with the *Reichsführer*-SS. The necessity of liquidating all Bolshevik chiefs [*alle Bolschewistenhäuptlinge*] and commissars speaks for it.[8]

Ten days later, on 13 March 1941, the decision had been taken: in the basic directive for the war in the East, Himmler was 'entrusted, on behalf of the Führer, with special tasks resulting from the struggle which has to be carried out between two opposing political systems'.[9] Thus the engagement of *Einsatzgruppen* ('Special Forces') of the *Sicherheitspolizei* (Security Police, SiPo) and the *Sicherheitsdienst* (Security Service, SD) became possible in principle – with the assistance of the High Command of the *Wehrmacht* and without the Commander-in-Chief of the Army, Field Marshal von Brauchitsch, having offered any resistance to the restricting of his authority. Until the end of April 1941, the Quartermaster General of the Army, General Wagner, and the head of the *Reichssicherheitshauptamt* (Reich Security Head Office), SS-*Gruppenführer* Reinhard Heydrich, were working on an agreement about the powers of the *Einsatzgruppen*.

This decision can, of course, in no way be equated with the decision to exterminate the Russian Jews. On 17 March Hitler had once more stated the objective to the Chief of the General Staff of the Army, General Halder: the 'intelligentsia' engaged by Stalin *must be* eliminated.[10] The powers of the *Einsatzgruppen*, as formulated by Wagner and Heydrich, were in line with this. In the rear Army areas they allowed only the 'securing' of materials and 'especially important individuals (leading emigrants, saboteurs, terrorists, etc.)'. For the rear Army Group areas the task was broadly formulated as 'the investigation and combating of activities hostile to the Reich'.[11]

In March 1941, no resistance having been forthcoming, Hitler expressed his ideas on how the war against the Soviet Union was to be waged in front of approximately 250 high-ranking *Wehrmacht* officers, mainly troop commanders of the Eastern Army. What was new here was the demand that the *Wehrmacht* itself should take a part in the war of annihilation: 'The troops must defend themselves with the same methods as those with which they are attacked. Commissars and GPU members are criminals and must be treated as such.'[12] However, the officers accepted Hitler's demands without protest. After the war some of those involved stated that there had been protests from von Brauchitsch. A careful analysis of the sources available shows that this was not the case.[13]

In the following weeks Hitler's demands were translated into orders by the High Command of the *Wehrmacht* and the Army with the result that the *Wehrmacht* was fully drawn into the war of annihilation. According to the Commissar Order, the troops were to shoot captured Red Army commissars and some of the civilian commissars on the spot. According to the Barbarossa Directive, the military courts were deprived of their jurisdiction for all offences committed by Soviet civilians. 'Suspect elements' were to be

3

executed at once. Moreover, ideologically motivated offences committed by German soldiers against the Soviet population were to remain exempt from prosecution. Before the first shot was fired, the circle of potential victims had grown enormously. Where originally 'only' the liquidation of the 'Bolshevik leaders' had been mentioned, with the Commissar Order it extended to all the commissars, and with the Barbarossa Directive to all those who resisted in any way. This provided the basis for the subsequent policy of extermination. In this context it is significant that, at least in the case of the Commissar Order, the Army leadership initiated the expression of Hitler's demand as a formal order and also introduced aggravating elements in the formulation of the Barbarossa Directive.

Judging from the surviving records, by the beginning of June 1941 there had been no suggestion that Jews should be among the victims. On 30 March Hitler had avoided arguing in terms of National Socialist racial dogma. The inclusion of the Jews in the annihilation policy was mentioned for the first time in orders on the treatment of Soviet prisoners of war, which were issued during the first weeks of the war in the East. The Chief of the General *Wehrmacht* Office in the High Command, General Reinecke, was also in charge of the Prisoner of War Department in the OKW. From at least 28 June onwards, only a few days after the beginning of the campaign in the East,[14] he was negotiating with Heydrich about the selection and execution of certain groups in the prisoner-of-war camps by *Einsatzkommandos* ('Special Units'). A draft of the agreement of 28 June shows how the circle of victims was enlarged once more. Not only were commissars and functionaries of all ranks to be 'eliminated', but also 'all persons who could be established as being agitators or fanatical Communists' and 'all Jews'.[15]

This agreement came into force on 17 July 1941. The Army's theatre of operations was expressly included, although only the Army High Command had direct authority to issue orders. In this case, however, the Army leadership was not immediately prepared to widen the responsibilities of the *Einsatzgruppen*. On 24 July, Quartermaster General Wagner by express order forbade the *Einsatzkommandos* to participate in the 'selection' of prisoners of war; although in practice he did allow it to happen: 'politically intolerable elements, commissars and agitators' were to be shot. The Jews were to be separated from the other prisoners and made available to work at the front. This decision shows that the Army leadership, unlike that of the *Wehrmacht*, was prepared to participate in exterminating the *political* enemy, but not in the extermination of the 'racial enemy'.[16]

Reinecke's approval of the liquidation of *all* Jews among the prisoners of war is remarkable – all the more so as a detailed analysis of the decisions made during the first weeks of the Eastern campaign shows that Heydrich initially proceeded cautiously in employing the *Einsatzgruppen*. Some commanders of *Einsatzgruppen* and *Einsatzkommandos* stated after the war that, in his briefing of June 1941, Heydrich had passed on Hitler's order to eliminate all Jews. Contemporary sources cast considerable doubt on these statements.

Four *Höhere SS- und Polizeiführer* (Higher SS- and Police Leaders) were assigned to the Reich Commissariats planned for the occupied territories. There they were to have the same responsibilities as the *Einsatzgruppen* in the Army's theatre of operations. Because of an organizational mishap, Heydrich was able to pass on his directives to them only in writing. These directives have survived, and from them we can see that Heydrich did not exceed the demands of the Commissar Order and Barbarossa Directive in essential points. All party functionaries of higher, middle and 'radical lower' rank were to be executed, as well as all 'other radical elements' and 'all Jews in state and party positions'.[17]

The fact that the four *Einsatzgruppen* commanders as well as the Higher SS- and Police Leaders were asked expressly to observe the agreement between Wagner and Heydrich scrupulously and thus 'ensure the most loyal co-operation with the *Wehrmacht*'[18] also suggests that Heydrich was proceeding carefully. This agreement was formulated relatively openly. The general execution of all *Jews* in the rear Army areas, as happened later, was certainly not permitted by the agreement.

Furthermore, Heydrich had demanded in his oral briefing, and repeated in a further order to the *Einsatzgruppen*, that the local population should be induced to perpetrate pogroms against the Jews – 'however *without trace*'.[19] A detailed report from the Commander of *Einsatzgruppe* A, Dr Stahlecker, dated October 1941, reveals the reasons. The Security Police, wrote Stahlecker, were to 'make no immediate appearance in the quite unusually hard measures taken, which were to arouse attention in German circles as well. Outwardly it had to be shown that the local population themselves had taken the first measures on their own . . . as a natural reaction against decades of suppression by the Jews'.[20] On the one hand, this was meant to overcome any scruples that the German troops might have and, on the other, it left the *Einsatzgruppen* a way out in case their murderous activities should meet with too much resistance.

Indeed, Heydrich could not be sure that the *Wehrmacht* would tolerate mass executions on a large scale. When SS *Einsatzgruppen* had started to exterminate the Polish ruling classes during the invasion of Poland in 1939, this had caused considerable unrest among the troop commanders. The murders in Poland and doubts about the chances of victory against France made a *coup d'état* seem likely for a short time. Heydrich and the *Einsatzgruppen* commanders – and of course Hitler as well – could not be sure in the spring of 1941 that the attitude of the generals had changed to such a degree that they would tolerate similar murder activities.[21]

In the report mentioned above, Stahlecker wrote that, 'according to the basic orders', the *Einsatzgruppen* 'had had the aim of eliminating the Jews *as far as possible*'.[22] This appears to be much closer to the truth than the claim that Hitler had ordered Heydrich to execute all Jews in all occupied Soviet territories, for the *Wehrmacht* was still a powerful factor which could not be disregarded completely. The *Wehrmacht*'s final loss of power and its *Gleichschaltung* (complete co-ordination with and subordination to Nazi doctrine) only began with the loss of German hopes in 1941, the winter before Moscow.

The reports of the four *Einsatzgruppen* commanders to the Reich Security Head Office[23] reveal surprise that from the beginning the co-operation of the Army presented so few problems. The SS commanders stressed that they had succeeded in establishing 'extremely good relations' with the departments of the *Wehrmacht*, that co-operation was proceeding 'extremely satisfactorily and without friction' and that it was 'generally good, in individual cases ... excellent, almost cordial', 'extraordinary' and 'especially successful'.[24]

Although the agreement between Heydrich and Wagner limited the activities of the *Einsatzgruppen* to the rear areas, they were in fact usually permitted to follow immediately behind the front.[25] Sections of the commandos could often advance with the tank spearheads. The departments of the *Wehrmacht* also provided further assistance, including the introduction of compulsory identification of Jews by Army commanders, the registration of Jews, the supply of transportation and support of 'combing-out activities' in Jewish districts. In at least one case a firing squad was supplied.[26]

There were only isolated cases of criticism and resistance in subordinate units, which found no support among the commanders of the Army Groups and individual Armies.[27] On the contrary, some Army commanders in whose areas extensive mass executions took place issued orders demanding understanding for their activities on the part of the soldiers. The Commander of the 6th Army, Field Marshal von Reichenau, wrote on 10 October 1941 that it was the historical task of the Army 'to free the German nation, once and for all, from the Asian–Jewish threat'. Therefore the soldiers needed to 'have full understanding for the hard but just retribution against subhuman Jewry [*Untermenschentum*]'.[28] The Commander of the 17th Army, General Hoth, and the Commander of the 11th Army, General von Manstein, used similar arguments.[29] In Manstein's rear Army area, *Einsatzgruppe* D had shot 11,000 Jews at Simferopol. The High Command of the Army also contributed to the dissemination of this way of thinking. As Hitler found Reichenau's order 'excellent', Wagner recommended that Army commanders along the whole Eastern front should issue similar orders, which as a rule seems to have happened.

To conclude from the *Einsatzgruppen* reports, the *Einsatzkommandos* came up against more resistance in the prisoner-of-war camps under the Army's jurisdiction than anywhere else.[30] The camp commandants could refer to the fact that the Quartermaster General of the Army had forbidden the involvement of *Einsatzkommandos* in the screening of prisoners of war. But even here the full extent of ideological concurrence in the lower ranks was revealed. Many commandants ignored Wagner's order, which was binding on them, and passed over to the *Einsatzkommandos* the Jews and communists among the prisoners of war. In a way, then, it was merely an adjustment to the existing situation when, at the beginning of October 1941, the High Command of the Army lifted the ban and then also gave the *Einsatzkommandos* access to the prisoner-of-war camps under the jurisdiction of the Army. Some signs, however, point to this having happened as a result of pressure from the *Wehrmacht* leadership as well. The import of the decision to have the 'intolerable' prisoners of war selected and liquidated by the *Einsatzkommandos* of the SS is shown by the fact that between June 1941 and May 1944 at least 580,000–600,000 Soviet prisoners of war – that is, roughly one-tenth of the total figure of 5.7 million – were handed over to the *Einsatzkommandos*.

By April 1942 the four *Einsatzgruppen* were able to report to Himmler (according to incompletely preserved documents) the execution of at least 461,500 Soviet Jews.[31] Basically this had become possible only through the co-operation of the *Wehrmacht*. The question that this immediately raises is why the *Wehrmacht*, which had sharply criticized the activities of the *Mordkommandos* (death squads) in Poland in 1939/40, now not only tolerated mass murder of a totally new quality, but also to a large extent supported it.

In order to answer this question we must first go into the genesis of the 'Criminal Orders' – the Commissar Order and the Barbarossa

7

Directive – once more. The target group of these orders was, in the first place, the Communist functionaries and in a wider sense all those who did not want to bow to German rule. There was no mention of the Jews. Some high-ranking troop commanders had raised some objections to the Barbarossa Directive, as they feared some of the clauses would have negative repercussions on troop discipline.[32] In its essentials, however, this directive too was followed: Soviet civilians who were regarded as partisans were not brought before courts-martial but were executed on officer's orders – or were handed over to an *Einsatzkommando*. The Commissar Order, which showed an especially striking deviation from military tradition in that it demanded the liquidation of defenceless prisoners of war, was in general also carried out – as far as can be ascertained today. Statements by troop commanders that they had not passed it on or had forbidden its execution prove to be wrong in most cases. Only in one instance do sources verify that a divisional commander ignored the order.[33]

Both orders had been accepted by troop commanders primarily because in their traumatic fear of Bolshevism they believed that all means were justified in the battle against it. According to Reichenau's order (quoted above) in the Eastern campaign, the soldier had 'tasks that surpassed the traditional merely military attitude'.[34] Also to the more conservative armed forces, the measures taken against the Communist ruling elites appeared to be necessary in order permanently to secure Germany's hegemony of leadership in Eastern Europe. In the East, 'severity is mild for the future', the Chief of the General Staff, Halder, had jotted in the margin of his notes on Hitler's speech on 30 March.[35] The steps demanded, moreover, had the character of singular and exceptional measures that in this situation seemed justifiable. This was also important for another reason. Although ideological concurrence in the Army leadership did not go as far as in the leadership of the *Wehrmacht*, Army leaders were quite prepared to make ideological concessions while competing with ardent National Socialists in the High Command of the *Wehrmacht* and with the SS for a leading position in a future Great Germanic Reich. This increased their readiness to deviate from traditional military values, as did their assessment of the chances of victory. Brauchitsch and Halder, as well as Hitler and the leadership of the *Wehrmacht*, were convinced that the Eastern campaign would end victoriously after a few weeks. The Army would thus be involved in the war of annihilation for only a short time, and this short 'stretch of dirt' seemed tolerable if it helped to secure the position of the Army leadership in the state of the future.[36]

The attitude resulting from these factors was reinforced by the way in which warfare developed in the East. The Red Army's desperate resistance and the repercussions of the 'Criminal Orders' led to a brutalizing of combat that exceeded anything German soldiers had seen so far. Thus the fear of Bolsheviks appeared to be justified and legitimate, even more so in view of the partisan warfare which itself was largely a reaction to the 'Criminal Orders'. By mid-July Hitler had recognized the opportunity it offered. In a conference with the top leadership he declared that partisan warfare 'also had its advantages: it gives us the opportunity to exterminate whatever stands in our way'.[37]

In fact, a fear of partisans (present from the beginning) and the subsequent partisan warfare that developed – however slowly – behind the front were the most important factors in increasing the troops' readiness to co-operate with the *Einsatzgruppen*. The troop commanders readily left the task of leading the battle against the initially small partisan movement, and of obtaining information about it, to the *Einsatzgruppen*, thereby giving them the opportunity for manipulation. It now became apparent that the troop commanders fully accepted Hitler's equation of Bolshevism and Judaism. Reichenau and Manstein justified the 'necessity of severe retribution against Judaism' with the claim that the Jews were supporting the partisans and plotting insurrections.[38] The *Einsatzkommandos'* reports corroborated this, because they had realized from the outset that for mass murder a 'plausible' foundation that could allay any possible qualms was necessary. The first massacre reported to the Reich Head Security Office was labelled a 'punitive measure' and in other cases the Jews were mostly shot 'in retaliation' – because of partisan attacks, because of alleged or actual sabotage and because of 'Soviet atrocities'.[39]

Another factor contributed to the development of the situation that made the Final Solution possible. The lives of the Soviet populace did not only seem of so little value because the propaganda concept of the 'subhuman' (*Untermensch*) was already widely accepted, the worthlessness of Soviet lives was demonstrated to the German soldiers daily. Because of the ruthless exploitation of food resources to the advantage of the German population, large parts of the Soviet population were condemned to death by starvation. This was a consequence that, in April 1941, had been deliberately intended by the planners of the exploitation policy.[40] It particularly affected Soviet prisoners of war. In the summer of 1941 their marching columns were decimated by debilitation and execution of the weak. No later than September 1941 the mortality rate in some camps reached one per cent *per day*.[41] Under these circumstances it seems understandable that some camp commandants did not want to argue with SS-*Kommandos* about the lives of prisoners whose life expectancy amounted only to days or weeks.

Thus, by the late summer of 1941 a situation was reached in which it was possible for many hundreds of thousands of Jews and Communists to be exterminated by the *Einsatzgruppen* with the help of the *Wehrmacht*. The High Commands of both the *Wehrmacht* and the Army had contributed to the development of this situation by the formulation of the 'Criminal Orders', which, as a general principle, had included the *Wehrmacht* in the annihilation policy and had then extended the circle of prospective victims between February and July 1941 in an almost geometrical progression. The troop commanders, who not only carried out the 'Criminal Orders' but also made possible the liquidation of the Soviet Jews through their generally willing co-operation with the *Einsatzgruppen*, also contributed to the situation.

Himmler and Heydrich had come closer to their goal of the 'most extensive elimination possible' of the Jews in the Soviet territories much more quickly than they could have expected in the spring of 1941. The extent of co-operation from the *Wehrmacht* made clear to the National Socialist leadership that this source of power would not oppose a move against the German Jews and against Jews in the remaining German areas under Nazi authority. In my opinion, the fact that in autumn 1941 the Jews were formally deprived of all their rights and began to be deported to the East – into the *Generalgouvernement* (General Government) of Poland and the *Reichskommissariat Ostland* – was *also* a consequence of the development outlined here.

In 1941, however, even the innermost circle of the National Socialist leadership seems not have thought of a physical liquidation of all Jews. Goebbels' diary and other sources suggest that in August and September 1941 other considerations were paramount. These included a plan to deport the Jews (after the victory in the East) from the territory of the Reich 'still further East' – that is, to Siberia, where they were to perish due to lack of nourishment.[42] Military developments made that impossible. The deportations, however, went on and led to chaotic situations at their destinations, which were 'solved' by the first mass annihilations of German Jews. The driving forces here were probably local departments of the Security Police and the civilian administration.

The deportations having begun, the desire of some of the *Gauleiter* (regional party leaders) in the Reich to get rid of the Jews led to an escalation of the situation in the late autumn of 1941. The thoughts of the leaders responsible – apart from Hitler and Goebbels, *Generalgouveneur* Frank and *Gauleiter* Greiser should be mentioned – now concentrated more and more on the possibility of exterminating the Jews altogether.[43] The mass murders by the *Einsatzgruppen*, further measures of annihilation by Higher SS- and Police Leaders in the new Reich Commissariats Ostland and Ukraine, and the first mass liquidations in Warthegau made the Final Solution in its later form conceivable. The *Reichsminister* for the Occupied Eastern Territories, Rosenberg, expressed this in a speech on 18 November 1941, when he declared that the Jewish question could 'only [be solved] by a biological extermination of the whole of Jewry in Europe'.[44]

The Wannsee Conference Protocol of 20 January 1942 shows that at this time the method of effecting the Final Solution, as it was later practised in Auschwitz and other extermination camps, had not yet been considered.[45] The perspective is longer-range: the extermination of the Jews through forced labour in the East, and the liquidation of survivors. The technical problems of how to exterminate the European Jews totally within the space of a few years had not yet been solved. The treatment of the Soviet prisoners of war contributed to finding a solution.

A long time before the attack on the Soviet Union, the High Command of the *Wehrmacht* had apparently been ready to promise Himmler at least 100,000 of the expected Soviet prisoners of war as labourers.[46] At any rate, on 1 March 1941 Himmler ordered the Commandant of the Auschwitz concentration camp to build a prisoner-of-war camp at Birkenau for 100,000 prisoners – and these could only have been Soviet prisoners. At that time Auschwitz had approximately 8,000 inmates. The enormous extension planned was, among other things, to provide workers for a gigantic industrial complex that IG Farben wanted to construct with Himmler's assistance. Of the 'up to 100,000' Soviet prisoners of war who had been allocated to Himmler by the High Command of the *Wehrmacht* in 1941, 10,000 came to Auschwitz in October. They were supposed to build the prisoner-of-war work camp, but, apart from a few survivors, they were quickly exterminated. The Birkenau camp, completed in the summer of 1942, was now to serve another purpose: it was to be the largest extermination camp in occupied Poland. Majdanek, the concentration camp near Lublin in which well over 200,000 Jews were killed, was also originally intended to have been a camp for 150,000 Soviet prisoners of war.

At the end of January 1942, a little less than a week after the Wannsee Conference, Himmler realized that his plans for the Soviet prisoners of war had failed. Of the more than 3.3 million Soviet prisoners of war who had fallen into German hands in 1941, approximately 2 million had died or been executed. Of the tens of thousands of prisoners who had been brought in to work in the concentration camp, only a few had survived. Himmler consequently took the significant step of ordering the transfer of 150,000 German Jews to the concentration camp.[47]

The plan to use the labour power of Soviet prisoners of war in Auschwitz paved the way for the carrying out of the Final Solution in two ways. First, with the building of the prisoner-of-war labour camp at Birkenau, the infrastructure, including the railway connection, was created that made possible a 'turn-over' of well over 1 million Jews in Auschwitz. Secondly, camp commandant Höss and his assistant, Fritsch, 'tried out' the pesticide Zyklon B on roughly 900 Soviet prisoners of war who had been singled out by *Einsatzkommandos* as 'intolerable' and who had been sent to Auschwitz for execution.[48] Thus they found the means that made possible the murder of millions of Jews with a minimal investment of labour.

NOTES

1 Martin Broszat, 'Hitler und die Genesis der "Endlösung"', *Vierteljahrshefte für Zeitgeschichte*, 25 (1977), pp. 739–75. The following owes much to Broszat's article.

2 See Helmut Krausnick, 'Judenverfolgung', in Hans Buchheim *et al.*, *Anatomie des SS-Staates*, vol. 2, 2nd edn (Munich, 1967), p. 301; Heinz Höhne, *Der Orden unter dem Totenkopf. Die Geschichte der SS* (Frankfurt/M., 1969), pp. 371–7.

3 Statement by Dr Walter Blume, leader of *Sonderkommando* 7a, quoted by Krausnick, 'Judenverfolgung' (as in n.2), p. 301; Höhne, *Orden* (as in n.2), pp. 376–7, quotes a similar statement by Otto Ohlendorf, leader of *Einsatzgruppe* D.

4 Uwe Dietrich Adam, *Judenpolitik im Dritten Reich* (Düsseldorf, 1972), p. 312.

5 Broszat, 'Genesis der "Endlösung"' (as in n.1). See David Irving, *Hitler's War* (London, 1977).

6 For a detailed description of these orders, their genesis and implementation see my book *Keine Kameraden. Die Wehrmacht und die sowjetischen Kriegsgefangenen 1941–1945* (Stuttgart, 1978), pp. 28–61.

7 Memo by Thomas, 26 February 1941, Nuremberg Doc. 1456-PS.

8 Percy Ernst Schramm (ed.), *Kriegstagebuch des Oberkommandos der Wehrmacht (Wehrmachtführungsstab) 1940–1945*, vol. 1 (Frankfurt/M., 1965), p. 341.

9 For the complete text see Hans-Adolf Jacobsen, 'Kommissarbefehl und Massenexekutionen sowjetischer Kriegsgefangener', in Buchheim *et al., Anatomie des SS-Staates*, vol. 2, pp. 166–9.

10 *Generaloberst Halder, Kriegstagebuch. Tägliche Aufzeichnungen des Chefs des Generalstabes des Heeres 1939–1942*, vol. 2 (Stuttgart, 1963), p. 320.

11 For the text of the agreement as signed by Field Marshal von Brauchitsch, Commander-in-Chief of the German Army, see Jacobsen, 'Kommissarbefehl' (as in n.9), pp. 171–3.

12 According to Halder's record: *Halder, Kriegstagebuch* (as in n.10), vol. 2, pp. 336–7.

13 See Streit, *Keine Kameraden* (as in n.6), pp. 35–49, also for the following.

14 See ibid., pp. 87–105, also for the following.

15 [Reichssicherheitshauptamt]/Amt IV/IV A 1 c of 28 June 1941; *Bundesarchiv*/Koblenz [BAK]:R 58/272.

16 Streit, *Keine Kameraden* (as in n.6), pp. 99–100.

17 Chef der Sicherheitspolizei und des SD/Br.B.IV – 1180/41 gRs. of 2 July 1941: BAK:R 70 SU/15.

18 'Merkblatt für die Führer der Einsatzgruppen und Einsatzkommandos', BAK:R 70 SU/15.

19 Teleprint message by Heydrich (with reference to the orders he had given orally in Berlin on 17 June 1941) of 29 June 1941: BAK:R 70 SU/32; see his *directive* of 2 July 1941 (see n.17).

20 Action report by Stahlecker, Nuremberg Doc. 180-L, *Der Prozeß gegen die Hauptkriegsverbrecher vor dem Internationalen Militärgerichtshof. Nürnberg, 14. Oktober 1945 – 1. Oktober 1946* [IMG], vol. 38, p. 672.

21 Streit, *Keine Kameraden* (as in n.6), pp. 50–9 and 126–7.

22 Nuremberg Doc. 180-L, IMG, vol. 38, p. 687, emphasis added.

23 'Ereignismeldungen UdSSR', BAK:R 58/214–221.

24 See the quotations from the *Einsatzgruppen* reports given by Streit, *Keine Kameraden* (as in n.6), pp. 110–12.

25 See ibid., pp. 109–25, also for the following.

26 When *Sonderkommando* 4a killed 1,160 Jews near the Ukrainian town of Luck (in the 6th Army's area of jurisdiction) in mid-July 1941, it was assisted by a police platoon and an infantry platoon: 'Ereignismeldungen UdSSR', 16 July 1941, BAK:R 58/214.

27 See Streit, *Keine Kameraden* (as in n.6), pp. 119–21.

28 Nuremberg Doc. 411-D, IMG, vol. 35, pp. 84–6.

29 Nuremberg Doc. 4064-PS, IMG, vol. 34, pp. 129–31. Hoth's order quoted by Erich Hesse, *Der sowjetrussische Partisanenkrieg 1941 bis 1944 im Spiegel deutscher Kampfanweisungen und Befehle* (Göttingen, 1969), pp. 89–90. Hesse erroneously attributes the order to Hoth's predecessor, von Stülpnagel.

30 See Streit, *Keine Kameraden* (as in n.6), pp. 99–105, also for the following.

31 *Einsatzgruppe* A (up to February, 1942): 229,052; *Einsatzgruppe* B (up to 14 November 1941): 45,467; *Einsatzgruppe* C (up to December 1941):

95,000; *Einsatzgruppe* D (up to 4 April 1942): 92,000 (Krausnick, 'Judenverfolgung', as in n.2, p. 302).
32 Streit, *Keine Kameraden* (as in n.6), pp. 42–4.
33 ibid., pp. 83–7.
34 Nuremberg Doc. 411-D, *IMG*, vol. 35, p. 85.
35 Halder, *Kriegstagebuch* (as in n.10), vol. 2, p. 337.
36 Streit, *Keine Kameraden* (as in n.6), pp. 80–2.
37 Memo by Bormann, 16 July 1941, Nuremberg Doc. 221–L, *IMG*, vol. XXXVIII, p. 88.
38 See the orders mentioned above (n.28 and n.29).
39 Streit, *Keine Kameraden* (as in n.6), p. 125.
40 ibid., pp. 63–5.
41 ibid., pp. 128–37.
42 This and the following is based on Broszat, 'Genesis der "Endlösung"' (as in n.1), pp. 747–51.
43 ibid., pp. 752–3.
44 Quotation from the manuscript of a speech Rosenberg made on 18 November 1941 to newspaper editors (*Schriftleiter und Hauptschriftleiter*) in his ministry: *Politisches Archiv des Auswärtigen Amtes*, Bonn: Pol. XIII/25. According to the notes taken by *Legationsrat* (legation councillor) Großkopf, representative of the Foreign Ministry in Rosenberg's ministry, Rosenberg had been even more outspoken: 'Concerning the Jewish question Reichsminister Rosenberg remarked that the Eastern campaign would solve this question for Europe. The Jews [*das Judentum*], even if they numbered many million heads in Europe, would be utterly eradicated [*völlig ausgemerzt*] on this side of the Ural Mountains.'
  As late as May 1941 Rosenberg had not known anything about plans to annihilate the Jews in the immediate future. In a memorandum for Hitler of 29 April 1941 (Nuremberg Doc. 1024–PS, *IMG*, vol. 26, pp. 560–6) he referred to the 'temporary provisional solution [of the Jewish question] ... (forced labour for the Jews, establishment of ghettos, etc.)'; likewise in his draft of instructions for the *Reichskommissar* Ukraine of 7 May 1941; Nuremberg Doc. 1028–PS, *IMG*, vol. 26, p. 571. Rosenberg was then intended to play an important role in the mastery over the conquered Eastern territories, so he would have known about any plans, had they existed.
45 Leon Poliakov and Josef Wulf, *Das Dritte Reich und die Juden* (Berlin, 1955), pp. 117–19.
46 See Streit, *Keine Kameraden* (as in n.6), pp. 217–23, also for the following.
47 Himmler's order of 26 January 1942 to the Inspector of Concentration Camps, Glücks, quoted by Martin Broszat, 'Nationalsozialistische Konzentrationslager 1933–1945', in Hans Buchheim et al., *Anatomie des SS-Staates* (as in n.2), pp. 108–9.
48 Streit, *Keine Kameraden* (as in n.6), p. 25.

2

The German Army
and the
Ideological War against
the Soviet Union

JÜRGEN FÖRSTER

On 22 June 1941 Hitler began his war against the Soviet Union. He was not the only one who knew that this day also marked the prelude of the mass murder of Jews and Communists. Operation 'Barbarossa' cannot be compared to the earlier campaigns of the war. Its totally different character resulted from Hitler's determination to realize his idea of *Lebensraum* (*lit.* 'living space'), in which German expansion to the East, the extermination of Bolshevism, and the annihilation of Jewry were inextricably intertwined.[1] The war against Russia has to be viewed 'as the struggle for territorial conquest, a clash of ideologies and the *Rassenkampf* that it undoubtedly was'.[2] Hitler's aims were to be achieved through war, a war in which Germany would face the grand alternative: glorious victory or total destruction. Military operations for the sake of conquest, and mass killings of hostile groups to safeguard the acquired *Lebensraum*, were only different aspects of this single war of extermination. Alan Bullock has rightly pointed out that 'of all Hitler's decisions' the decision to wage war on Russia 'is the one which most clearly bears his own personal stamp, the culmination (as he saw it) of his whole career'.[3]

Contemporary German historiography has far too long been preoccupied with the 'German catastrophe' (Friedrich Meinecke) and has thus overlooked the Jewish and the Soviet catastrophe.[4] Not until the 1970s did historians begin to analyse the significant connection between the outbreak and course of war and the mass murder of 'undesirable elements' and 'inferior races'. This may also explain why many a veteran still doggedly perpetuates the myth that

15

the *Wehrmacht* was not involved in the annihilation policy in the East.[5] Despite the trail–blazing studies of Manfred Messerschmidt on the *Wehrmacht* and National Socialist Germany[6] and of Christian Streit on the *Wehrmacht* and the Soviet prisoners of war[7] and further documentary evidence that proves that the *Wehrmacht* was actively involved in the sinister business of eradicating 'Jewish Bolshevism',[8] some authors still attempt to exculpate the *Wehrmacht* from the mass murder of Jews, Communists, commissars, and prisoners of war. The difficult problem of establishing a convincing tradition for the ideological profile of the *Bundeswehr* (armed forces of the Federal Republic) cannot be solved by legitimizing a gravely compromised profession or by selective exploitation of the resistance legacy. Thus (to guard against one kind of misunderstanding), it is worth pointing out that to hold the *Wehrmacht* responsible for many crimes in Russia is very far from designating the German *soldier* a criminal.

The relationship between the *Wehrmacht* and Hitler in regard to the Soviet Union was determined in large measure by considerable consensus on both ideological matters and Germany's role in world politics. The military leaders did not merely comply with Hitler's dogmatic views, they were not mere victims of their own professional tradition. They, too, believed that the dangers of Russia and Bolshevism should be eliminated for ever. The adversary in the East was considered the enemy *per se*. Had it not been the evil influence of Jewry and Bolshevism that had caused the downfall of Imperial Germany in 1918? Thus, Operation Barbarossa assumed a higher justification and a different quality from the war against France. Moreover, 'the idea of the vital needs of the German *Volksgemeinschaft* [National Folk Community] provided the *Wehrmacht* with something like a "clear conscience" in its brutal conduct of the war in the East'.[9]

Hitler was not only the supreme commander of the *Wehrmacht*, but also self-proclaimed supreme ideological leader of the military. Hitler had demanded in February 1939 that the entire Officer Corps form his 'guard to the bitter end' to aid him in achieving specific ideological objectives. It was in the war against the Soviet Union that Hitler put the military establishment on trial and thereby tested his ideological leadership. It is interesting to note that Hitler reiterated this demand on 27 January 1944: 'If the worst should come to the worst, then what really ought to happen is that the field-marshals and generals should defend the flag to the last'.[10] Even at that time, when a great number of the generals assembled at his headquarters knew that the *Wehrmacht*'s coat of arms had been stained since 1941, Manstein took offence at Hitler's lack of confidence in his generals.

When the military preparations for Operation Barbarossa were already far advanced, Hitler demanded – first within the small circle of his advisers and then before a wider military public – that the commanders recognize the ideological nature of the struggle by liquidating the 'Jewish–Bolshevik intelligentsia'. While assigning to the Army the initial responsibility for the pacification of all territory in the East and entrusting the SS with 'special tasks' within the Army's area of operation, Hitler was determined to convert the *Wehrmacht* into an instrument of extermination alongside the SS by erasing the line between military and political–ideological warfare. On 30 March 1941 the Army and Airforce commanders-in-chief and their chiefs of staff from the Eastern Front were assembled at the Reich Chancellery in Berlin. Hitler stated openly in a long address that he wanted to see the impending war against the Soviet Union conducted not according to customary military principles, but as a 'war of extermination' against an ideology and its adherents, whether within the Red Army or in a non-military function.[11]

Hitler's comments did not fall on barren ground in the Army. Three days before his supreme commander had prescribed the methods to be used for eradicating 'Jewish Bolshevism', Field-Marshal von Brauchitsch, Commander-in-Chief of the Army, had demanded that his military commanders recognize the German–Russian war as 'a struggle between two different races, requiring their troops to act with all necessary harshness'.[12] Even more striking is the fact that the draft agreement between the Army and the SS of 26 March 1941 on the duties of the *Einsatzgruppen* in the operations zone was amended for the Balkan campaign by the Army High Command. It was the first time that Jews and Communists, and not only emigrants, terrorists and saboteurs, were explicitly singled out as Germany's enemies to be handled by the *Einsatzgruppen*.[13]

Although it was Hitler who wanted to transform Operation Barbarossa into a war of extermination against Bolshevism and Jewry, it was the *Wehrmacht* senior officers and their legal advisers who cast his ideological intentions into legally valid form. While these pre-invasion directives were being prepared by the relevant departments of the *Wehrmacht*, individual senior commanders spelled out the consequences of Hitler's demands of 30 March 1941 in addresses to their commanding generals and individual commanders or inserted relevant paragraphs in deployment directives. For example, General von Küchler, commander of the 18th Army, expressed the idea that Germany and Russia were, ideologically and racially, separated by a deep gorge. Like Hitler, Küchler defined the political commissars within the Red Army and the secret service personnel as criminals who should be court-martialled and sentenced. By those measures he hoped to drive a wedge between the criminal political leadership and the decent Russian soldier, as well as provide for a speedier and less costly advance.[14] Another general who justified the coming war on the same grounds as Hitler was *Generaloberst* Erich Hoepner, commander of Panzer Group 4 in the north, who had been a member of the military opposition in 1938 and who ended his days hanging by piano wire from a meat-hook for his part in the Bomb Plot of July 1944.[15] On 2 May 1941 Hoepner wrote:

> The war against Russia is an important chapter in the struggle for existence of the German nation. It is the old battle of the Germanic against the Slav peoples, of the defence of European culture against Moscovite–Asiatic inundation, and the repulse of Jewish Bolshevism. The objective of this battle must be the destruction of present-day Russia and it must therefore be conducted with unprecedented severity. Every military action must be guided in planning and execution by an iron will to exterminate the enemy mercilessly and totally. In particular, no adherents of the present Russian–Bolshevik system are to be spared.[16]

An examination of the orders of the day issued by the military commanders on the eve of the invasion of Russia clearly reveals that they too used Nazi vocabulary to a large extent. General Lemelsen, commander of XLVII Corps, for example, told his troops:

> We are on the eve of a great event in the war. The Führer has called us again to battle. It is now our task to destroy the Red Army and thereby eradicate forever Bolshevism, the deadly enemy of National Socialism. We have never forgotten that it was Bolshevism which had stabbed our army of the Great War in the back and which bears the guilt for all misfortunes which our people suffered after the war. We will always remember that![17]

At the centre of the Army's preparations for the struggle against the 'deadly enemy of National Socialist Germany' stood *Generaloberst* Halder, the Chief of the General Staff, not the Commander-in-Chief, von Brauchitsch, or General Eugen Müller, General Officer for Special Duties attached to the Commander-in-

Chief. Despite his title, since October 1940 Müller had been subject to Halder's directives 'regarding military jurisdiction within the Army and against the population of occupied territories'.[18] Since Halder was willing to let the troops participate in the intended ideological war, the Army High Command formulated its own draft that confined military jurisdiction during Operation Barbarossa to the maintenance of discipline and expected the troops to deal themselves with civilians impeding or inciting others to impede the *Wehrmacht*. In cases where such 'criminal elements' could not be shot 'while fighting or escaping', an officer was to decide whether they were to be shot. The Army High Command also took the initiative against the commissars in the Red Army. As 'bearers of the Jewish–Bolshevik world view' they were to be executed after being taken prisoner on the orders of an officer who had to identify the commissar in consultation with two other officers or NCOs.[19]

Whereas in the case of the limitation of military jurisdiction the legal branch of the High Command of the *Wehrmacht* had formulated the first draft, the initiative for the formulation of the Commissar Order clearly came from the High Command of the Army. Although the commissars within the Red Army wore uniform, they were regarded not as combatants, but as political functionaries. The Army High Command's fear that such hardliners might continue disseminating propaganda in the Reich if taken prisoner of war was a major factor dictating the shooting of political commissars of all kinds – a policy illegal by all international rules. It was precisely because officers and officials in the High Command recognized the abandonment of military law in favour of political expediency that they acknowledged the necessity of justifying these illegal measures by citing a distorted version of post-1918 German history and pointing to the need for the absolute security of the German soldier.

In formulating the final decrees of 13 May and 6 June 1941 the High Command of the *Wehrmacht* not only travelled this path but accepted even harsher concepts than those offered in the drafts of the Army High Command. The C.-in-C. of the Army, Field Marshal von Brauchitsch, made amendments both to the decree for the exercise of military jurisdiction and to the guidelines for the treatment of the political commissars before he passed the decrees on to the Army. On the one hand, he laid the burden for segregating and executing the commissars 'inconspicuously' on to the shoulders of any officer. On the other hand, he stressed the duty of all superiors to prevent arbitrary excesses of *individual* soldiers against the Soviet population. 'Timely action by every officer', Brauchitsch concluded the one amendment, 'must help to maintain discipline, the basis of our successes.[20] Concern for the discipline of the troops was obviously more important than scruples about illegal shooting of captive commissars or of civilians who were mere suspects.

These directives were supplemented by the 'Guidelines for the Conduct of the Troops in Russia' of 19 May 1941, which also reflected the military establishment's involvement in an ideological war in the East.[21] Bolshevism was defined as the 'deadly enemy of the National Socialist German nation. It is against this destructive ideology and its adherents that Germany is waging war'. The battle demanded 'ruthless and vigorous measures against Bolshevik inciters, guerrillas, saboteurs, Jews and the complete elimination of all active and passive resistance'. These guidelines make it clear that Jews were singled out as a hostile group long before the draft agreement of 28 June 1941 between the *Wehrmacht* and the SS that allowed for their selection and execution by the *Einsatzkommandos* in the prisoner-of-war camps.[22]

Responsibility for prisoners of war during the Barbarossa campaign was shared by the High Commands of the *Wehrmacht* and of the Army. Within the Reich, in occupied Poland and in the two civil administrative provinces of the newly conquered eastern territories, Ostland and Ukraine, responsibility was borne by the High Command of the *Wehrmacht*, and in the area of operations by the Army High Command. On 17 July 1941 the High Command of the *Wehrmacht*, having reached agreement with the SS, decreed that the armed forces were to

> get rid of all those elements among the prisoners of war considered Bolshevik driving forces. The special situation of the Eastern campaign therefore demands *special measures* ... While so far the regulations and orders concerning prisoners of war have been based solely on *military* considerations, now the *political* objective must be attained, which is to protect the German nation from Bolshevik inciters and forthwith take the occupied territory strictly in hand.[23]

After an initial separation of civilians and prisoners of war by *Wehrmacht* personnel according to nationality and political trustworthiness, the 'specially trained' *Einsatzkommandos* then took over further selection and liquidation. The SS guidelines provided for the elimination of commissars and functionaries of all ranks, agitators, fanatical Communists and all Jews.

Although the camps in the area of operations had been included in the *Wehrmacht* decree, the Army High Command was not yet prepared to allow the *Einsatzkommandos* to participate in the selection of prisoners of war. On 24 July 1941, the Army Quartermaster General, General Wagner, decreed the 'immediate isolation of politically intolerable and suspicious elements, commissars and agitators'. The camp commanders were to deal with them 'in accordance with the special directives', that is to say, to shoot them, in line with the decrees of 13 May and 6 June 1941. 'Asians (in terms of race), Jews, German-speaking Russians' were also to be separated from the other prisoners and kept far from the German border.[24] This practice was not always observed, but Wagner's order of 24 July 1941 indicates that at least the Army leadership was not prepared to annihilate the 'racial enemy' among the prisoners of war, although it had no scruples about exterminating political opponents. On 7 October 1941, however, the Army High Command revoked the ruling and gave the *Einsatzkommandos* of the SS access to their camps, thus adopting the practice obligatory in the *Wehrmacht* provinces since July 1941.

We know from documentary evidence that at least 500,000–600,000 Soviet prisoners of war were handed over to the SS between June 1941 and May 1944. However, Streit's assertion that they were all shot has been heavily criticized, not always on scholarly grounds.[25] On the other hand, the fate of the 3.3 million Soviet prisoners of war who perished (out of a total of 5.7 million Soviet soldiers taken prisoner by the German Army between June 1941 and February 1945) points to the fact that the mass death of the Soviet prisoners of war was caused not by execution following political or racist criteria, but by the priorities of the German exploitation policy, which condemned hundreds of thousands of prisoners to death by starvation and endemic diseases. Of course, some efforts were made to treat Soviet prisoners of war in accordance with international law, for example by Count Moltke and Admiral Canaris in September 1941 and by General Leykauf in December 1941. Less well known is that even Rosenberg, Minister for the Occupied Eastern Territories, advocated a change of German policy in a letter to Field Marshal Keitel on 28 February 1942. Although Rosenberg agreed with the German effort to conduct an ideological struggle against the Soviet Union, he demanded that prisoners be treated in accordance with the laws of humaneness. Rosenberg thought that the past ill-treatment of prisoners was responsible for the stiffened resistance of the Red Army 'and thereby also for the deaths of thousands of German soldiers . . . An obvious consequence of this politically and militarily unwise treatment has been not only the weakening of the will to desert but a truly deadly fear of falling into German captivity.'[26] This change of attitude towards the Soviet

prisoners of war cannot, however, be credited to moral considerations; it was caused by the necessities of war – in particular the
shortage of labourers. As far as the magnitude of the wholesale
death of the Soviet prisoners of war is concerned, it is indeed
comparable to the systematic annihilation policy of the *Einsatzgruppen* and other SS agencies, whose action reports claimed the SS had
liquidated a total of 2.2 million Jews.[27]

In order to understand the whole complex of the ideological
relationship between Hitler and the Army that enabled the Army to
be involved in the extermination policy, it is necessary to look at the
implementation of the so-called 'Criminal Orders': the Barbarossa
Directive of 13 May and the Commissar Order of 6 June 1941. After
receiving the instructions on those two decrees by General Müller
and his legal adviser, Dr Lattmann, the returning judge-advocate of
the 11th Army told the military commanders on 18 June 1941:

> Each soldier must know that he has to defend himself against all
> attacks in battle; that in cases of doubt he can either liberate or
> shoot arrested persons. Each officer must know that he can
> shoot or liberate arrested persons, but that political commissars
> must be segregated and liquidated. Each battalion commander
> must know that he can order collective punishments.[28]

This particular paragraph affirms that, in cases of attack upon the
armed forces where the individual offender could not be identified
quickly, the burning of villages and/or mass executions could be
ordered.

The idea of many law-abiding senior officers that they could 'ride
the tiger', that is, accept the ideologically motivated measures and
yet demand of the troops that they should remain decent, soon
proved to be an illusion. The inherent conflict between the ideological and the military attitude towards the Eastern foe becomes
evident in two orders issued by General Lemelsen, commander of
XLVII Panzer Corps. Just a few days after the beginning of
Operation Barbarossa he condemned the 'irresponsible, senseless
and criminal' shootings of prisoners of war, deserters and civilians:

> This is murder! The German *Wehrmacht* is waging this war
> against Bolshevism, but not against the united Russian peoples.
> We want to bring back peace, calm and order to this land which
> has suffered terribly for many years from the oppression of a
> Jewish and criminal group ... A Russian soldier who has been
> taken prisoner while wearing a uniform and after he put up a
> brave fight, has the right to decent treatment ... This instruc-

tion does not change anything regarding the Führer's order on the ruthless action to be taken against partisans and Bolshevik commissars.[29]

It would be incorrect to underrate or play down the effect the Commissar Order had on the conduct of the troops or to assume (as do Nolte, Streim and Walle[30]) that the *Wehrmacht* generally found ways to circumvent or ignore it. Are we really still to believe that the order was not implemented at all or that official reports were deliberately manipulated,[31] as former soldiers apologetically claim? The large number of executions listed by the intelligence officers speak in too clear a language. The documentary evidence, for example, contradicts the memoirs of both General Guderian and Colonel (ret.) Roschmann.[32] Guderian's Panzer Group 2 is reported to have shot 183 commissars up to the end of October 1941,[33] and the LII Corps, of which Roschmann was the Quartermaster, is reported to have executed at least 15 commissars and political army leaders (*politruks*).[34] Even in the one case where General Halder in his diary states that the 17th Panzer Division had ignored the order, the divisional records in fact point to the opposite.[35] In his action report, the intelligence officer of Panzer Group 3 tersely wrote that the execution of the Commissar Order did not entail 'any problem for the troops', and that 170 commissars had been killed up to the beginning of August 1941.[36]

At the same time, there was growing criticism among some field commanders of the practical result of the Commissar Order. They argued, as Rosenberg did later with regard to the ill-treatment of Soviet PoWs, that the execution of this order would inevitably lead to a stiffening of Soviet resistance. On 23 September 1941, the Army High Command requested an examination of the implementation of the Commissar Order, taking into consideration the development of the campaign. Hitler, however, refused any change. A similar request from the 16th Army was turned down in December 1941.[37] It was only in May 1942 that the pressure exerted by senior commanders showed results. The Commissar Order was suspended in the operations area in order to encourage the tendency of Soviet soldiers to desert.[38] One divisional commander instructed his soldiers not to shoot commissars or political army leaders as late as September 1942.[39]

Extermination on an even larger scale than the shooting of Soviet commissars was carried out by the armed forces during anti-guerrilla operations. Although many high-ranking officers deliberately mixed military and ideological measures, 'only a few individuals honourably admitted as much'[40] after the war. General Röttiger, who became the first Army inspector of the *Bundeswehr*, wrote in an affidavit submitted at the Nuremberg trial:

> I have now come to realize that the order from the highest authorities for the harshest conduct of partisan war can only have been intended to make possible a ruthless liquidation of Jews and other undesirable elements, by using for this purpose the military struggle of the Army against the partisans.[41]

Hitler himself had recognized the opportunity offered by Stalin's appeal for the merciless people's war against 'German Fascism' behind the front. On 16 July 1941, Hitler declared: 'The partisan war gives us the possibility to exterminate everyone who opposes us.'[42] Professionalism and ideology went together well. As long as the mass shooting of Jews and Communists was 'perceived and construed as a military measure against Germany's enemies, it did not require nazified zealots (though surely those were not lacking), merely conscientious and politically obtuse professional soldiers to carry them out'.[43]

German security policy in the occupied territories in the East was a complex matter from the very outset of the campaign. Military security and administration either overlapped or were jointly conducted by the Army and the SS. According to their pre-invasion agreement, the SS had been given a free hand to carry out their task of eliminating Communist functionaries, Jews and subversive elements without restraint within the area of operations. The Army's own plans for military security were determined from the beginning by the vast expanse of Russian territory. On the one hand, the Army High Command consciously aimed at avoiding measures that would make the Soviet population hostile towards the German invader. If they remained peaceful, worked and obeyed the given orders, then the suffering would be minimized by combating sabotage incidents with reprisal executions chiefly of Communists, Russians and Jews. On the other hand, the rapid pacification of the occupied territories was to be achieved by dealing ruthlessly with the hostile sections of the civilian population. The guiding principles were to be the 'absolute security of the German soldier' and the spread of terror 'so as to crush every will to resist among the population'.[44] Pity and softness were considered as weakness that constituted a danger to the German soldier. The orders of July 1941 mixed military and ideological, punitive and preventive measures. They accused the supporters of the Jewish–Bolshevik system of being responsible for the renewal of fighting in already pacified areas, and justified reprisals and collective punishment instead of taking hostages. The mass shooting of suspected civilians and the destruction of villages were seen as appropriate reactions to any unidentified instances of sabotage.

It was not only Hitler and the SS who construed a causal connection between 'Jewish Bolshevism' and the partisan movement. Military commanders, too, saw the Jews as natural supporters of the Communist system and acted accordingly. After a mop-up operation near Mirgorod in the rear area of Army Group 'South', for example, the 62nd Infantry Division shot the 'entire Jewish population (168 souls) for associating with partisans', in addition to executing 45 partisans.[45] Christopher Browning has convincingly proved that similar things happened in Serbia. In Sabâc, for example, 'central European Jewish refugees, mostly Austrians, were shot by troops predominantly of Austrian origin in retaliation for casualties inflicted by Serbian partisans on the German Army'.[46] The reprisal policy of the military commanders in Serbia was not merely in compliance with the guidelines issued by Field Marshal Keitel on 16 September 1941, which demanded massive reprisals and summary execution of civilians for attacks on German soldiers. But the military commanders had already carried out reprisal executions against Communists and Jews prior to Keitel's instruction, which did not mention Jews explicitly.

In Poland the Army had already acted with the utmost severity against insurgents, but in the war against the Soviet Union the 'elimination of all active and passive opposition' was determined on ideological grounds. Jews and Communists were in fact and *a priori* classified as suspected partisans and therefore shot. In the West it had not been obvious to the military that the Jews would be among Germany's enemies. The intermingling of ideological warfare with military action in the East, which Hitler had advocated and which the Army High Command had consciously accepted for what it assumed would be a short campaign, becomes especially clear in the well-known orders of the commanders of the 6th, 11th and 17th Armies – Field Marshals Reichenau and Manstein, and *Generaloberst* Hoth. They all called for the complete extermination of the Soviet war machine as well as the annihilation of the Jewish–Bolshevik system, and instructed their soldiers to show understanding for the 'necessity of harsh punishment of Jewry'. This could only be interpreted by the troops as justification of the mass executions carried out by the *Einsatzgruppe* C. Being even harsher than Reichenau and Manstein,[47] Hoth turned his soldiers' thoughts to German history, to the alleged guilt of the Jews for the domestic conditions

LIBRARY
College of St. Francis
JOLIET, ILLINOIS

after the First World War: 'The annihilation of those same Jews who support Bolshevism and its organization for murder, the partisans, is a measure of self-preservation.'[48] Manstein concluded his order with an appeal to maintain discipline and to preserve military honour: 'The two ideas could now, it seems, co-exist, in the name of the German "struggle for existence".'[49]

It is not possible to justify the ruthless reprisal policy of the German Army in Russia by citing the need for 'absolute security for the German soldier'. The considerable discrepancy between the number of 'partisans' killed and German casualties on the one hand,[50] and the minor difference between the numbers arrested and those later executed on the other, both point to the ideological basis of the *Wehrmacht* reprisal policy. Orders such as those of Reichenau, Hoth and Manstein 'made against the background of the general terror of offical directives concerning the conduct of the war in the East ensured that the anti-partisan measures conducted by the Army, let alone the SS, took on more the aspect of an extension of National Socialist racial policies than of operations conducted according to military rules and practice'.[51] The disproportion in the *Wehrmacht* reprisal policy is most strikingly demonstrated by one report of the 707th Infantry Division, deployed in White Russia. In one month it shot 10,431 'captives' out of total of 10,940, while in the claimed combat with partisans the division suffered only seven casualties – two dead and five wounded![52] Among the shot 'captives' were former Soviet soldiers, escaped prisoners of war and civilians arrested during mop-up operations.

If we agree with Gordon A. Craig that 'the extermination of the Jews is the most dreadful chapter in German history',[53] then we have to accept that the *Wehrmacht* wrote some pages of this chapter. However, I would not go as far as Christian Streit, who asserts that the Army's implementation of the 'Criminal Orders' contributed decisively to a situation arising in the autumn of 1941 in which the murder of the European Jews became possible.[54] It would be wrong to think that the Final Solution was unleashed because the feared opposition of the Army to the annihilation of Jewry did not materialize. The decisions affecting the fate of the Jews in Europe had already been taken without giving any thoughts to the attitude of the military. The murder of East European Jews was decided in connection with the military preparation for Operation Barbarossa. The decision to murder the European Jews as a whole was taken in the summer of 1941, when Hitler believed that Russia had finally been crushed.

NOTES

1 Karl Dietrich Erdmann, *Die Zeit der Weltkriege* (Stuttgart, 1976), p. 337.
2 Michael Howard in a review of Militärgeschichtliches Forschungsamt (ed.), *Das Deutsche Reich und der Zweite Weltkrieg*, vol. 4, (Stuttgart, 1983), in *English Historical Review*, 99 (1984), p. 843.
3 Quoted by J. P. Stern, *Hitler: The Führer and the People* (Glasgow, 1975), p. 216.
4 Konrad Kwiet, 'Zur historiographischen Behandlung der Judenverfolgung im Dritten Reich', *Militärgeschichtliche Mitteilungen*, 27 (1980), pp. 149–53.
5 See Rolf Elble, ' "Kommissarbefehl" – ausgeführt', *Soldat im Volk*, 11 (November 1984), p. 3 and Hans Roschmann, *Gutachten zu den Verlusten sowjetischer Kriegsgefangener in deutscher Hand von 1941–1945 und zur Bewertung der Beweiskraft des sogenannten 'Dokument NOKW 2125'* (Ingolstadt, 1982), p. 28.
6 Manfred Messerschmidt, *Die Wehrmacht im NS-Staat: Zeit der Indoktrination* (Hamburg, 1969).
7 Christian Streit, *Keine Kameraden: Die Wehrmacht und die sowjetischen Kriegsgefangenen 1941–1945* (Stuttgart, 1978).
8 Helmut Krausnick and Hans-Heinrich Wilhelm, *Die Truppe des Weltanschauungskrieges. Die Einsatzgruppen der Sicherheitspolizei und des SD 1938–1942* (Stuttgart, 1981); Jürgen Förster, 'Das Unternehmen "Barbarossa" als Eroberungs- und Vernichtungskrieg', and 'Die Sicherung des "Lebensraumes" ', in Militärgeschichtliches Forschungsamt, *Das Deutsche Reich* (as in n.2), pp. 413–47 and pp. 1,030–78.
9 Manfred Messerschmidt, 'The Wehrmacht and the Volksgemeinschaft', *Journal of Contemporary History*, 18 (1983), p. 735.
10 Quoted in ibid., p. 736.
11 Quoted by Matthew Cooper, *The Phantom War: The German struggle against Soviet partisans 1941–1944* (London, 1979), p. 6. See *Das Deutsche Reich* (as in n. 2), p. 427.
12 Quoted by Förster, 'Das Unternehmen "Barbarossa" ' (as in n. 8), pp. 416–17.
13 ibid., p. 423.
14 Quoted in ibid., pp. 445–6.
15 Cooper, *Phantom War* (as in n. 11), p. 21.
16 Quoted by Förster, 'Das Unternehmen "Barbarossa" ' (as in n. 8), p. 446.
17 Quoted by Omer Bartov, 'The Barbarisation of Warfare: German Officers and Soldiers in Combat on the Eastern Front, 1941–1945', PhD thesis, St Antony's College, Oxford, 1983, p. 170.
18 Quoted by Förster, 'Das Unternehmen "Barbarossa" ' (as in n. 8), p. 429.
19 ibid., pp. 435–6.
20 ibid., pp. 432 and 438.

21 Quoted in ibid., pp. 441–2.
22 See Streit in Chapter 1 of this volume, p. 3.
23 Quoted by Streit, *Keine Kameraden* (as in n. 7), p. 90.
24 Quoted in ibid., p. 100.
25 See Roschmann, *Gutachten* (as in n. 5), pp. 25–8; Alfred Streim, *Die Behandlung sowjetischer Kriegsgefangenen im 'Fall Barbarossa'* (Heidelberg, 1981), pp. 244–5; Joachim Hoffmann, 'Die Kriegsführung aus der Sicht der Sowjetunion', in *Das Deutsche Reich* (as in n. 2), p. 730, n. 71.
26 Quoted by Alexander Dallin, *German Rule in Russia 1941–1945: A Study of Occupation Policies* (London, 1957), pp. 417 and 421–2.
27 Krausnick and Wilhelm, *Die Truppe des Weltanschauungskrieges* (as in n. 8), p. 621.
28 Quoted by Förster, 'Das Unternehmen "Barbarossa"' (as in n. 8), pp. 438–9.
29 Orders of 25 June and 30 June 1941. Quoted by Bartov, 'The Barbarisation of Warfare' (as in n. 17), pp. 200–1.
30 Ernst Nolte, *Der Faschismus in seiner Epoche* (Munich, 1963), p. 437; Streim, *Die Behandlung sowjetischer Kriegsgefangener* (as in n. 25), pp. 52–3; and Heinrich Walle, 'Ein Rundgang durch die Ausstellung', in Militärgeschichtliches Forschungsamt (ed.), *Aufstand des Gewissens: Militärischer Widerstand gegen Hitler und das NS-Regime 1933–1945* (Herford, 1984), p. 96.
31 Affidavit of 12 April 1948 by Helmut Kleikamp, intelligence officer of the Army Group 'South' in 1941, Institut für Zeitgeschichte, Munich; Georg Meyer (ed.), *Generalfeldmarschall Wilhelm Ritter von Leeb: Tagebuchaufzeichnungen und Lagebeurteilungen aus zwei Weltkriegen* (Stuttgart, 1976), p. 61, n. 240.
32 Heinz Guderian, *Erinnerungen eines Soldaten* (Heidelberg, 1951), p. 138; Roschmann, *Gutachten* (as in n. 5), Annex 3.
33 Bundesarchiv-Militärarchiv, Freiburg i. Br.: RH 21–2/v. 638. For the reports of the other Panzer Groups see Förster, 'Die Sicherung des "Lebensraumes"' (as in n. 8), p. 1,064.
34 Bundesarchiv-Militärarchiv: LII. Korps, 16041/43–45 and 16041/47. Roschmann supports his assertion with the Quartermaster's records and leaves aside the reports of the intelligence officer.
35 Halder diary, entry of 21 September 1941. Quoted by Förster, 'Die Sicherung des "Lebensraumes"' (as in n. 8), p. 1,063; Bundesarchiv-Militärarchiv, Freiburg: RH 21–2/v. 658.
36 Bundesarchiv-Militärarchiv: RH 21–3/v. 423.
37 Bundesarchiv-Militärarchiv: RH 26–12/246.
38 See Förster, 'Die Sicherung des "Lebensraumes"' (as in n. 8), pp. 1,068–9.
39 Quoted by Bartov, 'The Barbarisation of Warfare' (as in n. 17), p. 205. See Hans Meier-Welcker, *Aufzeichnungen eines Generalstabsoffiziers 1939–1942* (Freiburg, 1982), p. 166 (20 June 1942).
40 Messerschmidt, 'The Wehrmacht and the Volksgemeinschaft' (as in n. 9), p. 736.

41 Quoted by Cooper, *Phantom War* (as in n. 11), p.56.
42 Quoted by Förster, 'Die Sicherung des "Lebensraumes"' (as in n. 8), pp. 1,036–7.
43 Christopher R. Browning, 'Wehrmacht Reprisal Policy and the Mass Murder of Jews in Serbia', *Militärgeschichtliche Mitteilungen*, 33 (1983), p. 38.
44 Orders of 12, 23 and 25 July 1941. Quoted by Förster, 'Die Sicherung des "Lebensraumes"' (as in n. 8), pp. 1,037–9.
45 ibid., p. 1,055.
46 Browning, 'Wehrmacht Reprisal Policy' (as in n. 43), p. 39.
47 See Cooper, *Phantom War* (as in n. 11), Appendices 4 and 5.
48 Quoted by Förster, 'Die Sicherung des "Lebensraumes"' (as in n. 8), pp. 1,052–3.
49 Messerschmidt, 'The Wehrmacht and the Volksgemeinschaft' (as in n. 9), p. 735.
50 See Timothy P. Mulligan, 'Reckoning the Cost of People's War: The German Experience in the Central USSR', *Russian History*, 9 (1982), pp. 31–3.
51 Cooper, *Phantom War* (as in n. 11), p. 56.
52 See Förster, 'Die Sicherung des "Lebensraumes"' (as in n. 8), pp. 1,055–6.
53 Gordon A. Craig, *Germany 1866–1945* (Oxford, 1978), p. 749.
54 Streit in Chapter 1 of this volume, p. 2.

3

Resistance and Resignation in Nazi Concentration and Extermination Camps*

FALK PINGEL

Between 1933 and 1945 over half a million detainees died in Nazi concentration camps. This figure is only an approximation. Still less certain is the number of deportees – overwhelmingly Jewish – who were killed in extermination camps set up expressly for the purpose. It has been estimated that at least 2.2 million Jews were murdered in Belzec, Sobibor, Treblinka and Chelmno; perhaps as many again were selected on arrival at Auschwitz and Majdanek for immediate despatch to the gas chambers.[1]

How, in view of such figures, could there be any question of resistance? How could resistance possibly be offered, and by whom?

The SS controlled the social interaction of concentration camp inmates, allowing them little room for initiative; but although this was intended to prevent mutual support, not to mention illegal activity against the guards, there were always some who stood up to the oppressive regime. Early tribute to this resistance was paid in the first report to appear in the English press when the camps were liberated.[2] Closer enquiry into the conditions that favoured resistance soon makes it clear that the attitude of concentration camp inmates cannot be studied without taking into account the way in which the camps themselves developed. To a more limited extent this also applies to the extermination camps in the narrower sense, although these had a shorter history, lasting only from 1941 to 1944.

Far from remaining static, between 1933 and 1945 the concentration camps underwent considerable changes in size, function and internal organization. These changes were connected with general developments in the National Socialist system of domination. Four periods can be distinguished:

*Translated by J. Sondheimer.

30

1 'Seizure of power' and stabilization of the system, 1933–1936;
2 Preparation for war and the *Blitzkrieg* of the early war years, 1936–1941;
3 'Total' war, 1942–1944;
4 Break-up and final overthrow of the system, autumn 1944 to May 1945.[3]

This study therefore begins with an outline history of the concentration camps and of the corresponding phases in the development of Nazi domination, from which the opportunities for resistance open to inmates at each period should become clear. The following sections deal with the social and political prerequisites for resistance and describe some of the forms taken by resistance. In the last section, special attention is paid to the problem of Jewish resistance.

I

THE HISTORY OF THE CAMPS AND
THE DEVELOPMENT OF RESISTANCE

The setting up of the first concentration camps, which began in March 1933, was a consequence of the mass arrests that followed the Reichstag fire and the outlawing of working-class organizations (the Communist Party, trade unions, the Social Democratic party) in the spring of that year. The connection with one of the aims central to the Nazi seizure of power is obvious. In the immediate aftermath of the Reichstag fire, on the night of 27–28 February 1933, the first to be arrested in their thousands and put into hastily contrived provisional camps were the Communists; after 1 May it was the turn of trade unionists and ultimately of many Social Democrats, not to mention artists, intellectuals and politicians from the middle class who refused to acquiesce in the National Socialists' bid for power. Although the camps soon had some inmates sent there ostensibly for non-political reasons – repeated criminal offences, for example – political opponents of the regime formed the great majority at this period. In the early days, up to 80 per cent were Communists. The camp population was therefore relatively homogeneous and for the most part united in its opposition to National Socialism. When it came to fundamental questions of attitude and conduct, this political consensus was of more importance than the disagreements (for example between Communists and Social Democrats) that still persisted from the Weimar period.[4]

31

Living conditions were admittedly harsh but for most inmates they were not as a rule unbearable. Maltreatment was usually experienced only by known individuals especially hated by the Nazis. Jews, who at this date formed little more than 10 per cent of the detainees, were particularly at risk. With the stabilization of the National Socialist regime, many of those arrested in the early months were allowed to leave. Thereafter, and until the end of this first period, the total population of the concentration camps fluctuated between 4,500 and 6,000. About 2,000 of these detainees were housed in the camp at Dachau near Munich, soon looked on by the SS as the model for all concentration camps. Dachau was the only camp that lasted from the beginning to the end of the Nazi regime.

Resistance at this period meant chiefly the protection of detainees singled-out for maltreatment, the nursing of their injuries, and attempts through co-operation to make life a little easier. An individual term of imprisonment, while not predictable, rarely lasted more than a year and everyone was thus able to live in hopes of eventual release. Political resistance in the true sense was possible only outside the camp, and here again it was the Communists who took a lead by forming underground groups and spreading information about the brutalities and acts of persecution perpetrated by the regime, with the aim of keeping opposition alive and to prevent public opinion from hardening into an attitude of indifference or even loyalty to the regime. At this juncture the Communists, like many Social Democrats and members of the bourgeoisie, still hoped for an early overthrow of the Nazi regime. The knell to such hopes was sounded in 1935 when, by means of intensive police round-ups, interrogations and informers, the *Gestapo* (Secret State Police) tracked down many of the resistance groups, with especially damaging effect on the Communist resistance, which until then had been remarkably successful in maintaining their clandestine organizations. Far from being overthrown, thanks to the *de facto* coalition formed by the National Socialist Party, big business, and the Army, not forgetting the conservative bureaucracy, the Nazi leadership was now in a position to pursue an aggressive foreign policy; as a consequence, the persecution on the home front became more intense.

The second period, starting in 1936, saw a noticeable worsening in the position of detainees. With arms production and war in prospect, new and much larger camps were set up, capable in some cases of housing up to 6,000 inmates. The most important, apart from Dachau which was correspondingly enlarged, were Buchenwald near Weimar, Sachsenhausen and Ravensbrück (the women's camp), both near Berlin, and Mauthausen near Linz, set up in 1938 after the 'takeover' of Austria.[5] The Four-Year Plan, evolved in 1936 and calling for industry and the armed forces to be placed on a war footing by 1940, added an economic incentive to the extension of the concentration camp system. In 1937 and 1938 assorted batches of so-called 'a-socials' (vagrants, prostitutes and persons deemed to be work-shy) and persistent criminal offenders were sent to the concentration camps where they were put to work, alongside the other inmates, in quarries, in factory workshops attached to the camps and on the construction of new camps.

The success of intimidation in foreign policy, as proved by the annexation of Austria and the Sudetenland, was accompanied by a stepping-up of economic and police persecution of the Jewish population. In 1937 there had already been an increase in the proportion of Jewish detainees in concentration camps; this upward trend reached a momentary peak as a result of the mass arrests following the pogrom of 9 November 1938, when more than 30,000 Jews were despatched to concentration camps in the space of a few days. The majority, however, were released within a few months with instructions to emigrate.

After the invasion of Austria the camps began to receive foreign detainees, although Austrians were regarded by the Nazis as 'Reich Germans'. Following the outbreak of war, the influx of prisoners from occupied countries brought about a rapid increase in the proportion of foreigners, and Germans gradually came to be in a minority. Polish prisoners, who formed the largest group of foreign nationals, were detained in concentration camps set up for the purpose on Polish territory: one was at Stutthof, near Danzig, another at Auschwitz, in the neighbourhood of the manufacturing town of Katowice.[6] When the war started, the camps had about 24,000 inmates; by 1942 this number had risen to around 60,000.

With rearmament and war, efforts intensified to structure the internal regime in Germany in accordance with the Nazi theory of race; as a consequence, the ideological test became increasingly exclusive and the categories of persons who failed it correspondingly more numerous. The 'enemy-concept' was broadened to include not merely the regime's long-standing and, as it were, 'official opponents' – the political and other representatives of the working-class movement – but also elements deemed to be ideologically and hence 'racially' inferior; whether or not they were actively hostile to National Socialism as a political system was immaterial.

The murderous face of this ideology first showed itself in the plan, initiated during the early months of the war, for the extermination of the mentally sick. These victims met their deaths in especially fitted-out establishments, but the intensified political and ideological persecution that followed the outbreak of war also made its mark on the concentration camps.[7] In the face of an ever-increasing camp population, food and living conditions deteriorated to such an extent that many inmates were doomed to die from that cause alone. Prisoners belonging to certain categories were all but starved and made to work till they dropped. This treatment was meted out in particular to prisoners with a history of stubborn resistance outside the camp, who were therefore considered an especial threat, and to those regarded by the SS as racially inferior. Worst affected were the Jewish and Polish prisoners. Out of 2,000–2,500 predominantly Jewish prisoners from Austria and Poland who were transported to a tented camp at Buchenwald in September 1939, only about 600 were still alive in January 1940. At Mauthausen, which the SS used as a punitive camp and where the regime was exceptionally harsh, the SS camp doctor registered 6,591 deaths 'from natural causes' in 1941, enough to have all but extinguished the camp within a year had not the original 8,000 or so inmates been more than replaced by some 16,000 new arrivals.[8]

In these years of rising mortality, behaviour was dictated by the sheer anxiety to survive. Prisoners concentrated their energies on the day-to-day struggle for food and on efforts to be allocated to a work detachment and barrack block, which would have given them some protection against maltreatment. Relations between prisoners had become vastly more complicated. Persons of differing nationality and social class and of widely varying political viewpoints were crowded together in their thousands under conditions of great material deprivation. It had become harder to reach a common understanding on the need to help prisoners especially at risk by giving them food taken from the rations of the better nourished or by finding them lighter work at the expense of those still strong enough for heavier tasks. It was now more common for prisoners to seek privileges for themselves, ignoring their weaker comrades, and to collaborate with the SS. Betrayals in return for material rewards were not unknown. At this particular time, when there was most need for solidarity and mutual support, the danger of betrayal was in fact much greater than in the earlier period. As far as social and material conditions were concerned, the years 1940–42 were thus the worst for many prisoners.

Gradual improvement set in only during the following period. The Nazis' lack of success with their concept of a *Blitzkrieg* against the Soviet Union and the heavy losses sustained at the front had made it necessary to call up more men for the forces. To fill their places in the arms factories, the SS turned increasingly to prison labour; this meant that some relaxation of the camp regime was unavoidable, at least in the case of prisoners doing work requiring advanced technical equipment – aircraft production, for example. Deaths for the year 1943 fell noticeably below the average and this trend continued in some instances well into 1944, although the local number of prisoners had leapt by mid-year from about 60,000 to over half a million. Of these new prisoners, by far the largest number came from occupied countries, mostly from the Soviet territories. Further extensions were needed to the concentration camp system. In the large camps these took the form of numerous annexes directly adjoining the industrial plants in which the prisoners were set to work.

The goal of political and economic expansion, pursued by the Nazi leadership at this period through the mobilization and shameless exploitation of material resources and a captive labour force, was not the only objective. Just as thoroughgoing was the ideological campaign on the home front, which was carried into all the areas under Nazi military control; for the Greater Reich at which the Nazis aimed was not only to be unrivalled in extent and military strength, it was also to be based on an internal order inherently different from that of a mere military dictatorship. War with the Soviet Union at last made it possible for the Nazi leadership to merge their conception of internal rule with their policy of expansion and to pursue both aims with equal vigour. For this was their chance, or so they surmised, finally to demolish Marxism as a political system and thus acquire a space, stretching from the North Sea to the Urals, in which to erect the National Socialist racist state, devoid of Communists and Jews. The attack on the Soviet Union was the point on which anti-Marxism, anti-semitism and the quest for *Lebensraum* all converged, just as Hitler had projected in his book *Mein Kampf*. In practice, he had been unable hitherto to give these aims equal priority, having been obliged to take some account of the various power groupings in the National Socialist system. In the war against the Soviet Union everything was at stake: achievement of the Nazis' Greater Reich or total defeat.

Concentration camps were involved in the mass extermination of the Jewish population right from the start. In August 1941 Himmler summoned Höss, then camp commandant of Auschwitz, to a personal interview and informed him that extermination equipment was to be installed at Auschwitz.[9] Death by shooting, the method employed by the *Einsatzgruppen* operating behind the front lines, was to be replaced at Auschwitz by the use of poison gas. The process was already known to the SS from its use in the so-called 'euthanasia' operations carried out on the mentally sick; some of the personnel involved were transferred to the occupied part of Poland, to apply their expertise to an extermination programme conceived on a much larger scale. The first experimental gassings probably took place at Auschwitz early in September. They were carried out in two rickety buildings made over for the purpose; the gas chambers proper, which were installed in two former farmhouses well away from the camp, did not become operative until 1942, the one in January and the other in June. From the start of 1942, trains carrying Jewish deportees arrived continuously at Auschwitz. They were met by doctors and other SS personnel, who immediately proceeded with the process of 'selection': as a rule, the old, the very young and the infirm went straight to the gas chambers, while anyone who still seemed capable of work was sent to the camp, in most cases to Birkenau, a section of the camp originally designed to receive more than 100,000 Soviet prisoners of war. With the Russian campaign going badly for the Nazis, the *Wehrmacht* had been unable to supply the SS with as many prisoners as anticipated; their place on the labour gangs therefore had to be filled by 'worker Jews', as they were known in SS terminology. This was still no protection against eventual gassing, since at Auschwitz there was also an internal process of 'selection' and anyone who became chronically ill and unfit for work was discarded by the SS an an encumbrance.

The history of Lublin-Majdanek was similar. The camp had been set up in 1941 to take Soviet prisoners of war; but like Birkenau, and for the same reasons, Majdanek soon began to receive prisoners of other types and became a standard concentration camp. It was used chiefly for Polish prisoners, Jewish and non-Jewish. From April 1942, the Jewish transports were subjected to 'selection'; at first, those singled out for death were shot, but here too gas chambers were soon installed, in September or October of the same year.[10]

The involvement of these particular camps in mass extermination arose from the fact that both were located within the territory of the *Generalgouvernement*, which formed the kernel of permanently installed extermination sites within the National Socialist power orbit. In occupied Soviet territory, extermination was carried out by the *Einsatzkommandos* or by the employment of mobile gassing chambers: under this system the Jewish victims were penned into a van-like structure on the back of a lorry and gassed by fumes led in from the motor's exhaust.[11] The front inside the Soviet Union was never stable enough for the Nazis to risk setting up permanent installations there, because of the time they would have taken to destroy. This was why extermination sites were concentrated in the *Generalgouvernement*, so that 'the entire Jewish operation may be completed with all possible speed, without having to be held up even for a day by difficulties of any kind'.[12]

Between late 1941 and mid-1942, three more camps were set up in the Lublin district. They had no connection with the camps already mentioned and were the responsibility of the local SS police chief, Odilo Globocnik. With a labour force of less than 500, Globocnik built the three camps – Belzec, Sobibor and Treblinka – for the sole purpose of gassing the Jewish population. All that they contained was a series of gas chambers and the crematoria in which the corpses were burned, with just a few barrack blocks to house the SS personnel and their prisoner assistants; the latter, numbering a few hundred, were deportees who had been picked out by the SS and made to help in processing the transports and burning the bodies. Belzec, Sobibor and Treblinka were thus not in fact camps but factories whose output was death. From the outset, because they were eyewitnesses to the extermination process, the assistants were themselves killed off at varying intervals, sometimes after only a few weeks.[13]

The development of the concentration camp system in this third period was as full of contradictions as the war aims themselves. The rigour with which the occupied countries were kept under control had the result that anyone who aroused even the suspicion of sympathizing with the resistance was sent to a concentration camp and thereby withdrawn from the civilian labour force; such people were then supposed to be brought back into productive work as part of the captive labour force. But some of these camps had in addition been given the task of exterminating part of the subject population. No notice was taken of the argument that the labour force was being deprived of needed recruits, except in so far as a proportion of the Jews in Auschwitz and Majdanek did not proceed directly to the gas chambers. Instead they were sent to the camps, where they were so brutally treated that the majority had no chance of survival. With trainloads of fresh deportees constantly arriving, there were always replacements. Birkenau was usually so full that the SS could not hope to organize work for all the inmates.

The tendency for conditions of confinement to improve during the third period thus did not extend to Jewish detainees, whose situation was worsened by the threat of mass extermination and by moves to herd them into a small number of camps; in October 1942

Himmler had given orders for all Jewish detainees held in concentration camps on Reich territory to be sent to Auschwitz or Majdanek. Auschwitz, where standards of living differed according to the status of the detainees, reflected with particular clarity the contradictions in the Nazi war aims. Inmates of the old main camp belonged to a relatively privileged class, made up of non-Jewish detainees who took a share in the camp administration or had jobs in the most sought-after workshops, whereas the best that the mass of detainees in Birkenau could hope for, in a war of all against all, was to keep hold, at least for a time, on their literally naked existence. It is hardly surprising that resistance was stronger in the main camp than in Birkenau, or that conditions in Birkenau produced widespread resignation.

The resistance-minded prisoners saw to it that changes for the better were turned to their advantage. Thus when the SS ceased to make distinctions in their treatment of prisoners working in the arms factory, which up till then had in some cases been quite marked, this was followed by a lowering of the social and material barriers that in the past had often been a cause of misunderstanding. By degrees, groups that had been distinct started to come together. Underground circles, whose membership as a rule was exclusively party political or national in composition, became willing from 1943 onwards to set up joint steering committees to agree on all sorts of illegal activities. Coming from a body of this kind, decisions to help particular classes of detainees were less likely to arouse jealousy or suspicion. As resistance activity became international, its objectives were broadened to include sabotage and preparation for escape attempts, with the aim of establishing contact with resistance groups outside the camp and if possible to make the public aware of the crimes being committed inside them. These considerations applied with particular force to Auschwitz and Majdanek, where news of the defeats inflicted on the German armies, first on the Eastern front and later in Italy and the West, aroused hopes of liberation and provided the inmates with a real incentive to step up their resistance, so much so that in the final phase of the camps' existence it was even possible to contemplate an armed uprising – the impetus coming in this instance from prisoners in the extermination camps.

A retrospective glance at the evolution of the camp system and of the inmates' attitudes shows that resistance passed through several distinct stages, broadening in scope from one period to the next.

At the start, resistance took the form of assistance given by one individual to another: sharing a food parcel with someone not in receipt of extra nourishment from this source (which was usually forbidden to Jewish and Soviet prisoners), taking the place at work of a fellow-inmate too exhausted to carry on, and so on. Such actions were of course not aimed directly at the enemy, the SS; but, by thwarting the intentions behind the strict regulation of camp life and the attempt of the SS to distinguish between various categories of detainee, they kept alive and strengthened the inmates' will to resist. These individual gestures can therefore be counted as having paved the way for active resistance, as did the collective activities whose immediate aim was to foster a sense of community and dispel mutual distrust: theatrical productions, secret study circles in which inmates instructed one another in the history of their own countries and their resistance movements, clandestine memorial services for victims of the Nazi regime.[14]

Activities of this kind figured at the start of every resistance group, surrounding it with the cloak of solidarity and security that was needed as a protection against betrayal by fellow-prisoners and discovery by the SS. The resistance of the first period limited itself as a rule to actions whose purpose was to ensure that, as far as possible, detainees left the camp in a fit state to continue the struggle against National Socialism and with their will to resist unbroken. In the second period, even this minimum of illegal activity was very difficult to sustain, because of the blight cast on attempts at co-operation by the increasing acuteness of the struggle for survival. Furthermore, many detainees were not free from prejudices – nationalist, political or social – which were played upon by the SS, who openly favoured inmates they classed as German and Aryan. It should be stressed that in camps inside Germany it was German Communists who, having been pioneers in the formation of resistance groups, also acted as intermediaries between resistance cells formed by other nationalities, which were often operating in isolation, and so helped to form the habit of co-operation that during the third period established itself by degrees in all the camps. In this second period, however, individual groups still tended to be more interested in protecting themselves and their own identity than in joint action with other groups.

The mention of groups shows that we have already reached the second stage, when resistance ceased to be simply a matter of individuals coming to the aid of fellow-prisoners in trouble; such behaviour doubtless recurred, but its effect would always be limited. The only way for individuals to succeed in thwarting the intentions of the SS for any length of time was by seeking the protection of a larger group and the benefits it afforded: cover for illegal activity, a supply of food adequate to the needs of the group as a whole, and access to the work detachments offering most scope for resistance. Several forms of resistance – escape and sabotage for example – could scarcely be attempted without help from other people, if they were to have any prospect of success.

The second stage of resistance was therefore also marked by a tendency for groups to be formed on conspiratorial lines. For obvious reasons, these could not be highly organized, especially at first. Members of the same political party who were already known to each other before their detention might get together and discuss joint action. This led in time to regular meetings and ultimately to the formulation of specific objectives. In the early days, when the camp community was more or less homogeneous and had little reason to be afraid of internal enemies, such discussion could be fairly informal. In the socially divided camp of the second period, however, banding together in groups became essential not only for undercover work but equally for anyone with an active concern for his own survival. Only in the final phase, with the camps and the SS system both on the point of collapse, could the resistance movement abandon some of its caution and identify itself in the camp more or less openly as the enemy of the SS, since by this time it commanded at least the passive support of the prisoners as a whole.

Then, and only then, did the conditions become ripe for the third stage of resistance: an open trial of strength with the SS in the form of armed revolts. It is probable that, towards the end, more and more prisoners suspected the existence of underground circles and tacitly accepted their role in the regulation of camp affairs. Even so, the resistance groups could not as a rule contemplate going into action until the regime seemed, from the close approach of the fighting, to be at its last gasp, for it was only then that they could be sure of attracting the necessary support from prisoners not previously in the know.

II
SOCIAL AND POLITICAL CONDITIONS
FAVOURING RESISTANCE

Sustained resistance depended on the possession of precise information about the way the camp was organized, the number of guards and their tours of duty, the military situation outside the camp, and so on. Groups preparing to resist therefore had to gather such information. Here they were helped by opportunities actually created by the SS, since to cut down on the number of guards the SS entrusted certain supervisory and disciplinary functions to the prisoners. Each block and work detachment had at its head a prisoner known as the block senior or *Kapo*, and the prisoners' hierarchy was topped by the camp senior. Prisoners were also used to perform administrative duties, such as maintaining the card index of prisoners' names or assigning prisoners, on SS instructions, to work detachments and to transports destined for a camp where labour was short. Prisoners working in the kitchens or the clothing store could keep themselves and their comrades supplied with extras in the way of food and clothing; articles of value (jewellery taken from prisoners on admission, for example) could be acquired in similar fashion and used to bribe SS men to cover up escapes, and so on. So, as well as having advantages for the prisoners who performed these duties, the system was potentially of benefit to the camp as a whole. It had its disadvantages, however. Prisoners who performed these duties ('*Funktionshäftlinge*' as they were called) had to act on instructions from the SS and were therefore in danger of being regarded by their fellow-prisoners as SS lackeys. In Auschwitz, for example, they were in the position of deciding between life and death, because when an SS doctor gave orders for a specified number of prisoners to be gassed, it was left to the hospital orderlies and their *Kapos* to pick out the victims. This example of collaboration with the SS, as distinct from co-operation for the benefit of fellow-prisoners, shows the system in its other aspect. In the second period of the camps' history this aspect tended to be uppermost, because, with the political prisoners forming a smaller proportion of the camp population, the SS turned for preference to prisoners in the 'criminal' category, on the assumption that they could more easily be manipulated.

Prisoners in contact with the resistance therefore had to weigh the pros and cons carefully before they accepted particular responsibilities. It was in any case exceedingly difficult to conceal illegal activities from the SS and treacherously inclined *Funktionshäftlinge* without cover from a like-minded group, especially when the positions were filled by prisoners indifferent to the aims of the political resistance and ready to ape the terrorizing tactics of the SS.

During the early years of the war in particular, political prisoners had to contend with other groups, belonging usually to the criminal category, who were as interested as they were in occupying positions of responsibility but who intended to use them, often enough, to improve their own lot. Aware that these positions were frequently exploited for purposes not conducive to the common good

41

and that they were the object of contention between rival groups, many prisoners were positively opposed to the system: they felt themselves doubly oppressed, in the first place by the SS, in the second by their prisoner assistants. Even where the assistants in fact belonged to the resistance, many prisoners remained in ignorance of their illegal activity and so could not appreciate that they themselves stood to benefit from action taken by *Funktionshäftlinge* under cover of their official duties. If, on the whole, fewer prisoners were beaten, if the treatment prescribed by the SS for different categories of prisoners was applied in a milder, less discriminatory form, if medicines intended exclusively for the benefit of SS personnel found their way to sick prisoners, these were the kind of gradual improvements that in the end made it possible for this or that individual prisoner to stay alive. There were prisoners, however, who refused to seek such positions on principle, having no desire to carry out responsibilities under a system created by the SS. Indeed, how far anyone joined in camp activities in general was also at bottom a moral problem, since this again involved conforming to conditions laid down by the SS. When faced with this particular dilemma, there were some prisoners who remained so undecided between conformity and resistance that they ended by being more or less permanently excluded from the camp's collective life.[15]

That there would be differences in the capacity of detainees to survive and resist was clear from the moment of admission. Many were shocked beyond belief by what they experienced during their first few days in the camp, by the total absence of justice and by the complete disregard for human personality made so evident in the arbitrary beatings and other forms of inhuman and degrading treatment. The idea that people could do such things, and equally that they could be endured, was outside their experience. It helped, of course, to have a sound physical constitution, but this by itself was not enough to carry a newly admitted prisoner through the rigours of the early days. Psychological stamina was just as important, since it determined how far prisoners were able to endure the contempt, the slights to their dignity, the feelings of personal isolation that they experienced in their encounters with the SS. Appeals to more experienced prisoners for explanation of this behaviour, or indeed for protection, again met with a rebuff; for this was proof that the newcomers had not yet been initiated into the camp's narrow and closely guarded network of communications and hence represented a danger to anyone who took their part. Help had to be sought secretly, not in full view of the SS. Finding the conduct of the SS and of their fellow-prisoners equally unpredictable, newcomers were left so completely disoriented that, unless they very quickly managed to get their bearings, both their physical and emotional state would soon deteriorate.

Very few newcomers possessed the particular mental and practical skills needed to help them adjust to camp life. Experiences, aspirations and modes of behaviour that prior to detention had contributed to self-esteem might now make them vulnerable. The first lesson to be learned was how to behave without attracting the notice of the SS, because this was always dangerous. Some conformity with camp rules was required before it became possible to attempt even the smallest infringements. To withstand the daily pressures of camp life, prisoners needed practical skills, or at any rate the aptitudes, social and physical, that would enable them to work in a team, become accustomed to heavy labour or earn them a place, by reason of their linguistic or technical knowledge, in the munitions factory or on the staff of the camp.

Prisoners' ability to stand up to camp conditions, and their degree of success in making the necessary adjustment without abandoning ideas of resistance, depended to a large extent on their experiences prior to detention. Newcomers already involved with an illegal group (political or religious) naturally started off in a better position than most, because they could count on being recognized by contacts in the camp. Initiated by them into camp life and the right way to behave, they soon became fairly sure of their bearings. Groups involved in the resistance tried to see to it that prisoners they could trust were employed on duties in the 'reception' area, where they could support newcomers shown by their admission forms to be one of themselves.

The group contacts that were so important as a means of integration into camp life nearly always arose from prisoners' previous social and ideological connections. Newcomers, as we have seen, were apt to be unsure and to act in ways that made them conspicuous; it was precisely for this reason that experienced prisoners seldom came openly to their aid. For them to depart from this rule there had to be some unusual circumstance or some special link with the prisoner in question. The ties that bound prisoners together were of greatly varying character and did not have to be political. For example, prisoners in the criminal category – precisely the ones the SS preferred to place in positions of responsibility – banded together in small but closely knit groups under whose patronage much-desired privileges such as extra food or a good sleeping place were reserved for individual prisoners from the same milieu as themselves. Small groups of this kind could in some

43

circumstances set the tone of an entire block or work detachment. Prisoners in the criminal category tended to regard the *Funktionshäftling* system as a variant of the pecking order they were used to in ordinary prisons, and to exploit it in the same way. Since it was the most assertive, and regrettably enough often the least scrupulous, among them who volunteered their services to the SS, competition from this source presented the most dangerous threat to prisoners anxious to use the system to mitigate the arbitrary character of the SS regime. In the concentration camp context, determination to hold one's own was thus not necessarily synonymous with resistance: it could lead equally well to the manipulation of SS rules by prisoners for the purpose of their own survival, regardless of the cost to others. The will to survive was of course no less essential to anyone engaging in resistance, but the logic of resistance also dictated a preparedness to sacrifice one's life for the sake of achieving some specific goal.

Group contacts and anti-Nazi opinions were undoubtedly among the factors most instrumental in enabling prisoners to achieve the required conformity with camp regulations without incurring the danger of having to collaborate with the SS. Both were often facilitated by prisoners' political or religious convictions. The goals set by a person's principles are often the clue to their actions. So if prisoners valued their goals so highly that they had to pursue them even while in detention – or indeed precisely for that reason – they had a built-in protection against surrendering to apathetic resignation. How far in practice such beliefs were a helpful influence in the concentration camps depended on their context. For example, the inner strength and coherence of the small band of Jehovah's Witnesses attracted admiration from many prisoners who did not share their convictions; yet members of the sect were forbidden by their religious beliefs to take any part in active opposition to the SS, since they interpreted the Nazi regime as a sign that the end of the world, to which their creed looks forward, was near. On the other hand, they could be steadfast in their refusal to take part in arms production, and in their rejection of military service, which was generally the original reason for their detention, and were prepared to endure brutal punishment on that account. The taking of life is strictly forbidden to Jehovah's Witnesses as one of the cardinal principles of their beliefs.

The political beliefs most likely to arouse and sustain attitudes of resistance were obviously those that inspired the most positive conviction that the National Socialist system must and could be overthrown. From the outset, Communists were among the most active opponents of the SS. In several camps, Buchenwald and Sachsenhausen in particular, Communists are known to have struggled long and hard with prisoners in the criminal category over the share-out of positions as *Funktionshäftlinge*; in the bigger camps on Reich territory they had largely succeeded at the start of the third period in gaining the upper hand.[16] At this date the SS themselves had a positive interest in seeing that work detachments were kept up to scratch and that the camp bureaucracy gave at least the superficial appearance of being run under efficient supervision. As a rule the only prisoners willing and competent to fill the bill belonged to the political category, and the SS were prepared to take the risk of making it easier in this way for pockets of resistance to be formed. But political prisoners could never be sure of their safety in such positions. In Sachsenhausen, a *Gestapo* commission that had been called in to investigate suspected sabotage in 1944 received information from informers that led to the discovery of the practical help being given by political *Funktionshäftlinge* to Soviet prisoners of war, whose state initially was one of extreme material privation. As a result of this investigation 27 prisoners were shot and another 102 were sent to the penal camp Mauthausen; many of these had belonged to the hard core of the resistance and had been employed at Sachsenhausen in posts of special importance.

For obvious reasons, prisoners of other nationalities were more likely than Germans to adopt a line of resistance that united prisoners of widely divergent political opinions against the common enemy of their fatherland. Their resistance was therefore not so heavily inclined to the left as in the German groups, which had only a few middle-class members until after the outbreak of war. The first resistance groups to be formed in Auschwitz originated in Polish circles that were both nationalist and conservative and that included officers of the Polish army. In view of this strongly nationalist orientation, it was more than usually difficult at Auschwitz to set up an international co-ordinating committee; the first moves in that direction were made in 1943 by two Austrian Communists and a member of the Polish Socialist Party, Jozef Cyrankiewicz. Veterans of the Spanish Civil War were quick to resume contact with one another in the camps, where they helped to encourage the habits of co-operation they had acquired as members of the International Brigades; this was especially so at Mauthausen, where most of them were congregated.

It was particularly important for foreign prisoners who were activists to see themselves as part of a wider movement, extending far beyond the camp and steadily gaining ground against National

Socialism, rather than as an abandoned and impotent minority, powerless to challenge the tyranny of their present masters, the SS. As a result, they tended to be more eager than German prisoners to advocate forms of resistance carrying the greatest risk – sabotage, mass escapes, open revolt, for example. Polish prisoners in Auschwitz and Majdanek lost no time in making contact with resistance and partisan groups outside the camps, with a view to providing cover for escape attempts, smuggling out information about the concentration camps and the extermination sites, or organizing reinforcements in the event of an uprising. By contrast, contacts between the German resistance and camps on Reich territory were rare.[17] In several camps the planning and execution of armed uprisings was helped by Soviet prisoners of war, many of whom made their military expertise available to the underground movement.

To sum up, three factors were of overriding importance in helping newcomers to recover from their initial shock, to find their bearings, and, finally, having threaded their way through the maze of fragmented and competing hierarchies, to identify the SS as the real enemy to be attacked: practical capability, group contacts, and moral and political principles. The first two were neutral so far as values were concerned, and were chiefly important in the struggle for survival, but the third determined the side they would take in that struggle, whether they would continue to be concerned for their fellow-prisoners or would ignore the common good and fight only for themselves.[18]

Where these factors were lacking, prisoners' chances of being able to withstand the pressures were greatly reduced. Unable to find ways of eking out the meagre rations, they became undernourished, their pace of work slackened and they could not concentrate. This made them an easy target for bullying and maltreatment, which further undermined their power to resist. With no one to protect them, they were assigned to the toughest work detachments or to transports destined for camps where conditions were known to be harsh. Such prisoners became so emaciated that all they could do was to take whatever food was offered to them and go through the motions of working while they could still move and hold a tool in their hands. Constantly pushed around and beaten, they declined into a state of total apathy and inertia, a sign that death was not far off: in camp slang they were known as '*Muselmänner*' (*lit.* Mussulmen). In the spring of 1944 the SS themselves reckoned that out of 67,000 prisoners at Auschwitz as many as 18,000 were 'invalids' – their name for prisoners dying of starvation. The fate of these '*muselmänner*' was in the hands of others, of those who allocated the extra rations and the places on the least hazardous work detachments. Given the circumstances, when the choice lay between prisoners who could use such opportunities to further the cause of resistance and prisoners apparently too far gone even to rally their strength for the fight against the SS, the result was a foregone conclusion. The policy of the resistance was always first and foremost to strengthen their own group and to support prisoners from whom help could be expected in return. By increasing their influence in the camp, it was argued, the circle of those they could help would be correspondingly enlarged. However, the situation at Auschwitz was such that the entire camp could never be covered in this way. Realization of this fact forced the many who were excluded to become resigned and so hastened the process of their decline.

III
FORMS OF RESISTANCE

It might be expected that resistance began most typically as a spontaneous reflex, when a prisoner was first confronted with an example of camp brutality. Yet this was not the case. Just as it was necessary to become accustomed to camp life, so it took time for a would-be resister to recognize where his real opportunities lay. On first being admitted, someone might well come spontaneously to the aid of a prisoner being ill-treated, but he did so not knowing it was forbidden. Swift punishment followed, and like all newcomers he learned that actions regarded as normal in the outside world were treated in the camp as punishable offences. Very few prisoners were so uncompromising as to act in total disregard of camp regulations, and their resistance was inevitably of short duration, since the SS could not allow such behaviour to continue unchecked.

Take for example, the case of Paul Schneider, a Protestant clergyman sent to Buchenwald when he persisted, despite several warnings from the *Gestapo*, in speaking out in his sermons on behalf of persecuted victims of the regime. In Buchenwald he still refused to desist. When consigned by the SS to an underground cell, Schneider raised his voice and delivered his sermon to the prisoners as they assembled in the yard for roll-call, just as though he was standing in the pulpit of his church at home. In the end he was killed by the SS.[19]

Although anyone who had come through the first few weeks was aware that to act on impulse was dangerous and that support from other prisoners was unlikely to be forthcoming, there were times, even in the life of experienced prisoners, when the defences they had erected against the daily brutalities of camp life were pierced by some unforeseen occurrence and they could no longer contain their emotions. At such moments, when the outrage became too much for an individual to bear, resistance came close to desperation. As illustration may be quoted the case of the prisoner on a work detachment in Buchenwald who witnessed the killing of his brother by a member of the SS. If the victim had been anyone else, he would no doubt have closed his eyes to this piece of brutality (and had probably done so in the past). But because it touched him so closely, he singled out this one murder from the others being daily committed – in 1941, when this incident took place, deaths at Buchenwald totalled 1,500 – and denounced the SS man as a murderer, first to the head of camp security and then to the camp commandant. But any hopes of finding in the camp's superiors a court of appeal against the arbitrary action of an SS officer were doomed to disappointment: the arbitrary and unpredictable conduct of the SS was one of the means by which the prisoners were kept under control, because it made them permanently on edge. The complainant was removed to the punishment cells, where he died; the remaining members of the work detachment, all of whom had witnessed the incident, were killed.[20] By making the punishment collective, the SS ensured that no one imitated the individual's courage in protesting. What was done by one was judged to be the responsibility of all. Another reason for the punishment, of course, was the desire of the SS to protect themselves against subsequent inquiries. The prisoner in question had acted entirely on his own and in total disregard of the precautions with which protest in concentration camps had to be hedged. He failed to make any impression on the SS, except in so far as the lives of more prisoners were endangered.

The fact is that, for resistance to be effective over the long term, a high degree of integration and conformity was required, which in turn necessitated so many compromises that there was little outlet for spontaneous outbursts. The resistance did not as a rule dare to display itself openly as an example to previously uncommitted prisoners, which no doubt helps to account for its failure to imprint on the memories of many prisoners the names and deeds of 'heroes' to be handed down to posterity.

From time to time, however, *Funktionshäftlinge* felt compelled, despite their involvement with the resistance, to show the SS that an individual's endurance and his capacity to compromise had their limits. Cases of this kind usually arose when a prisoner whose duties were connected with the administrative routine of the camp was ordered by the SS to carry out in person the sentences on individual prisoners. Harry Naujoks, for example, the German Communist who was camp senior at Sachsenhausen, refused to hang a prisoner recaptured after a failed escape attempt, and Karl Wagner, camp senior at Allach (a subsidiary of Dachau), consistently disobeyed SS orders to administer corporal punishment. Both were Communists and prisoners of long standing, who before their detention had been tenacious in their active opposition to the regime. There is no denying that the attitude of the SS in such cases was ambivalent. While others who behaved like Naujoks and Wagner paid for it with their lives, these two lived to tell the tale.[21] Wagner, it is true, was locked up in the punishment cells and transferred to the main camp (Dachau); but he benefited there from the protection of his comrades and even managed to be reinstated as *Kapo* of a construction detachment. Both were helped by the fact that they based their protest not merely on a personal sense of moral indignation, which they invoked against the SS, but on a definite strategy regarding the performance of camp duties. Wagner, indeed, was able to demonstrate that the resistance–conformity dialectic could be stretched still further. On the one hand, as a senior prisoner with building experience he was useful to the SS; on the other, he made use of his skills to delay completion of a gas chamber in Dachau and thus limited the camp's immediate capacity to carry out exterminations. Here we find the factors of moral strength, disciplined political conviction and specialized technical skills all coming together and giving rise to actions that were undisguisedly to the advantage of prisoners and contrary to the intentions of the SS.

Evasion by SS men of extermination orders was all too rare; after all, their presence in the camps was optional and they were free to leave. Prisoners of course had no such option, but even in Auschwitz there were some who held out in this extremity. One such was Dr Hautval, a French woman doctor who refused to give lethal injections to prisoners unfit for work. Even comrades from the organized resistance could not support her in this attitude, but, having landed in the camp because she had helped Jews in France, Dr Hautval was determined not to have any direct share in responsibility for their deaths. By a stroke of luck, her refusal was accepted by the SS doctor, who had already been involved in a number of compromises with the resistance movement. Steadfastness of this order, however, was shown only by a tiny minority who had been

49

steeled for it by previous involvement in resistance activity and by the strength of their convictions.

At Auschwitz, examples of bravery stood in direct contrast with the everyday emotions of desperation and fear, as can be seen from the following incident, also involving lethal injections, administered in this instance by an SS hospital orderly to those unfit for work. One day, a prisoner who had the job of removing the bodies, noticed that his father was about to be injected, but from fear of being murdered in his place made no attempt at rescue.[22]

The greatest triumph for prisoners was to break through the isolation of the concentration camp. Escape, sabotage and revolt all represented an achievement of this sort, although in different ways, and each of these will now be considered in detail.

Concentration camps had been in existence for only a few months when two detainees succeeded in making their escape and drew attention to what was happening through articles published in newspapers abroad. On the night of 8–9 May 1933, the Communist *Reichstag* deputy Hans Beimler broke out of his prison cell at Dachau with the help of tools provided by a fellow-detainee and party member. Beimler's report on 'Murder camp Dachau' was published in Moscow while its author was still in hiding in Germany. This report was followed by the publication in Czechoslovakia in 1934 of an article by Gerhart Seger, a Social Democrat who had escaped from Oranienburg, near Berlin, the previous year.[23] For all their significance and the attention they attracted, these daring exploits were rarely repeated in the years that followed. The risk of recapture, which carried with it the high probability of death from violent maltreatment or, at a later date, through formal execution, was too great. Moreover, as the Nazi regime became established and tightened its grip, the chances of finding concealment in the population outside were correspondingly reduced. All this goes to explain why little is heard of escape attempts by German prisoners up to and including the early years of the war.

Foreign prisoners, by contrast, took a different attitude from the outset, for they could count on finding shelter in the indigenous population (Polish prisoners in Auschwitz and Majdanek were in this position) or in Reich territory in nearby forced labour camps (this applied in particular to the French, but also to Russians and Poles). Although no continuous statistical record of escapes exists, enough is known to suggest that from 1942 onwards escape attempts were increasing to an extent that posed serious security problems to the camp authorities. In the last period of the camps' existence, the chances of success for Soviet and Polish prisoners may have stood as high as fifty/fifty. The worst placed were Jewish prisoners. For them it was virtually impossible, in Reich territory at least, to find help: thus out of nine Jews who took part in escapes from Dachau between October 1944 and March 1945, only one managed to get clean away, whereas out of an overall total of 99 involved in such escapes, 44 were successful.[24]

It goes without saying that not all escapes were politically motivated. At Auschwitz and Majdanek, however, the connection between escape and resistance was especially close. The resistance group that had formed round the nucleus of a few Polish officers, which was the first to emerge as an entity, had made contact early on with the local Polish resistance. Information about the camp – its layout, personnel and procedures such as 'selection' – could therefore be smuggled out and items such as medicaments for the prisoners smuggled in. Quite extensive publicity was given, unfortunately without the desired effect, to several escapes of Jewish prisoners from Auschwitz early in 1944. Some of these were individual ventures, others were organized by the resistance, but in all cases the aim was to alert the Jewish population and their organizations in Europe and America to the exterminations taking place in Auschwitz and if possible to produce counter-measures from the Allies. A report compiled by two escapers, Alfred Wetzler and Rudolf Vrba, actually gave figures for the number of gassings to date, assembled from information gathered in the camp by experienced prisoners. It was possible to convey the report to the Pope's representative then in Slovakia, and thence by a roundabout route to the government of the United States. It is true to say that as a result the most comprehensive extermination programme ever attempted at Auschwitz, the gassing of the Hungarian Jews, was brought to a halt; the pressure brought to bear on the Hungarian government following these public disclosures was so great that in July 1944 it was decided to send no more transports to Auschwitz. On the other hand, the idea of bombing the extermination sites from the air met with no response from the Allies. When it came to military priorities, the resistance was unable to effect any alteration.[25] The consequences were suffered not only by the prisoners in Auschwitz but equally by the combatants of the Warsaw uprising and their comrades in many other concentration camps, who at the end of the war hoped in vain to see the Allied armies thrusting forward to the camps in order to liberate the inmates. The gas chambers at Auschwitz remained in operation until November 1944 when, with the fighting coming closer, the SS began to dismantle the crematoria with the obvious intention of sending sections of them to concentration camps further from the front, where they could be put to fresh use.

Proof that resistance in the camps, far from being narrowly conceived, embraced the aim of weakening the Nazi regime in general, is most clearly provided by the prisoners' efforts at sabotage. No one's circumstances were improved by engaging in sabotage, which on the contrary carried high risks for those who attempted it. Anyone detected in sabotage could expect to be punished by death and the same often applied to other members of his work detachment.

The most obvious openings for sabotage arose in camps where prisoners were employed on the manufacture of vital but complex pieces of equipment needed for the war effort, as for example in the carbine works at Hamburg-Neuengamme and Buchenwald, in the Heinkel aircraft factory at Sachsenhausen and at Dora, the concentration camp on the edge of the Harz mountains. Dora was originally a subsidiary of Buchenwald. It had been set up as a place in which production of aircraft, essential to the war effort, could be continued in bomb-proof shelters carved out of the southerly slopes of the Harz, when the normal sites became too vulnerable to air attack. By 1944 concentration camp prisoners at Dora were producing two of the key weapons in the armoury of the Third Reich – high-speed fighter planes and V-rockets. Because of its central importance to arms production and its greatly increased size, in October 1944 Dora became an independent camp, with its own ring of smaller satellites, containing all told about 30,000 prisoners.[26]

The easiest forms of sabotage were to waste or mislay materials or to work at an unnaturally slow pace. What was harder was to produce defective finished articles, whose faults would be detected only when they were brought into use at the front. Even so, prisoners in Mauthausen managed without attracting notice to produce rifle parts whose tempering was defective, ensuring thereby that rifles made from them would soon cease to function. However, in instances of sabotage depending on specialist technical knowledge it was often easy to pinpoint the workshop of origin, with obvious risk to the prisoners concerned.

A number of camp workshops turned out so many rejects that special commissions of inquiry were appointed to track the suspected sabotage to its source. As their reports make clear, the SS admitted that production was being seriously impeded by the prisoners. The detailed picture, however, is too complicated to allow a definite figure to be placed on the shortfalls and defects for which sabotage alone was responsible. Under the stress of the war's approaching end, production plants were hastily removed to temporary accommodation, to be started up again with inadequate resources and unskilled personnel. These external cicumstances were sufficient in themselves to bring about a marked deterioration in quality. It should be enough to point out that even the so-called 'miracle weapons' of the Third Reich, which according to propaganda were to be decisive in winning the war, had to be produced in emergency shelters and by prisoners, because the war had exhausted all the normal sources of civilian labour. Two factors – a too hasty start on production and sabotage by prisoners – were thus equally responsible for the fact that the output of V-rockets contained so many duds and that the weapon's destructive power fell short of the military's expectations.

The keenest advocates of really effective sabotage were undoubtedly to be found among the foreign prisoners. Their more cautious German comrades were apt at first to be sceptical, since they feared that the thorough investigations conducted by the *Gestapo* in cases of suspected sabotage, and the collective punishments administered, might lead to the complete exposure of the network which in some camps formed a link between groups of German political prisoners, the resistance, and key positions in the camp's administration. That these fears were justified was proved by the events at Sachsenhausen, to which reference has already been made (p. 45 above) and by what happened at Dora once the *Gestapo* had succeeded (chiefly by means of informers and torture) in exposing several strands of the resistance network: no less than 125 prisoners were executed, amongst them 99 Russians, 16 Poles and 7 Germans, the latter all Communists who had belonged to the inner ring of prisoners directing camp affairs. This happened as late as March 1945.

During 1943 even the prisoners could not remain unaware that the Nazi regime had exceeded its capacity to expand and was having to pull back on nearly every front, as could be gathered in particular from the constant stream of new foreign detainees, amongst whom a significantly large number were prisoners of war. The closer approach of the fighting posed with increasing urgency the question of what would happen to the prisoners if the camps themselves became engulfed in the battle zone. In Auschwitz and Majdanek the most obvious course was to capitalize on existing contacts by joining forces with local partisans in an effort to liberate the camp and the surrounding area. However, the different groups of Polish partisans operating in the Lublin district failed to unite in a common action on behalf of the camp's inmates, with the result that the SS were eventually able to evacuate the camp without hindrance.[27] Inside Auschwitz, the SS managed to trap the contact man between the camp and the partisans whilst he was carrying incriminating material, which meant that the contacts previously established failed to achieve their purpose. Equally abortive was an attempt to smuggle out some of the resistance leaders to organize help from outside; this failed because the prisoners were betrayed by an SS man on whose help they had felt able to rely. A few of those implicated managed to kill themselves before they could be interrogated. The rest were executed. In consequence, the resistance movement in Auschwitz was so greatly enfeebled that open acts of defiance during the final phase were out of the question.[28]

Prisoners detained in camps on Reich territory had just as much reason to prepare themselves against the danger of being caught defenceless as the front line came ever closer, and hence of being killed at the very moment when their liberation was in prospect. They were helped by the fact that prisoners were employed on arms production, which made it possible to accumulate by stealth a very modest store of weapons and ammunition. Plans for an uprising were most fully advanced at Buchenwald, where an international committee headed by German Communists, which had been in existence since 1943, made use of the cover provided by units with official duties in the camp – security, fire protection, etc. – to train an unofficial task force to be the spearhead of an open revolt.

Taking Buchenwald as an example, it should become clear that prisoners prepared to resist continued to face difficult decisions right up to the end. Prisoners in other camps were in a similar situation and reacted in similar ways, but the circumstances at Buchenwald were comparatively speaking more favourable: in other camps the organs of the resistance were less firmly established or else were deprived of continuous leadership, whether by premature evacuation of the camp or by the *Gestapo*'s punitive measures, as was the case at Auschwitz, Sachsenhausen and Dora.

In the camp's last days, however, the distinction between resistance and resignation ceased to be clear-cut even at Buchenwald. Here, as elsewhere, the SS anticipated the arrival of the battle front by starting on a piecemeal evacuation of the prisoners, who were made to march over long distances to other camps, inevitably suffering many casualties on the way. It was therefore virtually impossible to prescribe a uniform line of conduct: was it better, from the resistance point of view, to be included in the march or to be left behind in the camp? The transfers caused the break-up of existing networks, and most of the prisoners left behind were too ill to march and therefore too feeble for active resistance. Conversely, the number of prisoners in camps at the receiving end – which in the winter of 1944–5 briefly included Buchenwald itself – leapt dramatically: at Buchenwald by about 40,000 between December 1944 and February 1945. Disoriented, half-starved, and belonging to no regular work detachment, the new arrivals at Buchenwald were an unknown quantity, so much so that the prisoners' leaders found it hard to determine which of them could safely be relied on in an uprising. On 4 April 1945 the resistance committee nevertheless decided to disobey an SS order summoning all Jews to assemble in the yard used for roll-call. The fact that Jewish prisoners, invariably the ones to receive the worst treatment, were singled out in this way was ominous and enough to cause the prisoners in supervisory positions to withhold their co-operation. On the next and following days the SS were obliged to assemble the evacuation transports by force. The tension between the prisoners' and the SS leadership was further intensified when orders were given for a batch of 46 prisoners to be produced, amongst whom were some the SS rightly suspected of being pillars of the resistance. Rather than hand them over, the prisoners' committee decided to conceal all 46 in the camp; and, out of all the camp's 50,000 inmates, not one came forward to betray their whereabouts. In face of this, the SS did not dare to carry out their original threat of shooting members of the camp security unit if the wanted prisoners were not found.

With this evidence that the SS was open to compromise, the majority view in the prisoners' leadership turned against the idea of going ahead with an armed uprising, although it still had advocates among the French and Soviet prisoners who were next on the list for evacuation. As a substitute, greater efforts were made to delay the departure of the transports by any means short of force. The result was that about 28,000 prisoners left Buchenwald up to the time of its liberation. Those who remained tried by various means to pass information to the US forces as they drew closer, in the hope of encouraging them to speed up their advance and so bring pressure to bear on the SS. Eugen Kogon, one of the 46 prisoners in hiding, was smuggled out with the help of an SS officer and an SS doctor with the idea of sending a telegram to the camp commandant warning against further evacuations; this he did in the name of an English parachute unit he chanced to encounter. It likewise soon became possible to establish a secret radio contact with the American army. On 11 April, when the operations of forward American units could at last be seen from the camp, and the SS, with the exception of a few sentries, had departed, the prisoners occupied the watch towers, cut through the cable carrying current to the electrified fence and overpowered such SS men as remained. Even after the liberation, the prisoners' committee successfully exerted its authority to maintain order in the camp and to ensure that food was fairly distributed, with the result that 21,000 prisoners came out of Buchenwald alive.[29]

At Dachau, where for years the most important of the duties allocated to prisoners had been in the hands of German Social Democrats, an international prisoners' committee was formed only shortly before the camp's liberation. Dachau was used as a receiving camp for evacuation transports from other camps, Buchenwald included, right up to the end. On arrival, as the Dachau prisoners could not fail to notice, some of these transportees died of hunger, either in the camp itself or even at its gates; there was not enough food to go round, so the camp authorities simply left them to their fate. Therefore, when the authorities gave orders that Germans, Russians and Jews were to be sent away from Dachau, it was obvious to many prisoners that it was better for them to stay. With the classification of transportees according to nationality, the split between the prisoners inevitably widened. The camp committee lacked the weight to dissuade the camp police (composed of prisoners) from carrying out its task of assembling the transports, with the result that about 8,000 prisoners were forced to leave. However, with every day that passed the SS grip on the camp was growing weaker, and it was a help to the prisoners when constant air raid alerts ruled out the possibility of further evacuations. As at Buchenwald, efforts were made to enlist outside support. An outside work detachment, to which a number of experienced German prisoners had recently been added, succeeded in escaping in its entirety. One of its members reached an American unit and told its commander of the desperate situation in the nearby concentration camp. Others joined a group of people from the town of Dachau who were willing to surrender the place to the Allies without a struggle. On 28 April they overpowered the local Nazis in the belief that a similar action was being mounted in Munich, from which they expected reinforcements. In this they were deceived. With the revolt thus isolated, the SS found it easy to suppress it. Three of the escapers were killed only one day before the camp was liberated, having been caught just outside the wire where they were trying to clear a passage for prisoners escaping to freedom. American units finally reached the camp on 29 April.[30]

Especially desperate was the plight of camps in which, once the SS had relinquished control, there were no prisoners' organizations competent to fill the power vacuum, and to make arrangements, at least on an emergency basis, for the systematic share-out of food, care of the sick and prevention of private acts of revenge. Bergen-Belsen, for instance, passed its last days in a state of complete anarchy. It had been as good as abandoned by the SS. For months it had acted as a receiving camp for prisoners incapable of work and for evacuees already half-dead on arrival. Before that, Bergen-Belsen had been used almost exclusively for Jewish detainees. There was no internal political organization that might have intervened to impose some discipline. Everyone was left to fight for his own food and his own living space. 'There are no more roll calls. There is no more work. All we can do is die', as it is said in a diary relating to this period. It was thus the chaos of a camp in an advanced state of disintegration, a camp that even the Nazis eventually surrendered without a struggle, that greeted the British troops who entered Bergen-Belsen on 15 April, their first encounter with a major concentration camp.[31]

At Sachsenhausen, where the resistance movement had been fundamentally weakened by the Gestapo's investigations, evacuation was almost total. When Red Army units reached the camp they found only 3,000 prisoners, most of them unable to walk. Since the end of January about 20,000 prisoners had been transferred to other camps; a further 30,000 and more had been evacuated only two days before the camp was liberated. By now it is virtually impossible to reconstruct their fate. Deaths were not as numerous as in the mass evacuations from camps in Polish territory, but even so thousands were shot by the SS, either because they gave up from exhaustion or else for trying to escape. It was May before the main body of evacuees met up with units from the American and Soviet armies.

The reactions of prisoners on the evacuation marches – or death marches, as they called them – once again ranged from resistance to resignation. Physical endurance undoubtedly became a deciding factor, but there were also many prisoners who lacked the resolution and alertness to seize on the right moment to escape; for those who did, the prospects of success were greatest if they had had the forethought to wear extra clothing beneath their prison dress and to come to an agreement with other comrades. One person who managed to escape in this way was Hermann Langbein, an Austrian and a veteran of the Spanish Civil War, who belonged to the innermost ring of the resistance in Auschwitz and was being transported in the autumn of 1944 to a subsidiary of Neuengamme. Today Langbein is one of the few who can still bear witness to the

57

facts of extermination and resistance. It was otherwise for the very many whose strength deserted them as they trudged along the road swarming with prisoners and military transports:

> Each moment some miserable being would drop out of the column and sit himself by the roadside. I shall never forget that man and the way he sat. An SS man comes up to him, revolver in hand, and taps his shoulder. Without turning round, he gets up and follows the SS man. The men with the shovel bring up the rear. A shot, and the SS man and the men with the shovel come back. When I looked at this man, who knew he was going to die, his face was expressionless. The same scene was repeated every 50 metres.[32]

Evacuation fell hardest on the prisoners from the main camp at Neuengamme. Here the hold of the political prisoners on the most important administrative functions had always been relatively tenuous. No contingency plan had been made in the event of the camp's dissolution, although prisoners knew something of the situation elsewhere – for example at Bergen-Belsen, to which some small evacuation transports had already been sent. The risks attendant on an impromptu uprising with only a scant supply of weapons were considered too great – a view not shared, however, by a group of Soviet prisoners. The camp was still being evacuated, column by column, up to 29 April. Most of the prisoners – around 10,000 – were taken aboard three ships moored in the Bay of Lübeck. On 3 May the ships were bombed by English planes, operating, they thought, against their routine targets. Two ships were sunk; 7,000 and more prisoners lost their lives.[33]

IV
RESISTANCE IN THE FACE
OF EXTERMINATION

As we have seen, prisoners in concentration camps whose resistance was linked with the prospect of liberation took time over their preparations, which included cadre formation, consultation and detailed planning. Prisoners deported to extermination centres, by contrast, had almost no chance of preparing themselves in this way. The extermination centres were camouflaged by the SS to present the appearance of work or transit camps. The gas chambers were fitted up to look like shower rooms. The SS and their assistants tailored their behaviour to match, in case of possible resistance. In the initial phase of the extermination programme this deception undoubtedly worked. But during 1942 there came reports from Auschwitz, and more especially from Treblinka, spread by successful escapers and the underground grapevine, that in these camps kidnapped Jews were immediately put to death. After a time, therefore, many must have suspected what lay before them. Yet it was hard for individuals to be certain of the exact point – whether it was the selection process (in Auschwitz and Majdanek) or the moment of disembarkation from the train – from which there was virtually no return: for who could know of the procedures in such detail? From the moment of arrival on the station platform there was precious little scope for individual initiative, given the close surveillance, the narrowness of the fenced-in enclosures and the haste with which the operation was frequently conducted. Whether the deportees knew it or not, the time to decide for or against resistance was already past. Only a few hours or even minutes were needed to unload and strip the deportees before the doors of the gas chambers closed behind them; it was hardly the time for impromptu decisions, if earlier and more favourable opportunities and concealment had been passed by. To make a proper study of resistance to extermination one thus needs to start by examining to what extent Jewish populations in the ghettos made efforts to resist their disenfranchisement and to evade capture. Such an investigation falls outside the scope of this present study, which can therefore deal with only one aspect of Jewish resistance.[34]

One line of escape was to try jumping from the train, which was feasible if the carriages were insecurely fastened and the guards appeared inattentive. As a rule this was possible only for deportees who were on their own. However, the transports tended to be made up of family units, and collective escapes were usually out of the question: how could a mother leave her children or a grown-up son his parents? On the station platform, in the anteroom to the gas chambers, the dilemma was the same. There are several accounts, it is true, of protests and of desperate attempts to galvanize fellow-deportees into making a last-minute stand: at Auschwitz one SS man was actually killed as a result. But usually the guards were quick to isolate the would-be protesters, who were at once taken away to be shot. Our information about such happenings is necessarily sparse, which makes it inadequate as a basis for generalized conclusions. The internal structures and specific conditions that gave rise to active Jewish resistance in the face of extermination emerge more clearly from three episodes which occupy a unique place in the record of concentration camp resistance. These are the revolts that took place in the extermination camps of Sobibor and Treblinka and the resistance mounted by the cremation detachment at Auschwitz-Birkenau.

The number of prisoners employed and held captive in extermination centres was relatively small, ranging from about 600 to at most 1,000 depending on the camp; there was little to choose between conditions at the different sites. They had every reason to be well-acquainted with the extermination machinery, being themselves a part of it, and no reason to doubt that sooner or later they would be among its victims. They were familiar with the internal workings of the camp, and indeed, in some cases, with the personal habits of their SS keepers, who were accustomed to use prisoners as servants. After a while the SS abandoned their original intention of killing off the special detachments at three-weekly intervals in favour of retaining the services of teams inured to their gruesome task. As a result, the prisoners might form part of the detachment for months at a time and were able to build up between them a considerable body of experience.

There thus came into existence a nucleus of experienced prisoners, who evolved plans for an uprising timed to avert the threat to their own lives, whenever that might present itself. In Treblinka and Sobibor these ideas gradually matured into plans for a mass breakout, in which perhaps 10 per cent of the prisoners were involved. The deciding moment, for prisoners in both camps, came in 1943 when the number of deportation transports began to dwindle and the SS showed obvious signs of preparing to wind up the camp.[35] So when the prisoners were ordered to exhume the gassed corpses, originally thrown into pits, and then to burn them, it was clearly with the intention of erasing all traces of the crimes to which they themselves were the last witnesses. A small but strong steering committee had been formed at Treblinka at the earliest opportunity – the beginning of 1943 – and included, amongst others, senior *Funktionshäftlinge* and a former officer of the Czechoslovak army. On hearing that the cremations were all but completed, the core leadership fixed the uprising for 2 August 1943. At Sobibor, recruitment of a strong nucleus was a harder and more protracted process. The prisoners there had in fact received a stark warning of the fate they could expect when, at the end of June 1943, 'worker' prisoners from the now dissolved extermination camp at Belzec were brought to Sobibor and killed; messages sewn into their clothing showed that the Belzec prisoners had been deceived by the SS into believing that they were being transferred to a work camp. The situation was changed by the allocation to the work detachment in September of a group of Red Army officers who had been spared extermination. As well as contributing the necessary military expertise, they showed from the start their determination not to be killed without a struggle. On finally receiving news through one of the security staff of the rising in Treblinka, the group fixed the revolt for 14 October.

In both camps there were hitches in the prepared plan, with the result that open fighting broke out before the prisoners could be adequately armed and with members of the SS leadership still at large. For whatever reason – betrayal, as was apparently the case at Treblinka, or unforeseen conduct by the SS – the prisoners had to storm the security fence on the spur of the moment, without having a chance to take up their prepared positions and losing the advantage of mutual support. The steering committee thus lost control of the operation at the critical moment of open attack on the guard posts. Many lives were lost in consequence; and at Sobibor inmates housed in some of the camp's outer settlements were completely cut off and could take no part in the uprising. At Treblinka, although the majority actually succeeded in leaving the camp, many of the fugitives were shot, the SS having called in reinforcements from the Police and the Army. Nevertheless, out of the 500–600 prisoners who took part in the Treblinka uprising, close on 150 got clean away, and of these 52 are known to have survived the war. At Sobibor some 300 prisoners – representing about half the total – broke out, of whom about 100 were shot while escaping or recaptured. Part of the sad ending to this brave and resolute chapter in the history of resistance has still to be recorded: there were partisan groups who refused from anti-semitic motives to shelter the fugitives; worse still, some of those who took part in the uprisings are known to have been shot by partisans or to have perished in a pogrom conducted in Poland after the war.[36]

At Treblinka, although the SS did not rebuild a part of the camp burnt down by the rebels, the gassing installations – so far as they were still intact – continued in operation to the end of August. The camp was then destroyed, along with the surviving members of the work detachment. The end of Sobibor followed still more directly on the uprising. After these two revolts, the SS did not dare to continue with exterminations using the same methods as before; even at Majdanek, no more gassings were allowed. But this did not save 42,000 Jews still being held in the cluster of camps around Lublin. Early in November, and within the space of a few days, all 42,000 – 18,000 from Majdanek alone – were shot; even for the SS *Einsatzkommandos*, this action was without precedent.

But the extermination programme was still not at an end. New gas chambers and crematoria constructed at Auschwitz in 1943 had considerably enlarged the camp's lethal capacity. After the other sites had been dismantled, Auschwitz acted as the central extermination site for the Jewish population throughout the Nazi domain. The prisoners who worked in the extermination section were known at Auschwitz as the 'special detachment'. Because the extermination complex formed part of a large concentration camp, these prisoners were less isolated than their counterparts in the extermination camps; they therefore attempted to harmonize their plans for a breakout with the resistance in the main camp. As at Sobibor and Treblinka, the members of the Birkenau special detachment intended to activate their plan for an uprising as soon as they had reason to fear that their own liquidation was imminent. After the gassing of the Hungarian Jews in May and June 1944, which was the largest single operation ever to be carried out at Auschwitz, the strength of the detachment, previously around 900 prisoners, was reduced: 200 were killed by the SS. As the fighting drew closer in the autumn of 1944 it seemed likely that further reductions would follow. A proposal from the special detachment for a general uprising was therefore put to the resistance group in the concentration camp. The reasons it came to nothing are once again indicative of the specific conditions that had to be present to make prisoners decide for open revolt: the risks of biding their time in the camp had to be no less than those attaching to an immediate uprising, and the prisoners under threat of imminent death had to possess the physical strength and the determination to devise and implement a plan. Considered as a whole, the prisoner population of Auschwitz was too fragmented for those conditions to be generally applicable. Moreover, there were all too many prisoners who, it could safely be said, were no longer capable of playing an active part in an uprising and who would have been killed off in their thousands, even without offering resistance. The camp was too large and too complex for the resistance movement to envisage a revolt as truly in the interests of the majority. Unlike the special detachment, the members of the resistance were not in imminent danger of liquidation and they were anxious to postpone an uprising at least until there was a realistic prospect of their forces being able to break through to the front or of joining up with partisans. At that time, even if the revolt succeeded, it would not have been feasible to bring such a large crowd of escaping prisoners out of the camp in safety. Since the members of the special detachment were determined to take action, they were therefore obliged to go ahead on their own.

Through their contacts with the resistance movement, they obtained gun powder smuggled out of a factory in which prisoners were employed. On 7 October 1944, members of the special detachment heard that their numbers were again to be reduced. Around midday one of the crematoria was blown up and set on fire, and prisoners began pelting the SS with stones and other missiles; but only one other cremation detachment followed suit, the prisoners in the two others remaining quiet. Whether it was a premature disclosure of the planned resistance, or an attempt by the SS to mislead members of the special detachment, that resulted in an ill-timed and badly co-ordinated attack, is still not clear. One section did succeed in breaking through the camp's defences, but its members were hunted down while still in the neighbourhood of one of the camp's outer settlements. There is no evidence that any of them survived. The two crematoria that had been destroyed were never reactivated.

Little is known about the social and ideological background of the prime movers in the uprising. A group of Greek Jews is said to have been involved, which seems plausible in so far as prisoners from this particular transport had already refused point-blank to carry out the duties of the special detachment. Also mentioned are a detachment senior of long standing, who was in contact with the resistance organization in the main camp, and two Polish-French Communists, who had been active in the French resistance.[37]

These risings on the part of Jewish work detachments attached to extermination sites are otherwise without parallel in concentration camp history; to fit them into the overall pattern of resistance, they have to be considered alongside the uprisings of 1943 in the ghettos of Bialystok and Warsaw, which took place in similar circumstance. The process of clearing out the ghettos had been going on for several months; those inmates not too apathetic to take an active interest in their own fate were by this time in no doubt that they were destined to be sent to Treblinka for extermination and they therefore tried to evade deportation for as long as possible. So, as more and more transports left the ghettos, a hard core was built up of inmates prepared to resist. Open resistance to deportation began in Warsaw in January 1943 and was the prelude to the general uprising in April, which thus preceded the revolts in the extermination camps. The prime movers in the resistance were young men with Zionist or socialist affiliations. The ghetto's traditional leaders, like many others in the community, tended by contrast to have little faith in armed resistance.[38] It can thus be seen that organized Jewish resistance was subject to a set of conditions that have already been identified as determining concentration camp resistance in general.

In the first place, groups had to be formed consisting of people whose political views, or ideologies in the broader sense, had confirmed them as long-standing opponents of National Socialism, often as the result of a process that had started before their detention. Next, the more such groups were drawn together by the risks to which they were exposed and by the hope of liberation, the more likely were they to unite in a common action. Lastly, it was crucial to the success of their plans that such groups should include men with experience in the handling of weapons (prisoners of war, partisans). Thus it is not surprising that the common factor of being Jewish was not by itself enough to produce a general disposition to resist. Indeed, differences of nationality, social class and political outlook had given rise among the Jewish population to very different forms of Jewish consciousness. Above all else, it was the experience of persecution that enforced an inescapable sense of community. Where Jewish religious belief acted as a motive for open resistance, it was usually in circles that had rejected the path of assimilation as followed by a large part of the Jewish population, especially in Western Europe, since the last century, and who could point in vindication of their choice to the Nazi regime.

The Jewish leadership in the ghettos tended to be in the hands of those who were reluctant to surrender the social and economic benefits of integration and who therefore clung as long as possible to the illustration that persecution and discrimination did not signify extermination and that openings would still be left for the Jewish population to earn a living. To the end, many of them believed there was more to lose than to gain by open resistance. And even when the reality was unmistakable, they lacked the fortitude to abandon, overnight, the values by which they had lived; still believing that it was their duty as ghetto elders to protect their community, they could not change their tune by calling for an open rebellion that must doom many of its members to despair or sudden death. Thus there was no one in the ghetto of Theresienstadt who was prepared to pass on information about the extermination camps that began to trickle in during 1941 and later became a steady stream. Transports continued to be sent to Auschwitz, although some of those responsible must surely have known what that name signified. A Czech prisoner named Lederer, who escaped from Auschwitz in 1944 with the intention of warning the inmates of the ghetto, met with reactions of horror and sympathy, but also with silence. The people he spoke to kept the information to themselves.[39] There were special reasons why the inhabitants of Theresienstadt were so strongly under the illusion that they would be allowed to survive the war, albeit in captivity. The SS used the ghetto as a show-piece, to delude visiting international commissions into believing that Jewish communal and cultural life was being preserved under National Socialism; all too many of the ghetto's inhabitants refused to see that a deception was being practised not only on people abroad but also on themselves. Even the ghetto's leading Zionists were taken in, to the extent that they actually imagined that by convincing younger members to comply they were paving the way for the subsequent emigration to Israel. For many the moment of truth came only when they were personally confronted with extermination as an inescapable reality. We shall therefore end by considering the psychological barriers to resistance.

In 1943 two transports of Czech Jews from Theresienstadt arrived at Auschwitz. They were not subjected to the selection process; the family groups were preserved intact; and the whole party was accommodated in a separate unit of the Birkenau complex. These deportees were permitted to wear their civilian clothing and they were not obliged to work in the camp's routine detachments. Up to a point they could continue to live as they had while confined to the ghetto. As before, the education given to the children was conceived as a preparation for Israel. Apart from the office of camp senior, Jews were not debarred from holding positions of responsibility; those chosen for these offices had often occupied comparable positions in Theresienstadt. In the camp, as in the ghetto, political tendencies were conspicuous by their absence. The other prisoners, excluded from this 'family camp', were jolted out of their everyday existence by glimpses of a life that conformed to an unprecedented extent to the conventions obtaining in the outside world and that to all appearances was quite alien to that of the concentration camp. But while its inmates regarded the family camp as a genuine continuation of their existence in Theresienstadt, the other prisoners remained suspicious of a concession whereby Jews were allowed a life style that in all essentials was rooted in the pre-Auschwitz past and not in the Auschwitz present. Eventually it was discovered by prisoners working in the camp secretariat that the index cards for inmates of the family camp were marked 'SB', an abbreviation for *Sonderbehandlung* (special treatment) and a euphemism for death. Even now, the warnings that found their way to *Funktionshäftlinge* in the family camp were not taken seriously. Blinkered by their ghetto traditions, these Czech Jews paid no heed to the evidence of the holocaust visibly before them – the incineration chimneys, the gas chambers – and refused to accept that the persecution was all-embracing. They interpreted their more comfortable existence, which so plainly differentiated them from the other prisoners, the ones waiting to be gassed, as a sign of their own exemption from extermination; or else they utterly refused to recognize extermination as a part of Jewish reality. The SS strengthened them in their convictions. Eichmann, who was in charge of deportations to the gas chambers, visited the family camp and allowed the children to put on a show for his entertainment. Freddy Hirsch, who carried great weight as head of the camp's educational programme, took this as confirmation that nothing would happen to them. When the day finally came that saw the first consignment being loaded onto lorries to be taken to the gas chambers, Hirsch committed suicide. The SS had probably promised to spare his life if he would exert his influence in the camp to calm the prisoners and connive in their deception. Urged by the resistance movement on the other hand to fight back, Hirsch was torn between the two and decided for neither. Left leaderless, only a handful of prisoners, mostly block seniors, tried to resist. In their isolation they were quickly overpowered by the SS, as was normally the case when individuals attempted to offer unpremeditated resistance.

Wanting at least to light a memorial beacon, the Birkenau prisoners thought of setting fire to the family camp. Its way of life had reflected social and material conditions with which they had long since ceased to be familiar; because of the contrast it presented to their own futureless existence, the family camp could not be allowed to pass into oblivion, as so many other transports had, without some gesture of protest. So for these prisoners the distinctive character of the family camp acted as an incentive to mobilize their energies for resistance; on the majority of the camp's inmates (the most influential included) it had had the opposite effect, since it deceived them into taking the appearance of better conditions for the reality. Unfortunately, as we now know, this was precisely the effect that Eichmann wanted. For a while he even entertained thoughts of inviting an international commission of the Red Cross to inspect the family camp, in order to counter rumours that deportees sent to Birkenau were being gassed.[40]

It seems scarcely credible that anyone could suppress for so long as the Theresienstadt Jews the knowledge of the extermination being carried out in Poland. Formed as a community by the religious tradition that was now being systematically subjected to persecution, Jews took refuge in the promises of that same religion and mobilized its resources of patience and long-suffering. Even the historical examples of resistance, which were equally a part of Jewish tradition, lacked the potency to rise up at this late hour and undo the process that had gradually removed from Jewish communities their civic rights, along with their freedom of movement and association, and that had placed shackles on their thinking. Their attitude is summed up in the following quotation, which is concerned with Jews from the Warsaw ghetto who were not prepared to take part in open resistance, but who enlisted themselves more or less voluntarily in the death transports going to Treblinka:

> There was a considerable number of devout believers who went to their death steadfast in their belief in the immortality of the Jewish People and its Holy Tora. For them Treblinka was but another link in the chain of Jewish martyrology, a historical episode of a class that comes and goes with systematic regularity in certain periods. Serenely they accepted their fate. They died sanctifying the Name of God.[41]

An individual's decision in favour or resistance as opposed to surrender, or indeed self-abdication, usually had a prehistory stretching back beyond the period of detention and the final stages of persecution. The line of conduct followed in extreme situations needed to have been tried out in circumstances that seemed more open and more equivocal than those in which the prisoner or deportee would eventually find himself called to take action. To guide his behaviour in camp, a prisoner had to fall back on experiences gained outside it, and it was this that made resistance hard. Not many came to resistance for the first time in the camp. Anyone who felt compelled to do so, breaking completely with their previous experiences and principles, was actually closer to despairing self-abdication, or to egoistic self-assertion, than to resistance.

NOTES

1   The totals given by Gerald Reitlinger, *The Final Solution. The Attempt to Exterminate the Jews of Europe 1939–1945*, 2nd edn (London, 1956), are irreducible minima and for Auschwitz in particular fall short of the real number of victims; see Raul Hilberg, *The Destruction of the European Jews* (New York, 1983). The numbers given here are based on

the work of a research group whose findings have been published under the title *Nationalsozialistische Massentötungen durch Giftgas*, ed. Eugen Kogon *et al.* (Frankfurt/M., 1983).

2 *New Statesman and Nation*, 5 May 1945; see also text of R. H. S. Crossman's interview with Eugen Kogon, erstwhile prisoner, in *New Statesman and Nation*, 23 June 1945. A year later Kogon produced the first analytical study of the concentration camp system, *Der SS-Staat* (Frankfurt/M., 1946), English version: *The Theory and Practice of Hell* (London, 1951).

3 For supporting evidence and a fuller discussion see my detailed study *Häftlinge unter SS-Herrschaft. Widerstand, Selbstbehauptung und Vernichtung im Konzentrationslager* (Hamburg, 1978); and Martin Broszat, 'Nationalsozialistische Konzentrationslager 1933–1945', in Hans Buchheim *et al.*, *Anatomie des SS-Staates*, vol. 2, 2nd edn (Munich, 1967), pp. 11–136.

4 The extent to which differences of opinion persisted and affected the daily life of the camp can be seen from Hans-Günter Richardi, *Schule der Gewalt. Die Anfänge des Konzentrationslager Dachau 1933–1934* (Munich, 1983); Hermann Langbein, . . . *nicht wie die Schafe zur Schlachtbank. Widerstand in den nationalsozialistischen Konzentrationslagern, 1938–1945* (Frankfurt/M., 1980), ch. 10.

5 In the setting up of Sachsenhausen, express notice was taken of the requirements of the *Wehrmacht*, which at the beginning of the war was counting on large-scale detentions; Pingel, *Häftlinge* (as in n.3), p. 62.

6 Publications relating to individual camps exist as follows. Sachsenhausen: *Dokumente, Aussagen, Forschungsergebnisse und Erlebnisberichte* (Berlin, GDR, 1974); Buchenwald: *Buchenwald, Mahnung und Verpflichtung. Dokumente und Berichte*, 3rd edn (Berlin, GDR, 1961); Ravensbrück: Ino Arndt, 'Das Frauenkonzentrationslager Ravensbrück', in *Studien zur Geschichte der Konzentrationslager* (Stuttgart, 1970), pp. 93–129; *FrauenKZ Ravensbrück* (Berlin, GDR, 1971); Dachau: Günther Kimmel, 'Das Konzentrationslager Dachau. Eine Studie zu nationalsozialistischen Gewaltverbrechen', in *Bayern in der NS-Zeit*, vol. 2 (Munich, 1979), pp. 349–413; Mauthausen: Hans Marsalek, *Die Geschichte des Konzentrationslagers Mauthausen* (Vienna, 1974).

7 Under the code name '14f13' the concentration camps, like the mental homes, were visited by special commissioners on the look-out for sick prisoners suitable for transfer to the 'euthanasia' or death centres; Klaus Dörner *et al.*, *Der Krieg gegen die psychisch Kranken* (Rehburg-Loccum, 1980); Karl-Friedrich Kaul, *Die Psychiatrie im Strudel der 'Euthanasie'* (Frankfurt/M. 1979).

8 Pingel, *Häftlinge* (as in n.3), p. 98f.; H. Marsalek, *Mauthausen* (as in n.6), pp. 105ff.

9 Statements obtained from Höss for the Nuremberg trial, Nuremberg Doc. D–749 and PS 3868; see his narrative account written in prison at Cracow, *Kommandant in Auschwitz*, ed. Martin Broszat (Stuttgart,

1961), pp. 153ff. On the history of Auschwitz see Hermann Langbein, *Menschen in Auschwitz* (Vienna, 1972).

10 Józef Marsalek, *Majdanek. Geschichte und Wirklichkeit des Vernichtungslagers* (Reinbek, 1982).

11 On the activities of the *Einsatzgruppen*, see Helmut Krausnick and Hans-Heinrich Wilhelm, *Die Truppe des Weltanschauungskrieges* (Stuttgart, 1981).

12 Note from the head of Hitler's Chancellery, SS-Oberführer Viktor Brack, to Himmler, 23 June 1942, Nuremberg Doc. NO–2o5.

13 Adalbert Rückerl (ed.), *Nationalsozialistische Vernichtungslager im Spiegel deutscher Strafprozesse*, 2nd edn. (Munich, 1978); conversations with the one-time commandant of Sobibor and Treblinka reported by Gitta Sereny, *Into that Darkness. An Examination of Conscience* (London, 1974).

14 On the place occupied by prisoner work detachments in the system as a whole see Falk Pingel, 'Die Konzentrationslagerhäftlinge im nationalsozialistischen Arbeitseinsatz', in Wacław Długoborski (ed.), *Zweiter Weltkrieg und sozialer Wandel* (Göttingen, 1981), pp. 151–63.

15 Strikingly illustrated by the reflections of an Auschwitz prisoner, Jean Améry, *Jenseits von Schuld und Sühne* (Munich, 1970).

16 Dachau was the only camp where the influence of the Social Democrats was predominant; on the challenges to their role see Langbein, . . . *nicht wie die Schafe* (as in n.4), ch. 10.

17 Individual instances are cited by Pingel, *Häftlinge* (as in n.3), p. 203. French prisoners in the Natzweiler concentration camp near Strasbourg were in contact with the resistance; Kryzysztof Dunin Wąsowicz, *Resistance in the Nazi Concentration Camps 1933–1945* (Warsaw, 1982), p. 267.

18 Anna Pawelczynska, *Values and Violence in Auschwitz. A Sociological Analysis* (Berkeley, 1979).

19 Leonhard Steinwender, *Christus im Konzentrationslager* (Salzburg, 1946); and *Der Prediger von Buchenwald* (Berlin, 1954), pp. 190–1.

20 Kogon, *SS-Staat* (as in n.2), pp. 114–16.

21 For further examples see Langbein, . . . *nicht wie die Schafe* (as in n.4), pp. 223 ff.; Pingel, *Häftlinge* (as in n.3), pp. 192–4.

22 Pingel, ibid., p. 303; Langbein, *Menschen in Auschwitz* (as in n.9), p. 244.

23 Hans Beimler, *Im Mörderlager Dachau* (Moscow, 1933); the book also appeared in England under the title *Four Weeks in the Hands of Hitler's Hell-Hounds*. Gerhardt Seger, *Oranienburg. Erster authentischer Bericht eines aus dem Konzentrationslager Geflüchteten* (Karlsbad, 1934); the Social Democrat deputy-in-exile reported further on his experiences in *Konzentrationslager. Ein Appell an das Gewissen der Welt* (Karlsbad, 1934).

24 Pingel, *Häftlinge* (as in n.3), p. 204.

25 Vrba commented on the matter after the war. Rudolf Vrba and Alan Bestic, *I Cannot Forgive* (London, 1964); the whole question has now

been thoroughly investigated by Martin Gilbert, *Auschwitz and the Allies* (London, 1981).

26 On the history of the camp see Manfred Bornemann and Martin Broszat, 'Das KL Dora-Mittelbau', in *Studien zur Geschichte der Konzentrationslager* (Stuttgart, 1970), pp. 155–98; Manfred Bornemann, *Geheimprojekt Mittelbau. Die Geschichte der deutschen V-Waffen-Werke* (Munich, 1971). The many studies of production and resistance at Dora made in the GDR have been gathered together by Götz Dieckmann and Peter Hochmuth in *KZ Dora-Mittelbau, Produktionsstätte der V-Waffen – Kampffront gegen faschistischen Terror und Rüstungsproduktion* (Nordhausen, no date).

27 Inside the camp, support for the attempted breakout by force had repeatedly been voiced; the inactivity of the partisan groups therefore gave rise to much bitterness; Marsalek, *Majdanek*, pp. 226–7 and 240.

28 On and after 18 January 1945 about 60,000 prisoners left the camp and were set to march in the direction of the concentration camps at Gross-Rosen (in Upper Silesia), Buchenwald, Dachau and Mauthausen. About 15,000 did not survive these marches; Shmuel Krakowski, 'Death Marches and the Evacuation of Nazi Concentration Camps', unpublished ms., Yad Vashem, Jerusalem.

29 *Buchenwald, Mahnung und Verpflichtung* (as in n.6), pp. 501–3; Kogon, *SS-Staat* (as in n.2), pp. 336–8; as a corrective to the exaggerated credit claimed in particular by former Communist inmates of Buchenwald, who underplay the dependence of their own bid for freedom on the proximity of the US army, see Langbein, . . . *nicht wie die Schafe* (as in n.4), pp. 366–8, and compare further with the account given by the then head of the international camp committee, Bartel, in Christoph Klessmann and Falk Pingel (eds), *Gegner des Nationalsozialismus. Wissenschaftler und Widerstandskämpfer auf der Suche nach historischer Wirklichkeit* (Frankfurt/M., 1980), pp. 243–5.

30 Michael Selzer, *Deliverance Day. The Last Hours at Dachau* (London, 1980).

31 Eberhard Kolb, *Bergen-Belsen* (Hanover, 1962), p. 282; on arrival at Bergen-Belsen a woman prisoner from one of the Neuengamme evacuation transports wrote as follows:

Bergen-Belsen is an extermination camp. The ones who are still alive have become wolves. The SS are not content to inflict pain and death. They defile their victims. They take away everything a person needs – food, drink, water to wash in, a place to sleep. Then when someone goes mad from being so deprived and attacks his weaker comrades, they give him a free hand. With these shameless methods they bring their hateful work to its conclusion . . . [Fritz Bringmann, *KZ Neuengamme*, Frankfurt/M., 1981, p. 103].

32 ibid., p. 102.

33 The history of this attack has been reconstructed by a journalist, Günther Schwarberg, who interviewed former British airmen responsible for bombing the ship (without knowing the identity of the passengers) – his article appeared in the West German magazine *Der Stern*, 1983, no. 10; see also Rudi Goguel, *'Cap Arcona'. Report über den Untergang der Häftlingsflotte in der Lübecker Bucht am 3 Mai 1945* (Frankfurt/M., 1972).

34 On this in general see primarily: *Jewish Resistance during the Holocaust*, Proceedings of the Conference on Manifestations of Jewish Resistance (Jerusalem, 1971); Yuri Suhl (ed.), *They Fought Back: The Story of Jewish Resistance in Nazi Europe* (London, 1968).

35 In a directive dated 19 July 1942 Himmler had ordered that deportations to camps under Globocnik's control should cease from 31 December 1942.

36 One of the survivors published an account of his experiences: Yankiel Wiernik, *A Year in Treblinka – An Inmate who Escaped Tells the Day-to-Day Facts of One Year of his Torturous Experience* (New York, 1946); Miriam Novitch, *Sobibor Martyrdom and Revolt: Documents and Testimonies* (New York, 1980).

From Belzec there were no known survivors; it is probable that there were no major efforts at resistance. At Chelmno, too, there was no success in forming a solid core of resistance. Jaakov Grojanowski, who was determined to put up a fight, accordingly decided in January 1943 to escape on his own initiative. He was able in this way to warn his own Jewish community, and managed eventually to reach Warsaw, where he passed on information about the extermination centres to Dr Emanuel Ringelblum, a leading light in the ghetto resistance; Shmuel Krakowski, 'Das Vernichtungslager Kulmhof (Chelmno)', unpublished ms. Yad Vashem, Jerusalem.

37 Langbein, *Menschen in Auschwitz* (as in n.9), pp. 221–3; *Amidst a Nightmare of Crime. Manuscripts of Members of Sonderkommando* (Oswiecim, 1973). At Auschwitz, too, the partisan movement outside the camp was hesitant about supporting an uprising; Dunin, *Resistance* (as in n.17), p. 262.

38 The conduct of the Jewish Councils has been criticized by Isaiah Trunk, *Judenrat. The Jewish Councils in Eastern Europe under Nazi Occupation* (London, 1977); on this see also the literature referred to in n. 34.

39 Hans-Günter Adler, *Theresienstadt 1941–1945. Das Antlitz einer Zwangsgemeinschaft*, 2nd edn (Tübingen, 1960), pp. 154–6; and see in general Walter Laqueur, '*The Terrible Secret. An Investigation into the Suppression of Information about Hitler's Final Solution*' (London, 1980).

40 This description is based for the most part on an interview given to me by Erich Kulka, who at the time in question was a prisoner in Birkenau; Kulka's wife and son, however, were inmates of the family camp; see Pingel, *Häftlinge* (as in n.3), pp. 214–16; Hans-Günter Adler, *Die*

71

verheimlichte Wahrheit. Theresienstädter Dokumente (Tübingen, 1958), p. 307.

41 Yosef Gottfarstein, 'Kiddush Hashem over the Ages and its Uniqueness in the Holocaust Period', in *Jewish Resistance* (as in n.34), p. 466.

4

*Hitler's Final Solution and its Rationalization**

LOTHAR KETTENACKER

For many years, the front page of *The Times* carried a dictum by Lord Acton, taken from his correspondence with Bishop Creighton concerning the nature of the papacy at the time of the Reformation. The original version reads: 'Power tends to corrupt, and absolute power corrupts absolutely.' It is followed two sentences later by an equally remarkable statement which, no less than the more famous saying, indicates the deep gulf that existed between the political cultures of Britain and Germany: 'There is no worse heresy than that the office sanctifies the holder of it.'[1]

It is generally accepted that the genocide of the Jews, perpetrated in the name of an imagined German mission, represents the absolute and, at the same time, most corrupt form of the exercise of power. Equally undisputed is that the name of Auschwitz-Birkenau represents the lowest point in German history. The situation is less clear-cut, however, when we consider to what extent this enormous crime against humanity can ultimately be traced back to the person of the *Führer* and Chancellor Adolf Hitler. Were the more than five million Jews who were killed victims of a single, incomprehensible fanatical will, supported by a large number of accomplices, as thorough as they were deluded – or did the Jews get caught up in the machinery of a system of power that, never mind its ideological nature, had gone out of control? Conventional fascism of Italian or Spanish making, for example, did not produce this sort of monstrosity. Thus it can justifiably be argued that National Socialism acquired particular historical significance because of the Holocaust.[2] Without this, and without the Eastern campaign, which was characterized by a similar disposition towards genocide, fascism would

*Translated by Angela Davies.

probably not be as totally discredited as it is today. As far as I know, no German historian has yet seriously inquired whether the Final Solution would have been possible, or likely, without the man at the top, whose authority was constantly referred to by his major henchmen. Since German historiography has dared to approach the subject at all, it has for some time cautiously been circling around this unspoken question. The historians whom Tim Mason has called 'intentionalists'[3] – that is, Andreas Hillgruber, Eberhard Jäckel, and Klaus Hildebrand – answer with a categorical 'no'. The 'functionalists', by contrast, while recognizing Hitler's personal responsibility, suggest that the annihilation process was to a large extent the result of improvization dictated by the problems of implementing large-scale discrimination. Martin Broszat and Hans Mommsen are the main exponents of this line of interpretation.[4] Both positions, in spite of claims to exclusive validity, have helped to bring the debate about this dark chapter of German history into the open.

It is now time to move away from this dichotomy. The two interpretations need to be synthesized so that the discussion can continue on another level. Undoubtedly intention can be separated from realization as little as can, for example, the systematic rearmament and militarization of society from the world war that followed. Hans Mommsen is right in pointing out that the translation of Hitler's long-term objectives into the reality of genocide presents the real problem in untangling the complicated process that led to the Final Solution. Historians cannot be satisfied with Eichmann's stereotyped answer that it was all a matter of obeying orders[5] – especially as a single, definitive, written order by Hitler has never turned up, and, most experts now assume, never existed. On the other hand, it would definitely be misleading to see Hitler as merely an anti-semitic propagandist driven by circumstances and his bureaucrats ultimately to come to terms with the Final Solution whether he wanted to or not; as someone who did not wish to be bothered with the unpleasant details – a picture presented by Hans Mommsen in his contribution to this volume (Chapter 5) where he describes the Final Solution as the 'Realization of the Unthinkable'.

More important than any intentions that Hitler might have had towards the Jews is the early evidence of his mentality. He exhibits in the most extreme way the extraordinarily morbid nature of modern, and, as Hermann Graml has most recently shown, inherently destructive anti-semitism.[6] Eberhard Jäckel has summarized in one sentence all the expressions relating to parasites by which Hitler characterized the Jews in *Mein Kampf*:

The Jew is a maggot in a rotting corpse; he is a plague worse than the Black Death of former times; a germ-carrier of the worst sort; mankind's eternal germ of disunion; the drone which insinuates its way into the rest of mankind; the spider that slowly sucks the people's blood out of its pores; the pack of rats fighting bloodily among themselves; the parasite in the body of other peoples; the typical parasite; a sponger who, like a harmful bacillus, continues to spread; the eternal bloodsucker; the people's parasite; the people's vampire.[7]

Even if this vocabulary does not in judicial terms constitute criminal incitement to murder, it should have been sufficient reason for the prohibition on addressing public gatherings, which was placed on Hitler after his release from Landsberg Prison, never to have been revoked. Instead, this man was appointed Chancellor of the German Reich on 30 January 1933, because national conservative groups believed it was the best way to enlist mass support for the renewal of an authoritarian state. In fact, however, the appointment of a demagogue who had, among other things, publicly defended Nazi storm troopers legally convicted of murder,[8] objectively undermined the legal authority of the state to a degree hitherto unknown. This alone reveals the extent to which the rule of law, not to mention democracy, had been compromised by the end of the Weimar Republic. Even more, it indicates what that society would tolerate in the way of infringements of the law in the years to come. Hitler was only too aware that in its recruiting phase the movement had benefited from his anti-semitic propaganda, which served to denigrate political opponents. However, in his eventual rise to power racial anti-semitism proved to be an obstacle. Hitler's frequent remarks disparaging the bourgeoisie, and the conservative civil service in particular, reveal that he was reckoning on stronger resistance by the traditional elites to the systematic policy of discrimination undertaken after 1933. Thus the path to Auschwitz was marked, from the beginning, less by virulent anti-semitism in German society – later, in Jerusalem, Eichmann was to claim that he had by no means been a fanatical anti-semite in the 1930s[9] – than by a striking lack of solidarity with a threatened minority, and by a lack of resistance to a revolutionary regime in the process of radicalization and intent on introducing discriminatory measures. The development of domestic policy, no less than foreign policy, depended on the reaction of those affected, which marked the threshold of what was acceptable. Added to this was the dialectical dimension of policies that, fundamentally inspired by ideology, were rational only in their methods of implementation.

The National Socialists considered the Western democracies to be breeding grounds of Jewish influence, so it seemed as if anti-semitic measures could be used to a certain degree to extort good behaviour in matters of foreign policy. Conversely, foreign countries saw anti-semitic legislation as a measure of radicalization or consolidation of the National Socialist regime.[10] The anti-Jewish legislation introduced soon after the seizure of power had two further functions: first, it drove Jews out of business, which could be regarded as a substitute for the 'second revolution', that is, the social revolution demanded by the militants of the party;[11] secondly, it gradually transformed a free bourgeois society into a National Socialist *Volksgemeinschaft* by eliminating elements that were racially and ideologically 'impure'. This socialization process was insidious in the way in which it constantly had recourse to the law, which was used to enforce injustices in an ever more intimidating way. Gradually depriving a minority of its rights served to undermine the rule of law and, at the same time, corrupted any sense of justice. As early as 1920, the National Socialists' party programme had stated: 'Only members of the nation may be citizens of the State. Only those of German blood, whatever their creed, may be members of the nation. Accordingly, no Jew may be a member of the nation. Non-citizens may live in Germany only as guests and must be subject to laws for aliens.'[12] After the seizure of power, this course was followed with the utmost consistency; from the Prussian Ministry of the Interior's ruling of 17 February 1933 revoking the existing order to the police by which Eastern Jews were not to be expelled, to the instructions issued by the Ministry of Economics on 16 February 1945 about the 'treatment of *Entjudungsakten*' (files concerning Jewish affairs) which were not to fall into enemy hands.[13] Between these two dates, no fewer than 1,970 laws, decrees, orders and statutes were issued at national, state and municipal level – bearing witness to an indescribable fetish for order. The same bureaucratic thoroughness that was employed to deprive the Jews of their civic rights was later applied to their physical destruction at Chelmno, Treblinka, Sobibor, Majdanek, Belzec and Auschwitz. Even after the Final Solution had become reality, and so-called 'evacuation transports' were rolling towards the East, the discriminatory legislation by no means stopped: decrees were issued about prohibitions regarding the use of public telephones, obtaining permission to go on holiday, buying cakes from bakeries, subscribing to newspapers, receiving tobacco and egg ration cards, followed eventually by a restriction on the use of public transport.[14] In the end, the deportation of the Jews seemed no more than a logical consequence of the measures that had preceded it. When the murder campaign was in full operation, the 'Final Solution of the Jewish Question' was no longer allowed to be discussed in public, on the *Führer*'s orders. A confidential directive of 11 July 1943 from the Head of the Party Chancellery, to regional party leaders reads: 'Jews are, *en bloc*, being mobilized for the appropriate labour duties.'[15] The regime was concerned to provide a convincing alibi for what was actually going on.

The picture presented here of a legal machine grinding inexorably towards the factories of death seems to create the impression that the path to Auschwitz had been determined as early as 1933. However, historians agree that it was the outbreak of war in September 1939, and above all the conception of the Russian campaign as a war of wholesale extermination, that decisively shaped further developments. Precisely at this point, we see a disastrous mixture of intentional and functional factors determining the outcome of events. Discrimination against the Jews was no more an end in itself for Hitler than was rearmament. Both were necessary, well-thought-out stages in the process of attaining ultimate objectives that, for the time being, were not clearly defined – the solution of the so-called Jewish question, and the acquisition of *Lebensraum* in the East. The fact that Hitler had these objectives in mind simultaneously is indicated, first, by his prophecies of 30 January 1939 (which he later repeatedly cited) about the fate of the Jews if it came to another war, and, secondly, by the first steps towards translating the Final Solution into reality taken immediately after the outbreak of war. 'Today I shall once more be a prophet', he announced in 1939 on the anniversary of the seizure of power:

> If the international Jewish financiers inside and outside Europe should again succeed in plunging the nations into another world war, then the result will not be the Bolshevization of the world and thus a victory for Jewry, but the annihilation of the Jewish race in Europe.[16]

It would be pure speculation to regard this as an attempt to create an excuse, at this early stage, for the later physical destruction of the Jews. But it remains a possibility. In any case, it was more than a threatening gesture directed at the Western democracies, and designed to stop them from preventing the Germanic march eastwards against Jewish-Bolshevik Russia. If the Western powers did not stand in the way, it could be assumed that they would be obliged to take part in the evacuation of the European Jews in some form or other. If, however, it came to war in the West as well, Hitler saw no further reason to take international public opinion into account. After all, if this happened, it would vindicate the writing on the wall, to which he had repeatedly pointed, about a world conspiracy between Jewish finance and Jewish Bolshevism.

The strange pattern of alliances that emerged at the outbreak of war in September 1939 revealed the objective difficulties mounting up for the Nazi leaders bent on getting rid of the Jews once and for all. Deportation of the Jews overseas could no longer be contemplated, even if the emigration of German Jews had not completely dried up. The number of Jews in the German sphere of influence increased enormously with the Polish campaign. More than half of the German Jews had left Germany in time, but the approximately 330,000 who remained were joined by nearly 3 million Polish Jews.[17] They were mostly Orthodox, of an inferior social background, and did not have the sort of contacts abroad that many German Jews enjoyed. There could be no question of other countries absorbing these numbers of Polish Jews. But it was equally clear that they would not be allowed to remain freely in the Reich's new colonial hinterland. As early as 21 September 1939, Heydrich circulated a letter to all the leaders of the SS *Einsatzgruppen* mentioning a planned ultimate objective which was to remain top secret.[18] 'The first pre-requisite for achieving the ultimate objective', says the letter, 'is the concentration of the Jews from the country in the large cities.' These newly created ghettos were to be at railway junctions if possible, or at least close to railway lines. As far as possible, the areas designated for immediate annexation – that is, Danzig, West Prussia, Poznan and Upper Silesia – were to be cleared of Jews immediately. The first large-scale atrocities were in fact undertaken in these areas at the instigation of the *Reichssicherheitshauptamt* (RSHA – Reich Security Head Office) because it was feared that the introduction of a German civil administration and legal system could make the execution of these extreme policies more difficult.[19] However, these fears proved to be groundless because Hitler encouraged the governors appointed there to behave with the utmost ruthlessness towards the Polish population, and especially towards the Jews. He achieved this by making it absolutely clear that he expected his subordinates to report, within a few years, that their *Gaue* (regional party districts) had been 'Germanized'.[20] This did not mean the introduction of the German legal system; rather it meant aiming for as high a percentage as possible of German settlers and for the elimination of the Polish elites, especially of the Jews.

Hitler therefore made sure that his subordinates had special powers in the new areas, and that later, after Russia had been divided into several German dominions, the new governors were not subject to the control of the authorities in Berlin. Hitler explained to his confidants that 'a hard national struggle cannot be subject to legal constraints'.[21]

According to the RSHA, the Germanization of West Prussia desired by Hitler required the 'physical liquidation of all those Polish elements who (a) in the past had been prominent in any way in Polish affairs, or (b) were potential instigators of Polish resistance in the future'.[22] These broad categories included all Jews, who were considered to be destructive by nature, and whose annihilation could thus be justified as a preventive security policy.

Hitler and the Nazi elites did not trust the Army leaders to carry out this task; they were regarded, like the civil service, as depending too much on traditional interpretations of the law, even if this attitude was expressed only in the form of occasional complaints of passive resistance by commanding officers. Therefore, as early as 17 October 1939, Hitler ordered that the SS and the Police were to be exempt from military and ordinary jurisdiction respectively, without this provoking any protest from the Army High Command (OKH).[23] On the contrary, the delimitation of areas of authority, by separating military and political warfare, was welcomed. In view of the generals' acquiescence, the *Wehrmacht* can hardly be accused of Prussian militarism – rather it can be accused of the opposite, that is, abdicating its responsibilities and submitting too readily to an authoritarian state leadership. Hitler's order of 17 October 1939 turned the East, as it were, into the Wild West of the Reich, where law and order counted for little. At about the same time, Himmler was appointed Reich Commissioner for the Strengthening of Germandom in charge of all resettlement plans.[24] The extent of his overall powers can best be appreciated if one imagines that the American President instructed the Commander of the US Cavalry to take charge of the colonization of all the territories west of the Mississippi – with the explicit assurance that he would not have to answer for the methods used. When soon thereafter Hitler began to look even further east, he suggested, in passing, that the easiest way to pacify this huge area would be 'to shoot anyone who even looked askance'.[25] Of course, these Wild West methods seem almost humane in comparison with the deliberate course of action followed by the SS *Einsatzgruppen* against a defenceless civilian population. It was not simply a matter of breaking the law; lawlessness was elevated to a principle of the state, in the same way that anti-semitism, which existed in most societies at that time, attained legal status in the Third Reich. No wonder that Himmler was soon to dream of SS Marches in the East: the more the native population was decimated, the more the land became available for resettlement by German farmers and SS veterans.

The last phase on the path towards the Final Solution coincided with preparations for Operation Barbarossa – the attack on the Soviet Union. Hitler did not leave the *Wehrmacht* in any doubt about what was expected of it in the East. After the *Führer* had delivered a two-and-a-half-hour address to the commanders-in-chief on 30 March 1941, Colonel General Halder noted:

> The struggle of two world views: a scathing judgement passed on Bolshevism, which is clearly of a criminal nature. Communism a grave danger for the future. We must dissociate ourselves from soldierly comradeship. The Communist is not a comrade and will never be one. It is a fight to the death.[26]

On 13 May, Hitler ordered the restriction of military jurisdiction, thus creating the legal premisses for the fateful Commissar Order, which the Officer Corps was to implement.[27] According to this order, political commissars of the Red Army 'captured in battle or when offering resistance' were 'to be summarily executed on the spot'.[28] The justification given for the order was that most of the Red Army officers in question were said to be Jewish.

Only at this stage did the struggle against the so-called 'Jewish-Bolshevik intelligentsia' acquire the authority of a war aim, because, from then on, ideologically motivated anti-semitism could be declared a military necessity. Thus its full destructive potential could be realized. The rational legitimation of something inherently irrational played an important part in translating anti-semitic propaganda into the reality of genocide. This was an essential element in the process of gradual and insidious moral corruption, because it could not be taken for granted that the professional soliders of the *Wehrmacht* would necessarily have the 'correct' ideological attitude. Four SS *Einsatzgruppen* (A, B, C, D) were instructed to round up and kill all Jews in the rear of the fighting army as a precautionary measure during their mopping-up operations – after all, the Jews were considered to be the real supporters of the Bolsehvik system, and the core of the resistance to a permanent domination of the colonial hinterland. In fact, this argument was no more than a pretext, as is illustrated by the 'Reports to the Führer on Fighting the Partisans', in which the Jews murdered are listed separately. For example, under the heading 'Sympathizers and Suspected Partisans', Report No. 51 of 20 December 1942 lists 'captured: 16,553, executed: 14,257, Jews executed: 363,211'.[29] According to the most recent estimates, the four SS *Einsatzgruppen* alone, comprising only 3,000 men, killed a total of at least 535,000 people, mainly Jews, and mostly before the *Wehrmacht* was fully engaged in partisan warfare in the East.[30] The fact that this murder campaign took place in areas under Army command and with the full knowledge of the Army leadership has most recently been shown in Volume 4 of the West German quasi-official history of the war, which deals with the attack on the Soviet Union.[31]

All that remains in doubt is whether Hitler's order was passed on verbally by Heydrich to the leaders of the *Einsatzgruppen* on 17 June 1941 – that is, one week before the attack – as Helmut Krausnick assumes,[32] or whether it was given several weeks after the campaign had begun, when it became apparent that the Russian population's anticipated pogroms had not achieved the desired result. Alternatively, the order could have been given when the unrest created by the first random executions provided an excuse for treating the rest of the Jews as potential troublemakers. It would make sense if the precise nature of the instructions was left to the tacit understanding of what was meant by certain phrases in order to avoid any evidence that might have antagonized the Army leaders. Rosenberg's guidelines for the handling of the Jewish question in the occupied eastern territories advised: 'Any action undertaken by the local civilian population against the Jews is not to be prevented, so long as it is compatible with the maintenance of law and order behind the front lines.'[33] So long as the murder of Jewish citizens could proceed without any robbing and plundering, anything was acceptable. Rosenberg's ministry distinguished between resident Jews, who were to be 'segregated strictly from the rest of the population', and Jews who had migrated into the areas occupied by the Soviet Union and were to be 'eliminated by harsh measures'.[34] All written orders and regulations were worded in terms that could leave the non-initiated in doubt about the fate actually in store for the Jews. The official language of the regime not only camouflaged the final objectives, it also strengthened the petty officials' belief that they were carrying out certain tasks necessary for the war effort, the justification for and consequences of which were not for them to judge.

The fact that the Army leadership did not oppose the policy of extermination more strongly, and allowed the SS to carry on its own war against a defenceless population under the pretext that it was a preventive fight against partisans, must have been an important factor in Hitler's decision seriously to consider translating the Final Solution into reality – that is, concentrating all European Jews in Germany's sphere of influence in the East in order then to eliminate them by some means or other. The creation of Jewish ghettos in the East, which meant that for some time their fate appeared to be uncertain, made it easier to implement later measures, not only organizationally, but also psychologically. This is one explanation for the partial collaboration between the killers and their victims, which seems so incomprehensible to us today.[35] The order given to the SS *Einsatzgruppen* to exterminate the Russian Jews appears also to be an obvious point for dating the beginning of the end of the Western European Jews' ordeal. But can it be totally ruled out that Goering's order to Heydrich of 31 July 1941 to make all preparations necessary for an 'overall solution to the Jewish question in Germany's sphere of influence in Europe'[36] may have intended only the deportation of the Jews to the East, and not their immediate destruction? While settling the Jews in Madagascar, a scheme under consideration for some time,[37] seemed less and less feasible, the collapse of the Red Army, which in July 1941 was expected to be imminent, opened up the prospect of Siberia. Hitler's 'Table Talks' show that Siberia was at least a subject of discussion.[38] But what Graml pointed out in connection with the Madagascar Plan probably also applies to Siberia: physical destruction was to be given the appearance of a natural process.[39] It is striking that what was actually meant by the ambiguous term 'Final Solution' remained indeterminate until the time when all the organizational and technical preparations for the mass murder factories were complete. The double nature of this process alone suggests that the people closest to Hitler had no doubts about what was going to happen. But this approach distracts from the dialectic of the determining factors: the war in the East did not go according to plan; large numbers of Jews who arrived in the East had to be maintained from German supplies; the RSHA received more and more reports about psychological difficulties among the SS troops caused by shooting defenceless, unclothed people, including women, children and old people.[40] Hitler's frequently expressed wish to solve the Jewish question once and for all was an invitation to his technocrats to come up with more efficient, and more 'humane' methods of extermination. This explains why experience gained in the euthanasia programme (*Aktion T4*), and personnel who had worked on it, were used, and why eventually a departmental Party head in the *Führer*'s Chancellery, Viktor Brack, began to work on finding a poison gas that would take effect quickly and could solve the problem of the Final Solution in the most rational and economic way.[41]

We do not know for sure how interested Hitler was in the details of the preparations. But there is evidence that his chief collaborators, as assiduous as they were insecure, knew his obsession and kept him fully informed about everything relating to it – either to protect themselves, or to gain recognition.[42] In any case, it is clear that Hitler was determined to absolve himself and others by constant rationalizations, which none the less reveal nothing about the reality of the mass murders. Thus he said explicitly that the Jews had no right to survive a war they had plotted, or, in a cynical explanation given on 25 January 1942: 'I only say he [the Jew] must disappear. If he perishes in the process I can't help it. I can see only one possibility, total extermination, unless they [the Jews] go of their own accord.'[43] By that time, whole ghettos in Eastern Europe had already been evacuated to make room for new arrivals from Central and Western Europe. In most cases, Hitler spoke about the Final Solution in rhetorical terms, as if it were to take place in the future, presenting it as the judgement of an inexorable fate – at a time when the machinery of destruction had long been put into motion and was running smoothly.

It is generally accepted that Hitler expressed his wishes more or less unambiguously, and at times made crucial decisions. However, there is no consensus on whether a written *Führer* order, or even any single binding order authorizing the Final Solution, ever existed. Gerald Fleming has accumulated a great deal of convincing evidence that seems to suggest that while Hitler's wishes had the status of orders, if not of law, he himself did not want to be identified publicly with the execution of his plans, in order not to destroy the *Führer* myth among the people.[44] This is one explanation for the fact that it is so difficult to indict Hitler in a judicial sense on the basis of clear-cut documentary evidence. According to Martin Broszat, on the other hand, the last radical thrust was a result of the internal impetus of a system reacting to the pressure of circumstances.[45] But neither the existence of a decision-making process directed right from the beginning towards a specific end, nor the 'cumulative radicalization of the system' described by Hans Mommsen provides an adequate explanation.[46] Raul Hilberg has convincingly attempted to reconcile the intentional determining factors with those inherent in the system:

The individual measures and initiatives taken in the course of provisional planning quickly crystallised into a scheme of action directed towards a specific end. At the core of this crystallisation were Hitler himself, the pledges he had made to the world, and even more importantly, the wishes and expectations he expressed to his entourage.[47]

The activities unleashed by his ideas encouraged Hitler to become increasingly extreme, boosting his belief that he alone, historically unique, was capable of accomplishing the task. By the same token, Himmler, Heydrich and the new territorial rulers in the East could be sure that any anti-Jewish measures, particularly deportations, would meet with Hitler's full approval – even more, that this was the best way to prove themselves born leaders of strong character. An uncompromising attitude towards the Jewish question, more than any other criterion, was considered proof of ideological reliability. Unfortunately, party files relating to this topic have largely been destroyed. However, it would fit into the general picture if some regional party leaders and Lord Mayors pressed Bormann to relieve them of their Jews as soon as possible.[48] To rule over an area that had been cleared of Jews was the aim of every office holder. Frank, head of the *Generalgouvernement*, proudly reported to his officials on 25 March 1941 that the *Führer* had recognized their achievements in Poland and had promised him that the *Generalgouvernement* would be the first area to be freed of its Jews.[49] Goebbels pressed for the deportation of the Berlin Jews, but they enjoyed the protection of certain authorities in the capital who regarded them as an indispensable workforce within the armaments industry.[50]

At the notorious Wannsee Conference of 20 January 1942, at which the management of the Final Solution was discussed with the highest officials of the Reich departments, it was only the fate of the descendants of racially mixed marriages that was under discussion. The whole campaign was directed at no fewer than 11 million Jews, including those in neutral and enemy countries. Secretary of State Bühler advocated beginning with the largest concentration of Jews under German control, in the *Generalgouvernement*, 'because transport does not present a major problem here and factors concerning the deployment of labour will not stand in the way of these operations'.[51] Heydrich was fully satisfied with the result of the long-announced meeting, having feared much stronger resistance from the higher civil service.

However, the reality of the Third Reich was much more complex than it appears in the documents that aim to harmonize the diversity of options. The first reports about the Final Solution reaching the London Foreign Office in the summer of 1942 via the World Jewish Congress in Geneva present a somewhat different picture. The informer (a German industrialist called Eduard Reinhold Karl Schulte), who had access to the *Führer*'s headquarters, was identified only in 1983 by two American historians.[52] In the summary of the

Geneva telegrams, dated 21 October 1942, a name is mentioned that had never before been connected with the Final Solution, the Reich Minister for Food and Agriculture, Herbert Backe, who is alleged to have urged Hitler to order the physical destruction of all the Jews because of the difficult food supply situation. One section of the party, and above all *Generalgouverneur* Frank, is said to have opposed this step because many of the Jews in Eastern Europe were craftsmen and skilled workers who could not be replaced. The summary continues:

> In spite of this opposition, the plan submitted by Mr Backe was accepted by Hitler, and at the end of July the Führer signed an order according to which all European Jews on whom the Germans could lay hand, should be deported to Eastern Europe and should be destroyed. Our German informer assures us that he himself saw this order at the Führer's Head Quarters.[53]

The whole drift of previous research is put into question by this document, according to which a normal decision-making process *did* take place, culminating after all in a definite *Führer* order. However, the significance of this document should not be over-stressed any more than it was underrated at the time by officials at the Foreign Office. The story seemed to be so unbelievable that they did not even consider it necessary to inform the Vatican – the authority, so to speak, for moral indignation.[54] This document has not yet been fully examined, so initially we can only reflect hypothetically. The remarks that follow are therefore made subject to this proviso: they suggest that this is how it might have been, not, *nota bene*, that this is how it was.

The contradiction between the widely quoted minutes of the Wannsee Conference and Schulte's report disappears if we assume that, in the end, there were no differences in opinion about the Final Solution as such, but only about the economic priorities in carrying it out. As the extermination camps had been in operation for some time, any selection of people capable of working can only have been considered for the purpose of exploiting their labour. The fact that Goebbels had his way in the end and that he could proudly report to his *Führer* 'that most of the Jews have been evacuated from Berlin'[55] is further evidence for the assumption that within the Final Solution a last, possibly controversial, decision had been made not to spare any Jews on account of the war effort. This presumed dispute is of some historical interest, first because Jews could be saved in large numbers only by being conscripted for labour, and secondly because the whole process may cast new light on the evolution of

Nazi war aims. If Hitler decided to support Backe's radical position, it was because, at a time when the military situation was deteriorating rapidly, the significance of dogma increased at the expense of rational calculation. Ideology gained a momentum of its own. It could be summarized as follows: final victory and Final Solution – if both could not be attained, then at least the latter should be aimed for. Eichmann reports that the deportation of the Jews from Central and Western Europe was no longer considered merely 'important for the war effort', but from now on was classified as 'important and decisive for the outcome of the war'.[56] This was never Goering's position, for whom there was no doubt about the priority of the war effort. He is quoted by Frank in a speech to his officials on 25 March 1941 as having said categorically: 'It is more important to win the war than to persist with our race policy.'[57] In order to win over people like Goering, rational considerations were also brought into play that, even though they were clearly of secondary importance, should not be underestimated.

Raul Hilberg has shown that the need for justification on non-ideological grounds (however spurious its character) was an important ingredient in the psychology of the SS *Einsatzgruppen*.[58] Hitler had studied the causes of the collapse in 1918, and had come to the conclusion that the stability of the home front, and therefore of the regime, was to a large extent dependent on the general supply situation. He was constantly concerned with the lessons he drew from the past, but they seemed particularly relevant at a time when Backe was pressing him to agree to a reduction in the level of food rations. The Security Service (SD) report of 23 March 1942 states, with unusual clarity: 'According to concurrent reports from all over the Reich, the announcement of a reduction in food rations was greeted with great disappointment and led to considerable disturbances, especially among the workers.'[59]

Herbert Backe, who committed suicide in Nuremberg in 1947, was regarded as an extraordinarily efficient and responsible technocrat, with one over-riding interest: that the German people should be adequately fed in time of war.[60] This subject had occupied him continuously since 1936. He was much more competent than his boss, the *Blut-und-Boden* (*lit.* 'blood and soil') ideologist Richard Walter Darré. In May 1942, that is, precisely at the time being discussed here, Backe replaced Darré as *Reichsminister* in charge of food supplies. Since the beginning of the war, Backe, as Under Secretary of State, had generally been regarded as the chief organizer of food production and distribution, and had suffered because his achievements had not received sufficient recognition. He was tremendously egocentric, but a totally incorruptible Nazi, who, despite being the manager of a large state-owned estate, lived only on his official rations. Self-important Nazis he could not stand, but Heydrich, and above all Hitler, he admired greatly.[61] His sense of duty, like Heydrich's, knew no bounds. Even at the beginning of the war, Backe had instructed food distribution offices to exclude Jews from all supplementary food rations.[62] Born in Batum, Russia, of German parents in 1896, Backe grew up and was interned in Russia during the war, and became one of the most determined advocates of conquering the Ukraine in order to secure food supplies permanently for the German population.[63] He fully supported General Thomas' guidelines for the policy of economic exploitation in the East, in which the 'starvation of millions of people' was calmly accepted 'so that we can take what we need out of the country'.[64] The guidelines that Backe himself issued to local agricultural leaders in the East state: 'The Russians have been putting up with poverty, hunger and penury for centuries. Their stomachs are flexible – therefore, no misplaced sympathy.'[65] Backe certainly had the correct mentality for the Final Solution, a conclusion supported by other examples from his papers deposited in the Federal Archives.[66] It is also possible that his plea for the Final Solution was designed to prove to Hitler how implacable a National Socialist he was. In order to demonstrate how much the Reich's food supply had deteriorated during the fourth year of the war, he may thereby have provided a pseudo-rational argument for the most radical form of the Final Solution, something that Hitler was aiming for anyway. Within the ideological terms of reference, a weighing-up was permissible, especially when it was a matter of making a particular policy appear appropriate in all respects, ideologically as well as in terms of the necessities of war. The ruling elites of the Third Reich wanted the soundest possible justifications for their measures, even if their decisions had not actually been made on this basis. Hitler was particularly keen on statistics that, at first sight, seemed unchallengeable, and Backe, who had several opportunities to lecture the *Führer* in 1942–43, was an expert in this type of argument.[67]

The controversy about the extent of Hitler's personal responsibility has exhausted its potential for affording deeper understanding. The evidence for this is so overwhelming that the discussion must be considered closed. A debate that continues to focus on this issue inevitably leads to monocausal explanatory models, even where this outcome is not desired. Leaving the war aside for the moment – especially the totally unrestrained war in the East, which was undoubtedly the decisive factor in bringing about the Holocaust – at least three determining factors can be extrapolated from the preceding discussion.

First, the latent anti-semitism in German society must be mentioned, as well as a certain amount of confusion among the traditional conservative elites about the priorities of justice and legality, combined with what was called positive national feeling – which was, in reality, limited exclusively to private morality. There simply was no popular protest in favour of the Jews, not even the totally assimilated German Jews, as there was, for example, when attempts were made to remove crucifixes from Bavarian schools, or to dismiss a Protestant bishop. In both these cases, official plans were foiled.[68]

To this was added the rapid advancement of a new anti-bourgeois elite of efficient and uncompromising technocrats, who imagined that they could make the impossible possible, not least because of their certainty that they would always be backed up by Hitler. Evil was by no means as banal as Hannah Arendt suggests in her portrayal of the subaltern SS-*Obersturmbannführer*, Adolf Eichmann,[69] whose perception of duty was limited by the narrow bounds of a perverted sense of legality. He, and those like him, could be held responsible for 5.1 million Jews being killed instead of 3.5 million, but not for the principle of genocide as such. This was conceived and rationalized at a higher level, by ideological fanatics, racial biologists, eugenicists and the like, who were merely waiting for the 'go ahead' from their political leader. Technocrats of power like Heydrich and Backe, Himmler and Frank could not do without a rational justification for their actions. The common denominator of all justifications for the Final Solution was the need to stabilize the system – whether by securing the food supply or by destroying potential opposition to the regime. As Himmler declared to a meeting of generals at Sonthofen on 24 May 1944, the Jewish question was 'a considerable factor in the internal security of the Reich and Europe'.[70] It had been 'solved uncompromisingly, according to orders and rational judgements'. Allegedly, the bombing could not have been borne if the Jews had not been removed from the German cities.[71] *Generalgouverneur* Frank expressed a similar sentiment in September 1944: if the Jews had not been eliminated, it would have been like sitting 'on a volcano, which could have erupted at any minute'.[72] It was self-evident that, throughout the whole murder campaign, one remained 'decent', 'clean', even 'humane'. Or perhaps it was not so self-evident after all. Himmler took every opportunity to emphasize that the slightest irregularity, such as an SS man lining his pockets, would be punished severely: 'That could not be justified. It is underhand, whether it concerns 1 mark or a valuable piece of jewellery. It will cost him his head. It has nothing to do with the value, it is a matter of decency and principle.'[73] This was the most perfidious alibi of them all.

Hitler's part must now be briefly assessed. He was by no means merely the swaggering Utopian, who was out of touch with brutal reality. His leadership gave the regime its real driving force, and kept it constantly moving towards ever more exacting and radical objectives. This impression is confirmed by Goebbels, who refers to Hitler in his diary as the 'undismayed champion of a radical solution'.[74] He seriously believed that by annihilating the Jews he would be doing the world – or at least Europe – a great service. Nobody, as he saw it, had been prepared to take the necessary steps to achieve this end, in the sense of accelerating the process of natural selection.

Finally, it should be stressed again that this is not a plea for a fundamentally new interpretation of the Holocaust, explaining it as the result of food rationing during the war. This would be a complete misinterpretation of the arguments put forward. Laqueur is quite right to suggest that Hitler's decision had nothing to do with the German food situation, though he is probably wrong in dismissing all the evidence pertaining to this issue.[75] Whatever Hitler had in mind – and there can be no doubt that he wished for the destruction of European Jewry in one way or another – the actual extermination was not just a matter of his fiat in the way that he ordered the German attack on Poland or the invasion of Russia. For some time the Final Solution was less explicit than the term suggests; it was a gradual process by which Hitler's rhetoric was translated into concrete, ever more extreme actions. It has been argued that all the chief perpetrators felt the need to justify the monstrosity of the Holocaust in rational terms and that Hitler, though driven by his racialist obsession, remained to the last the arbiter of what superficially appeared to be an emergency situation, which, nevertheless, he himself had helped to bring about. The worlds of rationality and irrationality, of reality and unreality were closely interrelated. The more Hitler realized that the war might be lost – and there is evidence that it first dawned upon him as early as December 1941 – the more he concentrated his efforts on working out his own obsession in the guise of the supreme war lord given to the pursuit of destiny.[76] There was now no chance to execute a quick resettlement plan in the East, neither was it necessary, after Pearl Harbor, to take Anglo-Saxon (i.e. world) opinion into account: the points were set for the trains to Auschwitz. In his most destructive aims Hitler followed the same pattern that had guided him through his foreign policy adventures before 1939: total opportunism as a means of realizing ideologically fixed aims.

NOTES

This chapter is based on the German version of my inaugural lecture at the University of Frankfurt a.M. on 25 January 1984.

1 John Neville Figgis and Reginald Vere Laurence (eds), *Historical Essays and Studies by John Emerich Edward Dalberg-Acton* (London, 1907), p. 504.
2 See Klaus Hildebrand, *Das Dritte Reich* (Munich/Vienna, 1979), p. 88.
3 Tim Mason, 'Intention and Explanation: A Current Controversy about the Interpretation of National Socialism', in Gerhard Hirschfeld and Lothar Kettenacker (eds), *The 'Führer State': Myth and Reality* (Stuttgart, 1981), pp. 23–42. For the most recent historiographical survey as regards Hitler and the Holocaust see Ian Kershaw, *The Nazi Dictatorship* (London, 1985), pp. 82–105. As to Jäckel's position, see his ch. 'Hitler orders the Holocaust' in *Hitler in History* (Hanover and London, 1984), pp. 44–65.
4 Martin Broszat, 'Hitler und die Genesis der " Endlösung". Aus Anlaß der Thesen von David Irving', *Vierteljahreshefte für Zeitgeschichte* 25 (1977), pp. 739–75. As to Hans Mommsen's interpretation, see his contribution to this volume (Chapter 5). An intermediate position is taken by Ian Kershaw who is inclined towards a 'functionalist' approach but states categorically: 'Without Hitler as head of the German State between 1933 and 1945, and without his fanaticism on the "Jewish Question" as impulse and sanction, touchstone and legitimation, of escalating discrimination and persecution, it seems hardly conceivable that the "Final Solution" would have occurred' (Kershaw, *Nazi Dictatorship*, as in n. 3, p. 90).
5 See Jochen von Lang, *Das Eichmann-Protokoll* (Berlin, 1982).
6 Hermann Graml, 'Zur Genesis der "Endlösung" ', paper given at a conference of the *Militärgeschichtliches Forschungsamt* in Freiberg i. Br. in March 1984, unpublished ms.
7 Eberhard Jäckel, *Hitlers World View. A Blueprint for Power* (Cambridge and London, 1981) pp. 58–9.
8 See Paul Kluke, 'Der Fall Potempa. Eine Dokumentation', *Vierteljahrshefte für Zeitgeschichte* 5 (1957), pp. 2279–97.
9 Von Lang, *Eichmann-Protokoll* (as in n. 5), p. 137.
10 In this context, the *Kristallnacht* pogrom, coming only a few months

after the Munich conference, had a shattering effect. See Andrew Sharf, *The British Press and Jews under Nazi Rule* (London, 1964), pp. 171 ff., also A. J. Sherman, *Island Refuge* (London, 1973), pp. 170 ff.

11 As to the pressure from below for action see Karl A. Schleunes, *The Twisted Road to Auschwitz. Nazi Policy towards German Jews, 1933–1939* (Chicago/London, 1970), pp. 71 ff.; also Helmut Genschel, *Die Verdrängung der Juden aus der Wirtschaft im Dritten Reich* (Göttingen, 1966).

12 Jeremy Noakes and Geoffrey Pridham (eds), *Documents on Nazism, 1919–1945* (London, 1974), p. 38.

13 Joseph Walk (ed.), *Das Sonderrecht für die Juden im NS-Staat* (Heidelberg/Karlsruhe, 1981), p. 3 and p. 406.

14 ibid., decree nos. 287 (p. 360), 305, 306 (p. 363), 310 (p. 364), 326 (p. 368), 368 (p. 376), 377 (p. 378).

15 ibid., decree no. 493 (p. 493).

16 Max Domarus (ed.), *Hitler. Reden und Proklamationen, 1932–1945*, vol. II, Part I (Munich, 1965), p. 1058.

17 See 'Migration Statistics', Appendix I in Sherman, *Island Refuge* (as in n. 10), pp. 269–272. The SS were particularly interested in facilitating emigration. On their initiative, on 24 January 1939 Göring set up a special department in the Ministry of the Interior to co-ordinate emigration (the *Zentralstelle für jüdische Auswanderung*). It was followed on 4 July by the merger of all German Jewish organizations into the *Reichsvereinigung der Juden in Deutschland* (Reich Association of Jews in Germany), which from then on organized emigration and managed to get approximately 100,000 Jews out of Germany (i.e. the Old Reich). See Uwe Dietrich Adam, *Judenpolitik im Dritten Reich* (Düsseldorf, 1972), pp. 226–32; also Genschel, *Verdrängung der Juden* (as in n. 11), p. 262. As late as 20 May 1941 the *Reichssicherheitshauptamt* (RSHA) encouraged the Jews from Germany and from the Protectorate (i.e. Bohemia and Moravia) to emigrate via Spain and Portugal. In order to improve their limited chances, the RSHA (signed by Walter Schellenberg) instructed its subordinate offices to prevent French and Belgian Jews from getting away 'in view of the final solution of the Jewish Question which is undoubtedly in the offing', *Bundesarchiv*/Koblenz [BAK]: R 58/276/1.

18 Copy from Polish files, BAK: R 58/276/1. See also Martin Broszat, *Nationalsozialistische Polenpolitik. 1939–1945* (Frankfurt/M., 1965), p. 20 f.; Klaus-Jürgen Müller, *Das Heer und Hitler. Armee und nationalsozialistisches Regime 1933–1940* (Stuttgart, 1969), pp. 668 ff.; and Helmut Krausnick and Hans-Heinrich Wilhelm, *Die Truppe des Weltanschauungskrieges. Die Einsatzgruppen der Sicherheitspolizei und des SD 1938–1942* (Stuttgart, 1981), pp. 74 ff.

19 Krausnick and Wilhelm, *Truppe des Weltanschauungskrieges* (as in n. 18), p. 89 f.

20 See Henry Picker, *Hitlers Tischgespräche im Führerhauptquartier* (Stuttgart, 1976), p. 62. Also refer to my article on the so-called *CdZ-Gebiete* – the districts bordering on Germany and Austria and therefore subject

to civil rather than military administration (Alsace, Lorraine, etc.) – in Dieter Rebentisch and Karl Teppe (eds), *Verwaltung oder Menschenführung. Studien zur Innenpolitik des Dritten Reiches* (forthcoming).

21 Quoted in Krausnick and Wilhelm, *Truppe des Weltanschauungskrieges* (as in n. 18), p. 18.

22 Quoted in ibid., p. 88 f.

23 See ibid., p. 87.

24 Hitler's secret decree of 7 October 1939. See R. L. Koehl, *RKFDV. German Resettlement and Population Policy 1939–1945. A History of the Reich Commission for the Strengthening of Germandom* (Cambridge, Mass., 1957). See also Broszat, *Nationalsozialistische Polenpolitik* (as in n. 18), pp. 64–6.

25 Nuremberg Doc. L–221, *Der Prozeß gegen die Hauptkriegsverbrecher vor dem Internationalen Militärgerichtshof. Nürnberg, 14. Oktober 1945 – 1. Oktober 1946 [IMG]*, vol. 38. As to the connection between the war in the East and the Holocaust, see Andreas Hillgruber, 'Die "Endlösung" und das deutsche Ostimperium als Kernstück des rasseideologischen Programms des Nationalsozialismus' *Vierteljahrshefte für Zeitgeschicht*, 18 (1972), pp. 133–53.

26 Franz Halder, *Generaloberst Halder. Kriegstagebuch. Tägliche Aufzeichnungen des Chefs des Generalstabes des Heeres 1939–1942*, vol. 2 (Stuttgart, 1963), pp. 336 f.

27 See Jürgen Förster, 'Das Unternehmen "Barbarossa" als Eroberungs- und Vernichtungskrieg', in *Der Angriff auf die Sowjetunion*, vol. 4 of *Das Deutsche Reich und der Zweite Weltkrieg*, ed. by Militärgeschichtliches Forschungsamt/Freiberg i. Br. (Stuttgart, 1983), pp. 426–40.

28 Nuremberg Doc. NOKW–1076, published by Hans-Adolf Jacobsen, 'Kommissarbefehl und Massenexekutionen sowjetischer Kriegsgefangener', in Hans Buchheim *et al.*, *Anatomie des SS-Staates*, vol. 2 (Olten/Freiberg i. Br., 1965), pp. 225ff.

29 Nuremberg Doc. NO–511, quoted by Hillgruber, 'Die "Endlösung" und das deutsche Ostimperium' (as in n. 25), p. 148.

30 Krausnick and Wilhelm, *Truppe des Weltanschauungskrieges* (as in n. 18), p. 619. Wilhelm assumes that altogether 2.2 million people were killed during the first wave of executions in the East, i.e. before the extermination camps were set up. See also Raul Hilberg, *The Destruction of the European Jews*, new edition (New York, 1983), p. 767–8.

31 See n. 28 as well as Jürgen Förster's contribution to this volume (Chapter 2).

32 Krausnick and Wilhelm, *Truppe des Weltanschauungskrieges* (as in n. 18), pp. 150–72.

33 'Auszug aus den Arbeitsrichtlinien des Reichsministers für die besetzten Ostgebiete für die Zivilverwaltung, III. Richtlinien für die Behandlung der Judenfrage', BAK: R 26/IV/33b.

34 ibid.

35 See Hilberg, *Destruction of European Jews* (as in n. 30), pp. 630–5. See

also Isaiah Trunk, *Judenrat. The Jewish Council in Eastern Europe under Nazi Occupation* (New York, 1977).

36 Text and interpretation as a purely administrative formality in view of earlier decisions: Helmut Krausnick, 'Die osteuropäische Etappe der "Endlösung"', in Andreas Hillgruber (ed.), *Probleme des Zweiten Weltkrieges* (Cologne, 1967), pp. 212–24. A different interpretation is given, more in the sense of my question, by Adam, *Judenpolitik* (as in n. 17), pp. 308–16.

37 See Hans-Günther Adler, *Der verwaltete Mensch* (Tübingen, 1974), pp. 69–81.

38 Picker, *Tischgespräche* (as in n. 20), pp. 187 (4 April 1942) and 340 (29 May). In both instances Siberia is mentioned and then rejected as a dumping ground for Jews since the struggle for survival would only make them more dangerous.

39 See Graml, 'Zur Genesis der Endlösung' (as in n. 6).

40 See Hilberg, *Destruction of European Jews* (as in n. 30), pp. 218–19, who describes Himmler's visit to *Einsatzgruppe* B in Minsk and the disturbing effect the experience of the shooting of 100 Jews, carried out as a demonstration, had on him.

41 As to the now-established connection between the euthanasia programme and the use of Zyklon B for mass killings in concentration camps, see Eugen Kogon *et al.* (eds), *Nationalsozialistische Massentötungen durch Giftgas* (Frankfurt/M., 1983).

42 It is well known that Himmler kept Hitler fully abreast of the activities of the SS *Einsatzgruppen* by regular reports on *'Bandenkämpfung'*; see Hillgruber, 'Die "Endlösung" und das deutsche Ostimperium' (as in n. 25), p. 148. This also applies to a comprehensive report on the state of the Final Solution by the Inspector for Statistics of the SS of April 1943, published by Leon Poliakov and Josef Wulf, *Das Dritte Reich and die Juden* (Munich, 1978), pp. 240–48. See also Gerald Fleming, *Hitler and the Final Solution* (London, 1985), pp. 135–9. More revealing still are Himmler's notes either for or after his meetings with Hitler. On 19 June 1943, for instance, they say: 'Following my report on the Jewish question the *Führer* remarked that the evacuations of the Jews had to be carried out ruthlessly, regardless of any unrest within the next three to four months and had to be seen through', BAK: NS 19/1447.

43 Werner Jochmann (ed.), *Adolf Hitler. Monologe im Führerhauptquartier 1941–1944. Die Aufzeichnungen Heinrich Helms* (Hamburg, 1980), p. 229.

44 See Fleming, *Hitler and the Final Solution* (as in n. 42), pp. 28–30.

45 Broszat, 'Hitler und die Genesis der "Endlösung"' (as in n. 4).

46 See Hans Mommsen, 'Hitlers Stellung im nationalsozialistischen Herrschaftssystem', in Hirschfeld and Kettenacker (eds), *The 'Führer State'* (as in n. 3), pp. 43–72.

47 Hilberg, *Destruction of European Jews* (as in n. 30), p. 262.

48 Several cases though can be documented. Goebbels repeatedly urged Hitler to give his go-ahead for the 'clearance' of Berlin, which, when

eventually achieved in March 1943, pleased the *Führer*. See Broszat, 'Hitler und die Genesis der "Endlösung" ' (as in n. 4), pp. 751–7 and Willi A. Boelcke (ed.), *The Secret Conferences of Dr Goebbels, October 1939–March 1943* (London, 1967), p. 294. Baldur von Schirach made similar requests for Vienna but was frustrated by Hans Frank, head of the *Generalgouvernement* (German–occupied Poland) which served as the dumping ground for Jews from the West (Hilberg, *Destruction of European Jews*, as in n. 30, p. 141). In November 1941 Hitler felt it necessary to remind Schirach that it was his job not to solve Vienna's housing problems but to get rid of Jews and Czechs. See Helmut Heiber (ed.), *Akten der Partei-Kanzlei der NSDAP. Regesten* (Munich/Vienna, 1983), vol. 1, no. 15,406.

49 Werner Präg and Wolfgang Jacobmeyer (eds), *Das Diensttagebuch des deutschen Generalgouverneurs in Polen 1939–1945* (Stuttgart, 1975), pp. 335–8.

50 See Boelcke, *The Secret Conferences of Dr Goebbels* (as in n. 48), p. 240.

51 Text in Poliakov and Wulf, *Das Dritte Reich und die Juden* (as in n. 42), pp. 116–26. See also Eichmann's interrogation: von Lang, *Eichmann-Protokoll*, pp. 882–89. After all, Eichmann was the author of the notorious minutes. As to Heydrich's reaction, see Hannah Arendt, *Eichmann in Jerusalem. Ein Bericht von der Banalität des Bösen*, German edn (Hamburg, 1978), p. 149.

52 Richard Breitman and Alan M. Kraut; see *International Herald Tribune*, 11 November 1983; also *Der Spiegel*, no. 51, 19 December 1983.

53 Public Record Office/London [PRO]: FO 371/30921/C10833. These communications from Geneva via Berne, which contain the first message about the Holocaust reaching the West, are referred to in Bernard Wasserstein, *Britain and the Jews of Europe 1939–1945* (Oxford, 1979), p. 168, and, more specifically, in Walter Laqueur, *The Terrible Secret* (London, 1980), pp. 76–82. Laqueur dismisses the information concerning a controversy in the *Führer* Headquarters: 'Not all the additional information emanating from Geneva was helpful and some was quite wrong' (p. 82). The news that Himmler and Frank, two of the worst persecutors of the Jews, should have opted to oppose the Final Solution seems to him too incredible, though he blames the Western governments for adopting exactly the same attitude vis-à-vis the Holocaust.

54 The report received by the Central Department of the Foreign Office was not passed on to senior officials like Orme Sargent, Alexander Cadogan or Eden. I quote the minutes by members of the Central Department: W. D. Allen: 'There is nothing we can do short of winning the war. But possibly it might be useful for Mr. Osborne to pass the substance of the report on to the Vatican'; L. Harrison: 'I am still rather sceptical about the story and I am not much in favour of passing it on to the Vatican'; F. Roberts: 'I agree with Harrison' (PRO: FO 371/30921/C10833).

55 Boelcke, *The Secret Conferences of Dr Goebbels* (as in n. 48), p. 294, 2 March 1943.
56 Von Lang, *Eichmann-Protokoll* (as in n. 5), p. 152.
57 Präg and Jakobmeyer, *Diensttagebuch* (as in n. 49), p. 336.
58 Hilberg, *Destruction of European Jews* (as in n. 30), p. 276.
59 Heinz Boberach (ed.), *Meldungen aus dem Reich. Auswahl aus den geheimen Lageberichten des Sicherheitsdienstes der SS 1939–1944* (Neuwied/Berlin, 1965), p. 242.
60 See Anna C. Bramwell, *Blood and Soil. Richard Walther Darré and Hitler's 'Green Party'* (Abbotsbrook, Bourne End, 1985). I owe further valuable information on Backe's personality to Dr Bramwell as well as to Professor Horst Gies from Berlin, the foremost German expert on Richard Walter Darré (Backe's rival) and Nazi agricultural policy. However, the conclusion that Herbert Backe might well have been one of the protagonists of the Final Solution at a crucial moment is entirely my own.
61 Bramwell, *Blood and Soil* (as in n. 60), pp. 120–7. This also comes out in his personal memoirs written while awaiting his trial in Nuremberg and now part of his private papers kept at the BAK (Nachlaß Backe, No. 3/fol.1).
62 Walk, *Sonderrecht für die Juden* (as in n. 13), pp. 312, no. 47 (1 December 1939.
63 In the 1920s Backe wrote a Ph.D. thesis on wheat production in Russia trying to prove that the Russians were incapable of managing their own agriculture. The thesis argued strongly in favour of a German take-over of Russia and was consequently rejected by the University of Göttingen on political grounds. See BAK: Nachlaß Backe, No. 7/fol.1.
64 Quoted by Rolf-Dieter Müller, 'Von der Wirtschaftsallianz zum kolonialen Ausbeutungskrieg', in *Der Angriff auf die Sowjetunion* (as in n. 27), pp. 146f.
65 Quoted by Christian Streit, *Keine Kameraden. Die Wehrmacht und die sowjetischen Kriegsgefangenen 1941–1945* (Stuttgart, 1978), p. 65.
66 There is, however, as in the case of Hitler, only indirect evidence – such as, for example, a piece of outrageous anti-semitic rhetoric scribbled on the back of a menu dating from his visit to Italy (3–7 May 1943). It is not clear whether these are his own ideas or notes from somebody else's speech. 'Jewry in Europe must be exterminated ... We must return to the old anti-semitic slogans. The whole war is an anti-semitic war ...' etc. BAK: Nachlaß Backe, No. 5/fol.1, 38
67 See Backe's personal memoirs (Nachlaß Backe), pp. 41 f. Hitler always showed great interest in Backe's statistical tables, which he studied while Backe gave his reports.
68 See Ian Kershaw, *Der Hitler-Mythos. Volksmeinung und Propaganda im Dritten Reich* (Stuttgart, 1980), pp. 90–110.
69 Arendt, *Eichmann* (as in n. 51).
70 Speech in Sonthofen, 24 May 1944, in Bradley F. Smith and Agnes F.

Peterson (eds), *Heinrich Himmler. Geheimreden 1933 bis 1945 und andere Ansprachen* (Frankfurt/M., 1974), p. 203.

71　Speech in Sonthofen, 21 June 1944, in Smith and Peterson, *Heinrich Himmler* (as in n. 70), pp. 203 f.

72　Letter to Lammers, 23 September 1944, in Präg and Jakobmeyer, *Diensttagebuch* (as in n. 49), p. 914. See also p. 810 (4 March 1944): 'If we still had 2 million Jews roaming about in the country and on the other side only the few German men would not have been in control of the situation.'

73　Speech in Sonthofen, 21 June 1944 (as in n. 71).

74　Louis P. Lochner (ed.), *The Goebbels Diaries* (London, 1948), p. 103.

75　Laqueur, *The Terrible Secret* (as in n. 53), p. 82.

76　That there might be a link between the turn of the war and the Final Solution is also suggested by S. Haffner, *Anmerkungen zu Hitler*, paperback edn (Frankfurt/M., 1981), pp. 138–41. His thesis is quite convincing. As to Hitler's doubts about final victory in December 1941, see Joachim C. Fest, *Hitler: Eine Biographie* (Frankfurt/M./Berlin, 1973), p. 892.

5

*The Realization of the Unthinkable: the 'Final Solution of the Jewish Question' in the Third Reich**

HANS MOMMSEN

The history of the Holocaust defies simple explanations. Since the pioneering account by Gerald Reitlinger, which appeared in English in 1953,[1] researchers from many countries have produced detailed analyses of the persecution and liquidation of European Jewry.[2] The actual course of events has now been largely established, and the description of the deportations and exterminations is not subject to dispute among serious researchers;[3] at most, there is marginal controversy about the exact number of victims,[4] although this does not affect the overall assessment. Nevertheless, the horror of that culmination of inhumanity outstrips the capacity of historians to imagine and describe it. How could the unimaginable utopian dream, the extermination of more than 5 million European Jews, become unspeakable reality,[5] and with such appalling efficiency? Propaganda alone – the savage tirades of hate directed against Jewish fellow citizens and minority groups by Hitler, Goebbels, Streicher, the SS paper *Schwarze Korps* and the press – cannot explain why the many people who were directly or indirectly involved in the destruction of the Jews did not find some way to withhold their co-operation. References to manipulation by terror or to the compulsion to obey orders are also inadequate. The real problem in providing a historical explanation of the Holocaust lies in understanding the overall political and psychological structure that gave rise to it. Human nature shrinks from the depiction of the immeasurable barbarity that attended the activities of the SS *Einsatzgruppen* and the use of factory methods to destroy human life in Auschwitz,

*Translated by Alan Kramer and Louise Willmot.

Chelmno, Belzec, Sobibor, Treblinka and Majdanek. This is also true in an objective sense. When the subjugation and ill-treatment of human beings drives them to the edge of existence, reducing them to naked and hopeless desperation, then the last quasi-moral mechanisms governing human relations collapse in ruins. To the liquidators, but also to those who merely happened to come into contact with the business of murder, the victims had ceased to be human beings; they were classed lower than the most common criminals, whose individual identity was still recognized.[6]

In the immediate post-war years it was widely believed that the Final Solution was carried out by a very limited circle – by the sworn order of the SS, or indeed by an even smaller group consisting of the Death's Head Divisions, who provided the guards for the concentration camps.[7] However, recent research has tended to contradict this theory. Although the 'technical' implementation of the Final Solution was carried out by relatively small staffs, it would not have been possible without the co-operation of relatively large groups of officials. The claim that the *Wehrmacht* was entirely or even largely uninvolved has been exposed as untrue. It has been established that the OKW (Armed Forces High Command) and the OKH (Army High Command) actively participated in the preparation of criminal orders, and that Army units repeatedly provided essential support in the Soviet Union and other occupied countries in Eastern, South-eastern and Western Europe. Officials of the Reich railways and the *Reichsbank*, the diplomatic service, the civilian administrations in the occupied territories, the German and non-German police forces – all these contributed actively to the Holocaust in some form. The crucial question is why they were not aware of what they were doing, or why they were able to suppress with such strange consistency such knowledge as dawned upon them.[8]

An essential element in the explanation of the Holocaust was the removal of the inhibitions of the *Einsatzgruppen*, of the concentration camp guards involved in the extermination process, and indeed of all those who implemented the Final Solution. This loss of inhibition is not necessarily linked to anti-semitic and racial–biological indoctrination of the persecutors and the onlookers; we know, for example, that many of the officials responsible for the Final Solution were not primarily anti-semitic. Technocratic and subordinate attitudes could be as important as blind racialism or the mere parroting of national socialist anti-Jewish clichés. The motivation of each individual must therefore be assessed separately. In this connection, Hannah Arendt has spoken of 'the banality of evil';[9]

at a certain level, the destruction of human life – under orders to do so – was perceived as a skilled job like any other. It lay below the threshhold of social and, ultimately, moral behaviour towards individual human beings.

The example of Rudolf Höss (camp commandant of Auschwitz) has frequently been used to illustrate the divided morality of the SS thugs: he was able to combine the everyday business of organizing mass murder with scrupulous respect in the private sphere for all those secondary virtues incorporated in the apparently moral concepts of 'German order' and hygiene.[10] The speeches of Heinrich Himmler in October 1943 and January, May and June 1944 also contain the double standard that maintains that adherence to 'decent' practices – the forbidding of sadism, the avoidance of personal gain and the acceptance of 'personal responsibility' – can be used to justify criminal deeds.

This dichotomy between criminal acts and hypocritical and frequently cynical pseudo-morality was fundamental to the entire system, not just to Heinrich Himmler and the SS. True responsibility based upon ethics was eliminated, being replaced by a formalized canon of values devoid of any real content. Traditional concepts such as 'doing one's duty', 'loyalty', 'honour' and 'serving one's country' withered into execrable phrases, used repeatedly to justify the actions of the regime, as self-justification by its representatives, and to compel loyalty.[11]

There is no doubt that the liquidations that followed the deportation of the Jews were implemented with the utmost secrecy; Himmler, Heydrich and the other participants in the planning and realization of the programme knew full well why they kept any knowledge about the annihilation of the Jews from the German population, or more precisely from the pseudo 'public opinion' of the Third Reich.[12] On the one hand, the destruction of the Jews was described as a vital task in world history; on the other, it was to be kept secret from the world. The idea that traces of these crimes could be obliterated by opening up the mass graves and attempting to burn the bodies before the arrival of the Red Army was both absurd and utterly grotesque. This psychological reaction reveals that the veneer of ideological bigotry that covered the awareness of guilt was really very thin.[13]

The victories of the Red Army and the looming prospect of military defeat began to destroy the Nazi dream world of cynical power politics and megalomaniac schemes for the future. At the same time, pangs of remorse over the crimes they had committed, or something approaching a moral conscience, began to be felt.

Himmler's speech in Poznań on 13 October 1943, and his subsequent attempts to spread knowledge of the Final Solution – and thus the burden of responsibility for it – more widely, were symptomatic of this.[14] However, the diffused nature of decision-making in the Third Reich made it impossible to say afterwards that responsibilities had been delegated according to a set plan. The accused at the Nuremberg Trial of Major War Criminals were often not even willing to admit their knowledge. In many cases they shifted responsibility to the *Führer* and, except for Goering and perhaps Speer,[15] argued that they were merely carrying out orders. The flight from responsibility and the suppression of knowledge of criminal actions did not begin in 1945, however.

Despite a considerable degree of agreement among historians about the deportation and extermination process, opinions differ in analysing the causes of the Holocaust and are sometimes diametrically opposed to one another. In view of the vital importance of the subject in world history, this is not surprising. Many historians still believe that Hitler had envisaged the actual physical extermination of the Jews from the beginning and had set himself to achieve this as a long-term objective.[16] However, the carefully recorded statements of the future dictator on the subject do not provide conclusive proof of such an intention. Moreover, verbal expressions of this nature are not uncommon, being typical of radical anti-semitic wishful thinking since the late nineteenth century.[17] In fact, Hitler's actual instructions for action during the 1920s are rather more restrained.

Hatred of the Jews was indisputably fundamental to Hitler's *Weltanschauung*; opinions conflict, however, about how much influence he exerted on the detailed moves to force Jews out of German social and economic life and to deprive them of legal rights. There is a consensus of opinion that Hitler approved the cumulative intensification of persecution and that his attitude served as its legitimating authority. This does not mean that he actually initiated each step. As in many other aspects of domestic policy, he intervened only in isolated instances, frequently after receiving information from unofficial sources.[18] This is illustrated by his criticism of the sentence passed on one Markus Luftgas, which he thought too lenient; on Hitler's intervention, the sentence of imprisonment for hoarding food was replaced by the death penalty. However, there was a series of cases that demanded that he decide between rival, competing strategies. In these, he shrank away from making definitive, unambiguous commitments, and proved to be dependent on changing personal influences. Whenever he was confronted with a choice between two courses of action, he would favour the less extreme solution rather than play the part of revolutionary agitator.[19] The development of the Nuremberg Laws, for example, reveals that in the sections relating to 'Aryans' Hitler did not follow the party radicals but tended to support compromises, even if his attitude did not always remain firm.

From the intentionalist point of view there appears to have been an escalation in the measures of persecution against the Jews consistent with the interplay between the pressures of extremist groups in the Nazi Party (NSDAP) and the subsequent moves of the regime. However, it cannot be said that the illegal 'spontaneous' attacks on Jewish citizens, and the subsequent judicial measures to destroy the social and professional position of the Jewish community, were co-ordinated. The party had made extremely radical legislative proposals in spring 1933, but its initiatives were largely blocked by bureaucrats in the higher civil service (although those involved in the administration of justice were more prepared to conform). External economic and foreign policy considerations played a significant, but not decisive, role. The friction between the ministerial bureaucracy and the lower and middle-ranking party apparatus also slowed the pace of persecution. Thus, even those measures that satisfied the conventional demands of conservative groups for racial separation were considerably delayed and were mostly put into effect only after November 1938.

Many ordinary Germans gained the impression that the anti-semitic outrages that had accompanied the process of *Gleichschaltung* (Nazification of state and society) after March 1933 were declining, and that calm would return once the government took vigorous action to prevent 'spontaneous' attacks. This was certainly an illusion. The rabble-rousing tirades of the NSDAP, led by Julius Streicher's semi-pornographic paper *Der Stürmer*, influenced the political climate sufficiently to make people refrain from public contacts with Jews. They did not, however, generate the desired pogrom atmosphere, as was clearly proved in 1938. Radical anti-semitism gained its real political impact from the fact that the Political Organization of the NSDAP, which had previously been restricted more or less to welfare work, was increasingly diverted into the political arena. The higher civil service, still predominantly conservative despite efforts to Nazify it, endeavoured to make concessions to the NSDAP in the sphere of anti-semitism whilst evading party claims to control the administration, except in the municipal sector. It failed to perceive that it thereby opened the door to the abandonment of legal moderation in the conduct of state affairs and of the principle that the state should be under the rule of law. In Jewish affairs in particular, policy was set on a twisted road, which had no limits and no end.

After the Nazi seizure of power, those groups in the NSDAP that originated in the extreme *völkisch* movement – including the vast majority of the '*Alte Kämpfer*' – did not become socially integrated. Many of them remained unemployed, while others failed to obtain posts commensurate with the services they believed they had rendered the movement. The social advancement that they had hoped for usually failed to materialize. This potential for protest was increasingly diverted into the sphere of Jewish policy. Many extremists in the NSDAP, influenced by envy and greed as well as by a feeling that they had been excluded from attractive positions within the higher civil service, grew even more determined to act decisively and independently in the 'Jewish question'. The pressures exerted by the militant wing of the party on the state apparatus were most effective when they were in harmony with the official ideology. It was against Hitler's mentality openly to oppose these endeavours – with which he was in any case instinctively in sympathy – although he privately agreed to measures that counteracted them. Hitler was thus decisively responsible for the escalation of persecution. The initiative rarely came directly from him, however. He was not concerned with detailed moves to achieve the desired 'solution of the Jewish question'. This was connected not least with his visionary concept of politics, in which anti-semitism was less a question of concrete political measures than of a fanatical ideological approach. Consequently, the regime failed to develop a coherent strategy until Heydrich took control of Jewish policy into his own hands.

The genesis of the 'Nuremberg Laws' reveals the mixture of improvization and programmatic commitments that guided the policies of National Socialism. The militant wing of the NSDAP had long demanded a general ban on mixed marriages as well as the dissolution of existing ones. Preparations for legislation of this kind had begun immediately after the seizure of power, although the various departments concerned had not progressed beyond drafting various legislative proposals, for fear that anything more might undermine the legalist course. The same fate befell the plans announced by Secretary of State Pfundtner, which envisaged the creation of a special right of citizenship linked with the requirement to document 'Aryan' descent. In this case, the scheme was shelved partly because of the extreme demands of the NSDAP, which was pressing for the general adoption of its own much stricter rules on

'Aryan' descent; these excluded persons with one Jewish great-grandparent from membership of the party. The Reich Ministry of the Interior was also anxious to avoid serious repercussions for the German minorities in Poland, especially in Upper Silesia.

In the summer of 1935 there emerged the beginnings of a compromise between radical party circles and civil servants in the Ministry of the Interior, at least to the extent that the civil servants agreed to make certain concessions on the issues of mixed marriages and the restriction of the Jews' right to citizenship, on condition that attacks on Jewish businesses ceased and that there should be no compulsory confiscation of Jewish property. This compromise provided the background to Hitler's decision, on the occasion of the Nuremberg party rally, to use legislation to regularize the 'Jewish question' as a 'unique secular solution'. Hitler had originally summoned the *Reichstag* and the diplomatic corps to Nuremberg in order to make a solemn government declaration, using the Abyssinian conflict to announce Germany's own revisionist demands in foreign affairs. On the recommendation of Baron von Neurath, this plan was dropped on the evening of 13 September. As the passing of the Reich Flag Law was hardly sufficient to justify the special session of the *Reichstag*, the inner circle of party leaders decided to introduce a *Judengesetz* (Jewish law) to the *Reichstag* instead, mainly in the hope of improving the acutely strained relations between the party and the ministerial bureaucracy. There were no concrete suggestions about the substance of this legislation, and, in the night-long deliberations that followed, Hitler vacillated over which precise policy he should propose.

On the same night, the experts on Jewish affairs and citizenship in the Reich Ministry of the Interior were ordered to Nuremberg and instructed there and then to submit drafts for a Reich citizenship law and a law on mixed marriages. They were therefore unable to refer to the preliminary work that had been done within the various government departments. This explains why Gürtner, the Reich Minister of Justice, first learned about the 'Nuremberg Laws' only when they were announced. In the main, the laws did not really represent a qualitatively new stage of National Socialist Jewish policy. They contained little more than sweeping stipulations that could be interpreted in various ways. In the prescribed language of the regime, the laws offered German Jewry the opportunity to establish itself as a 'national minority'. Despite their discriminatory language, they did not go beyond a programme of segregating the Jews from the rest of the population, and were actually regarded as an acceptable 'legal solution' by many of those people most affected

103

by them. Only after the issue of provisions for the precise application of the laws, which mostly occurred at a much later stage, were
they used as an instrument for the further, systematic persecution of
the Jewish people.

The Reich Citizenship Law excluded Jews from the right to Reich
citizenship, which was due to be created as an addition to mere
nationality status. Loss of Reich citizenship had no concrete significance, apart from the loss of the right to vote; the issue of whether
the Jews should be deprived of German nationality and placed under
Alien Law, as the NSDAP had intended, was thus sidestepped.
Furthermore, the experts in the Reich Ministry of the Interior
succeeded in making both the Reich Citizenship Law and the Law
for the Protection of German Blood and German Honour applicable
only to full Jews and to those half-Jews who belonged to the Jewish
religious community and did not live in mixed marriages. They thus
did not fulfil the more extreme proposals of the NSDAP to include
'Grade 1 and Grade 2 persons of mixed descent'. On the other hand,
the First Ordinance to the Reich Citizenship Law prohibited Jews
from holding public posts, replacing the emergency regulations on
the civil service which had been in force since 7 April 1933.

In fact, the new Reich Citizenship Law never had any practical
significance. Certainly, Hitler did approve the Law on Provisional
Citizenship in March 1938 after the *Anschluss* (annexation of
Austria), thereby granting the population of Austria the right to
vote. However, he forbade further preliminary work on the
implementation of the law when serious disagreements arose
between the Ministry of the Interior and the Office of the *Führer*'s
Deputy over the racial and political criteria to be applied to each
citizen. The idea of submitting every German to a formal 'tribunal'
hearing before an official *Reichsbürgerbrief* (Deed of Reich Citizenship) could be issued actually raised serious doubts about Wilhelm
Frick's grasp on reality.

The Law for the Protection of German Blood and German
Honour was seen as particularly odious outside Germany because of
its discrimination against the Jews. On closer inspection, however,
it cannot be regarded as a victory by the NSDAP over the more
moderate ministerial bureaucracy. The Jews were prohibited from
raising the Reich flag, but this only confirmed the status quo and at
least protected them from being attacked for failing to honour the
swastika. The law contained the ban on mixed marriages that was
already *de facto* in effect, but refrained from decreeing that all
existing mixed marriages were automatically dissolved, as party
militants had demanded. It also made *Rassenschande* (sexual inter-

course between 'Aryans' and 'non-Aryans'), a category of offence developed by Nazi lawyers, into an offence punishable by law. Although in early summer 1935 Hitler had suspended the ban on the employment of 'Aryan' domestic servants under the age of 45 by Jews, he now gave in to pressure from high-ranking party officials and permitted the inclusion of this provision. In an attempt to find a precedent for it, Gerhard Wagner, the head of the Reich Medical Association and one of the leading rabble-rousers, had gone back to fifteenth-century regulations governing the employment of domestic servants; copies of these regulations were preserved in the NSDAP central archive. On the issue of the legal definition of the status of Jews, on the other hand, Hitler inclined towards accommodating the concern of the jurists in the Ministry of the Interior about the introduction of legislative measures that they regarded as too extreme. Although the provision stipulating that the law should apply only to full Jews was deleted, Hitler proposed that a press notice should be issued that would make this limited application clear.

It is therefore not surprising that the Nuremberg Laws produced an angry response from the NSDAP. Goebbels had the radio broadcast of the *Reichstag* session cut short before the bills were read out and instructed the party's press and officials not to discuss the laws until the provisions for their implementation had been decided upon. At a secret *Führer* conference in Munich on 24 September, Hitler adopted the position of the experts from the Ministry of the Interior: using the argument of Bernhard Lösener, the official responsible for racial affairs in the ministry, he spoke in favour of a more restricted legal definition of Jewishness and warned against creating a group of people who had nothing to lose. This meant that half-Jews who were not members of the Jewish religious community, and 'Grade 2 persons of mixed descent', would not be affected by the law. However, Martin Bormann persuaded Hitler to issue secret instructions that paragraph 6 of the First Ordinance to the Reich Citizenship Law, which would have ruled out any introduction of more sweeping regulations governing entry to public institutions, including the German Labour Front, and which he had just signed, was not to be applied.

Bormann was thus compensated for his defeat over the actual drafting of the Reich Citizenship Law. He also got his way on another issue later. The draft Law on the Acquisition and Loss of German Nationality, which had been prepared in early 1939 with the assistance of Hans Globke, contained a provision to strip the offspring of racially mixed marriages of their German nationality (instead, they were allowed a right of abode as long as they were permanent residents). This clause later provided a stepping-stone for the Eleventh and Twelfth Ordinances to the Reich Citizenship Law, which were issued in 1943 and indirectly sanctioned the deportation of the Jewish population. However, there was never a definitive regulation of the legal status of the Jews – the government departments opposed it for a variety of reasons and adopted delaying tactics, whilst Hitler showed no personal interest in legal regularization.[20]

On this issue it would seem that Hitler cannot be regarded as one of the extremists; instead, he tended to compromise between the position of the various departments and the demands of party officialdom. Specifically, his regard for public opinion made him recognize the merits of a policy of exempting from persecution those sections of the Jewish population that were largely assimilated, at least for the time being. He remained susceptible to arguments of this nature, although there can be no doubt that in principle he wanted to see persons of mixed blood removed from the German 'blood union'. Characteristically, as late as 1942 he decided against the deportation of the partners in 'privileged mixed marriages', who had previously been exempted from persecution, and also of people of mixed descent ('*Mischlinge*') in general.[21]

Hitler's conduct can be interpreted in various ways. Some historians believe that his decisions were determined by his conviction that the 'Jewish question' would be 'solved', possibly during a war, and that he acted throughout in pursuit of a plan that had long been decided. In this case, caution and tactical considerations – and even sometimes simple convenience – must be considered as determining factors in shaping his policies. This pattern of conduct is said to apply in particular to the field of foreign policy.[22] It was second nature to Hitler to make his decisions only when the situation seemed over-ripe, but it is certainly an exaggeration to claim that he waited upon events with the sure-footedness of a sleepwalker, as the propaganda would have us believe. Equally, he was not always, and not unconditionally, afraid to make decisions. His immediate and instinctive perception of impending dangers was rooted in a deep psychological insecurity, masked by a mixture of megalomania, joviality, harshness, determination and, not least, endless tirades of rhetoric. Ultimately, he would respond with restless activity and a flood of decisions, thus 'taking the bull by the horns'.[23]

As far as I can see, no such reactions have been documented in the Jewish question. None of the measures to restrict and then to deny Jews their civil and economic rights, and to make them into social pariahs, were directly attributable to initiatives of the *Führer* himself. This is true of the boycott campaign of April 1933; of the Nuremberg Laws (abhorrent though they were, their significance in the persecution of the Jews has often been exaggerated);[24] of the pogrom of November 1938, which was unleashed by Goebbels;[25] and of the subsequent 'Aryanization policy' promoted by Hermann Goering.[26]

To state these facts is not to claim that the events occurred without Hitler's approval and even encouragement. Nevertheless, given the ideological framework and the existence of machinery to trigger off 'spontaneous' anti-semitic outrages, they were first conceived by the rival satraps around Hitler, who were unscrupulously determined to outdo one another in implementing National Socialist policies, and thus to please the *Führer*. Only in retrospect have these measures acquired the appearance of being part of a systematic and cynical escalation of persecution. This can be demonstrated, for example, in the case of Goebbels. After the failure of his attempts to generate a pogrom atmosphere among the population in connection with the boycott campaign, he adopted the policy of legal measures against the Jewish community.[27] It is not likely that this change was the result of a tactical decision taken after consultation with Hitler. The *Führer* cared little for legal actions; he probably agreed to this course because it suited his objectives in foreign policy. However, it is also true that Hitler had little patience for the struggles of the rival departments as they strove to obtain, or to maintain, leadership in the Jewish question; he was instinctively in sympathy with the strong-arm methods favoured by the militant groups in the NSDAP, though he sometimes found it necessary to by-pass them.[28] Nor did Hitler interest himself in the detailed implementation of the anti-semitic programme; his few interventions do not reveal any practical plan. The propaganda aspect was of paramount importance for him, in this as in other issues. His conduct after the unsuccessful boycott campaign of 1 April 1933 reveals this clearly. He had approved Goebbels' initiative, had probably entrusted Streicher with the task of carrying out the boycott, and had defended the measures in the face of Cabinet criticism by claiming that there had been no other way to appease the 'anger of the people'.[29] Nevertheless, he was careful to distance himself from these events in public. He was fascinated by the idea, put forward by Goebbels at this time, of using German Jews as hostages for obtaining the good conduct of the Western powers in their foreign policy dealings with the Reich. This notion, which Goebbels had originally used as a propaganda expedient, was taken up by Hitler as a serious strategic argument. In later years it became a recurring *leitmotiv* in his public pronouncements.[30]

Hitler's threat to take bitter revenge on 'world Jewry' in the event of war, and to destroy German Jewry in retaliation, was thus made in the context of exerting propaganda pressure. Many authors have nevertheless deduced from these utterances that Hitler was firmly resolved to wage an all-out campaign of genocide against international Jewry. The repetition of this threat has been interpreted as the decision that set in motion the systematic extermination of those Jews in German hands.[31] There is absolutely no doubt that Hitler's own ideas did indeed involve the physical destruction of the Jews, but they also involved the destruction of other entire populations. He did not hesitate to demand the liquidation of large groups of Slavs, and expressly ordered that the besieged population of Leningrad should be left to starve to death.[32]

In the case of the Final Solution, Hitler maintained the taboo on public discussion of the issue until the very end. In this he was more consistent than Himmler, who spoke openly of the systematic liquidation of the Jews in the speeches mentioned above. This fact has led David Irving to assert that Hitler was not fully informed about the extermination programme before 7 October 1943 – and even then only informally – although it had been in full swing for over 18 months by that date.[33] In one respect Irving is correct: the actual measures for implementing this monstrous scheme never were discussed, either officially or privately, in the *Führer*'s headquarters. Hitler always kept carefully within the confines of the prescribed phraseology – to the effect that 'the Jews are, *en bloc*, being mobilized for the appropriate labour duties', as Bormann put it in a confidential directive to high-ranking party officials on 11 July 1943 in an attempt to counter rumours about the 'special treatment' of the deported Jews.[34] Himmler's use of this camouflage language – at its most striking in the reports of the SS statistician Richard Korherr[35] – reveals that the observance of secrecy and the use of prescribed terminology extended even to the internal correspondence of the *Führer*'s headquarters.

Hitler nevertheless continued to express his extreme racialist and anti-semitic opinions, which were nothing short of paranoid, in countless unofficial and official statements. Phrases typical of the language of *Der Stürmer* occur with great frequency: the Jews are described as a 'bacillus', as carriers of disease, and as dangerous vermin which must be destroyed. This terminology, which he shared with the militant anti-semitic wing of the party and the SS, remains constant throughout and did not become more extreme in response to the Holocaust. Typically, it remained within the frame-work of propagandistic metaphor. With the exception of his comment to a Slovak diplomat at the beginning of 1939 that 'Now we are going to destroy the Jews',[36] there are no known statements by Hitler that refer directly to the policy of genocide.

There are, however, some recorded remarks that appear at first sight to refer to the issue. The 'Table Talk' of 25 October 1941 contains Hitler's observation: 'By the way, it is no bad thing that we are rumoured to have a plan for the destruction of the Jews.'[37] The remark was made before the policy of genocide was systematically implemented (which began to occur only in March 1942 after preliminary steps had been taken in autumn 1941), so the comment must be interpreted in the context of proposals to settle the Jews in the Russian marshlands. Hitler wound up his remarks with the observation: 'Terror is salutary.' This was a reference to the liquidation programme of the *Einsatzgruppen*, which led to, but is not identical with, the subsequent Final Solution.[38] It is therefore not correct to infer from the passage quoted that Hitler was actually alluding the policy of the Holocaust. A similar picture emerges from the 'Table Talks' of 23 and 27 January 1942 and also from a note by Goebbels on 14 February 1942: 'The Führer once more expressed his determination to clean up the Jews in Europe pitilessly'.[39] These comments amounted to massive threats against the Jews and emphatic support for the deportation programme, but did not constitute admission of an actual intention to commit genocide.

It is also worth recalling Hitler's conversations with Marshall Antonescu and Admiral Horthy in mid-April 1943, when he evaded the straightforward comments of his Hungarian guests by resorting to standard anti-semitic rhetoric.[40] His reaction has been described by Martin Broszat, who emphasizes 'Hitler's ability to distort the facts and turn them upside down whenever he was faced with the reality of criminal actions.[41] The apparently reliable record of Hitler's reaction to the reproaches of Frau von Schirach[42] also reveals how he deliberately avoided any mention of the true facts, indicating an instinctively defensive attitude.[43] The statement that comes nearest to an admission of genocide is Hitler's secret speech to *Wehrmacht* officers and generals on 26 May 1944, in which he explained, in apologetic tones:

By removing the Jews, I eliminated the possibility of any kind of revolutionary nucleus or germ cell being formed. Of course, you could say to me: Yes, could you not have solved the problem in a simpler way – or not simpler, for everything else would have been more complicated – but in a more humane way?

This justification is strikingly similar to remarks made by Himmler only a short time before. Significantly, it is once more only the policy of deporting the Jews that is being admitted, not the policy of mass liquidation; the reference to an allegedly 'more humane' solution should be regarded as a possibly subconscious allusion to the liquidation. In any case, his ambiguous statements reveal that Hitler himself felt a compulsive need for self-justification, psychologically balanced as always by aggressive accusations directed against the alleged enemy. This was especially apparent after the subject was taken up in Allied news reports.[44]

The controversy provoked by David Irving over the question of how far Hitler was informed about the actual measures taken to implement the Final Solution – and this is the only point of real dispute – cannot easily be decided by examining the ambiguous statements of the *Führer*.[45] The question of whether or not Hitler was thoroughly briefed on the state of the genocide programme during Globocnik's visit to *Führer* headquarters on 7 October 1942 is not conclusive either.[46] Gerald Fleming, who disputes Irving's interpretation from beginning to end, nevertheless concludes that, despite the violent threats and prophecies in his speeches, Hitler used calculated cunning to disguise his own *personal* responsibility for events, especially for the implementation of the policies of destruction that he had nurtured for so long. In contrast to Irving, Fleming emphasizes that Hitler himself arranged the use of the camouflage language that was used whenever the policies of genocide were discussed.

Such an interpretation – also made by others[47] – seems to be both plausible and consistent with the evidence. However, it also raises a number of difficulties. Even within Hitler's closest circle of trusted friends, there is no sign that he was ever prepared to abandon his usual metaphors in his references to the 'Jewish question'. If such behaviour had been based only on machiavellian cunning, there would have been no reason not to speak directly when the perpetrators were discussing events among themselves. There is not a single reliable piece of evidence that this ever happened. Himmler's speeches, in which he revealed the policy of the Final Solution, contain only passing references to a 'military' order by Hitler; he may well have been referring specifically to Hitler's speech of August 1939.[48] In so far as the implementation of the measures of liquidation rested on an order, rather than merely a 'wish of the

Führer',[49] that order was the Commissar Order (*Kommissarbefehl*) of 1941 and Hitler's instructions on how it was to be carried out.[50]

In fact, we must conclude from these observations that Hitler gave no formal order to carry out the Final Solution of the 'European Jewish question'. Krausnick still believes that Hitler gave a secret order to exterminate the Jews in March 1941 at the latest, in connection with his intention to 'have the political commissars of the Red Army shot'.[51] However, it is crucial to distinguish between the partial destruction of the Jews of Eastern Europe, based on the Commissar Order, and the systematic policy of the Final Solution, in spite of the fact that the latter developed from the former. As will be shown in a different context, preparations for the systematic implementation of the Final Solution were begun only in late autumn of 1941 and were not based on a written order. There are also many internal reasons for believing that Hitler never gave such an order orally, either.

The exclusively metaphoric language in which the *Führer* discussed the 'Jewish problem', as well as his general reluctance to take decisions that might have caused public opposition and perhaps have had to be withdrawn, make it unlikely that he would have come to a binding decision. Remarkably, even in early 1942 Hitler considered reactivating the abandoned Madagascar Plan.[52] If one attributes such behaviour to a desire to dissemble even among his closest friends, then it would simply be evidence of the extent to which he shrank from referring openly to the factory-style destruction of human life. His conduct in this and other matters, however, appears to be due less to an extreme intellectual cynicism than to an ability to dissociate himself completely from reality.[53]

Hitler's speech to the *Reichstag* on 30 January 1939 is cited more than any other as evidence of his early intention to destroy the Jews systematically:

> Today I shall once more be a prophet. If the international Jewish financiers inside and outside Europe should again succeed in plunging the nations into another world war, then the result will not be the Bolshevization of the world and thus a victory for Jewry, but the annihilation of the Jewish race in Europe.[54]

This argument, repeated in the speeches of 30 January 1941, 30 January 1942, 30 September 1942 and 8 November 1942,[55] is complemented by Goering's report at the infamous meeting at the Reich Air Ministry on 12 November 1938, in which he quoted Hitler: 'If the German Reich comes into conflict with foreign powers

111

in the foreseeable future, it goes without saying that in Germany too our main concern will be to settle accounts with the Jews.'[56] Although at first sight the connection with the subsequent genocide policy may appear to be evident, the political motive behind this statement is in fact ambivalent. Such threats were intended primarily to exert pressure on the Western nations, particularly Britain and the United States. They are thus connected with the hostage argument, which had surfaced as early as 1923: in that year the radical anti-semite Hermann Esser had argued that, in the event of a French invasion, one German Jew should be shot for every French soldier who stepped onto German soil. Andreas Hillgruber has concluded that such statements revealed the radical, racial–ideological objectives of the regime in the coming war. This is to over-state their significance, although the potential for a 'war of racial destruction' that is discernible in them is not disputed.[57]

Hitler considered the 'Jewish question' from a visionary political perspective that did not reflect the real situation. The struggle against Jewry was for him an almost metaphysical objective; as his 'Political Testament' reveals, it eventually took on a chiliastic dimension.[58] Hitler had always sympathized with 'spontaneous' attacks on Jews. They reflected his belief that anti-semitic opinions could be used both for mass mobilization and for the integration of the party's supporters. A campaign of extermination, implemented with extreme secrecy and with an increasingly bad conscience (as in the case of Himmler), was not completely compatible with this concept. Time and time again Hitler argued – quite incorrectly – that it was the Jewish element in the population, and especially the Jewish elites, who were mobilizing resistance to National Socialism and opposing the triumph of the 'anti-semitic idea' in the world. The alleged need to 'remove' the Jews from German territory and to fight Jewry on the principle of 'an eye for an eye, a tooth for a tooth' can always be traced back to the chiliastic component of Hitler's otherwise fragile personal philosophy. By contrast, the spurious justifications of the *Einsatzgruppen* for the murder of the Jewish population – ranging from housing shortages and the danger of insanitary conditions through to partisan warfare[59] – reflect their need to justify a crime that went beyond the causal connection of racial–biological anti-semitism.

Throughout his career Hitler, out of a mixture of instinct and vanity, avoided any attempt to confront his ideological dream-world with political and social reality. He felt strongly that the inner consistency of his *Weltanschauung*, or of the 'National Socialist Idea' as he described it with typical formalism, would be damaged if

112

confronted with the complexity of the real world. Even during the *Kampfzeit* (the period before 1933; *lit.* 'time of struggle') he had adopted the habit of simply ignoring inconvenient realities. The refusal to accept disagreeable information increasingly became a dominant feature of his style of government. J. P. Stern has emphasized that Hitler's popularity was based on the fact that he turned his private sphere into a public one.[60] Political success and almost unlimited power enabled him to turn his subjective opinions on issues more and more into objective yardsticks for decision-making. Anti-semitic imagery spared him the need to reflect on the true consequences of his prophecies of the 'destruction of the Jewish race in Europe', a tendency that was reinforced after the invasion of the Soviet Union had committed him to an 'all or nothing' strategy. There was no middle ground between Hitler's daily work, crammed with military and armament production details, and the construct of ideas that formed his ideology and that bore no relation to reality. His passion for architectural planning was just another way of escaping into a dream-world once his supremacy as a military commander was threatened by unacknowledged defeats. Hitler's escape into the illusory world of film and opera formed part of the same syndrome.[61]

When confronted with the actual consequences of the destruction of the Jews, Hitler reacted in exactly the same way as his subordinates, by attempting not to be aware of the facts or suppressing his knowledge. Only in this way could he give free rein to his anti-semitic tirades and his threats to destroy the Jews physically whilst simultaneously avoiding nearly all direct identification with the policy of genocide that was actually being implemented. The collective repression of disagreeable facts and criminal actions is an inevitable adjunct of any kind of political irrationalism; under National Socialism, the mechanism of repression was perfected. In 'good' years it was moderated by foreign policy considerations and by Hitler's instinctive perception of how the population would react. Above all else, he feared public alienation from the regime, and it is no coincidence that he vowed repeatedly that the events of 9 November 1918 would never be repeated.[62] However, as the war took its course this last corrective disintegrated, and the criminal and destructive energies that lay at the root of Hitler's personality ultimately prevailed over tactical and political considerations.

The fact that the Final Solution tied down large quantities of materials, including vital transport capacity, and critically diminished the labour force that was so desperately needed, ought to have suggested the need for a modification of the deportation and murder programme. When Hitler was confronted with this problem, he usually responded evasively. In cases where he sensed a possible loss of prestige, as in the deportation of Jews from Berlin to Riga,[63] he ordered that the measures be delayed. However, the *Führer* did not stop Himmler and his thugs. As before 1939, he felt bound to stand by the party and the SS, institutions whose members took literally the 'grand' historical perspective presented them by Hitler. On the 'church question', Hitler was able to restrain Martin Bormann; on the 'Jewish question', he was the slave of his own public prophecies. Any retreat would have made him lose credibility in his own eyes, when his supreme guiding principle was to avoid any such development. At its root was his manic idea that, as bearer of the 'National Socialist Idea', he must not allow himself to contradict his own previous statements.[64]

The realization of the Final Solution became psychologically possible because Hitler's phrase concerning the 'destruction of the Jewish race in Europe' was adopted as a direct maxim for action, particularly by Himmler. Hitler, it must be conceded, was the ideological and political author of the Final Solution. However, it was translated from an apparently utopian programme into a concrete strategy partly because of the problems he created for himself, and partly because of the ambitions of Heinrich Himmler and his SS to achieve the millennium in the *Führer*'s own lifetime and thus to provide special proof of the indispensability of the SS within the National Socialist power structure.[65] Himmler's statements indicate that he intended to fulfil in one single, 'masterful', self-sacrificial act something that had actually been intended as a timeless programme.[66] He thus directed a large part of his energies towards a programme that, for Hitler, had only a low priority in comparison with the conduct of the war.

Himmler and Heydrich thus played a decisive role in implementing the Final Solution. Nevertheless, it must be stressed that a purely personalized interpretation would prevent full understanding of the issue. The eventual step towards mass destruction occurred at the end of a complex political process. During this process, internal antagonisms within the system gradually blocked all alternative options, so that the physical liquidation of the Jews ultimately appeared to be the only way out.

At this point it is necessary to recall the various stages of the National Socialist persecution of the Jews. It was certainly not carried out according to a carefully prepared plan; Karl A. Schleunes has justifiably spoken of a 'trial and error' method.[67] Only in 1941 did Heydrich succeed in eliminating rival contenders for control of the 'Jewish question'. Previously there had been constant infighting between departments and party offices determined to safeguard their own authority in the field. This infighting resulted in a continuous escalation in the persecution of the Jews. Seen from the perspective of the subsequent policy of genocide, the numerous individual moves against the Jewish community would appear to have been logical steps in one coherent plan. However, it would be inappropriate to seek any such degree of rationality in the motives of the men who initiated the specific measures.

It would also be an entirely improper simplification of this process to trace it back to ideological factors alone. Anti-Jewish initiatives gained their momentum because they were associated with other interests. A desire to enhance their own prestige and to extend their authority was an important motive for many National Socialists, especially the *Gauleiter*; their rival attempts to declare 'their' districts 'Jew-free' play a conspicuous role in the genesis of the Holocaust. Straightforward economic interests were usually involved as well: in the case of the *Gauleiter*;[68] in the case of Goebbels in relation to the pogrom of November 1938;[69] in the anti-semitic outrages in Austria directly after the *Anschluss*;[70] in the case of the Reich Security Head Office (RSHA) especially with regard to the attempts to establish an SS economic empire;[71] in industrial and banking circles as the 'spontaneous' and legalized 'Aryanization' measures and the exploitation of the labour of concentration camp prisoners offered advantages to many;[72] and among the commercial middle class which, especially in the early years of the regime, tried hard to intensify the repressive measures against their Jewish competitors.[73] The list could be extended at will: direct and indirect, legal and illegal gains at the expense of Jewish wealth and property were part of daily life in the Third Reich, which can accurately be described as a system of officially promoted corruption in this as in other respects.[74] It is scarcely surprising that Speer's construction department showed no reluctance to make use of Jewish dwellings in Berlin, and that Nazi officials at every level were prepared to claim Jewish property for their own private use without embarrassment.[75]

Another mechanism, equally effective in radicalizing the persecution of the Jews, was provided by the *Judenreferate* (sections for Jewish affairs) which were established in each government department after 1933. These sections felt the need to justify their existence by introducing cumulative anti-Jewish legislation. Numerous shameful restrictions were imposed on German Jews by means of administrative decrees that were usually both defamatory and economically superfluous. Moreover, they were issued openly;

every citizen could have found out about the inhuman treatment of his Jewish fellow citizens by reading the *Reichsgesetzblatt* (Official Gazette).[76] No less shocking is the willingness of the authorities to enforce this legislation down to the last detail, although their own primary motivation was not anti-semitic.[77]

The anti-semitism of the conservative nationalist civil service elite, although more moderate than that of the NSDAP, prevented them from resisting anti-semitic infringements even when they involved blatant violations of the law. The same is true of the *Wehrmacht*, the public administration and the courts. The majority of those involved in the legal profession were willing to adapt the administration of justice to the dominant ideology of anti-semitism, even before the legal basis for such behaviour had been created.[78] They contented themselves with the illusion that the regime would go no further than the complete segregation of the Jewish section of the population.[79]

In contrast to the conduct of a large proportion of the German upper class, anti-semitic feeling was less easily mobilized in the population as a whole. The boycott of April 1933 had been a complete failure in this respect. Similarly, the pogroms of November 1938 were greeted with overwhelming disapproval among the population.[80] There were scarcely any anti-semitic outbursts of the kind characteristic of Eastern European countries; only in Vienna after 18 March 1938 did anti-semitic outrages occur that had a comparatively broad basis of popular support. Anti-semitic resentment was traditionally directed more against non-assimilated Jews. It took years of systematic propaganda to transfer the stereotyped image of the East European Jew to the entire Jewish population and to indoctrinate the younger generation in particular with anti-semitism.[81]

The strategy of exerting pressure on German Jewry by unleashing popular resentment thus proved to have been ill-conceived. Goebbels soon turned instead to the systematic 'legal' elimination of the Jews from public life, a course of action that was to be justified by the fiction that their alleged preponderance in certain professions had to be rectified and a programme for racial segregation implemented.[82] Accordingly, the attacks of the storm troopers and NSDAP were gradually supplanted by 'legal' procedures; this was not so much the result of a deliberate strategy linking 'spontaneous' with legal actions, but was due rather to the fact that the Nazis had no clearly thought-out conception of how they should proceed in the 'Jewish question'.[83] At any rate, it had quickly become apparent that toleration of 'spontaneous' actions by party hotheads did not bring a 'solution' of the 'Jewish question' any closer. All the leading Nazi officials concerned with the issue – Heinrich Himmler, Reinhard Heydrich, Hermann Göring, Martin Bormann and Wilhelm Frick – were convinced until after the outbreak of the Second World War that a systematic policy of compulsory emigration offered the only real 'solution'.[84]

However, the exclusion of Jews from public and social life, begun in 1933 and increased until 1939 though with varying degrees of intensity, must also be accounted a failure from this point of view; it was simultaneously an incentive and a handicap for those Jews who wanted to emigrate. The regime's reluctance even to make the financial terms of emigration tolerable – the Reich Flight Tax (*Reichsfluchtsteuer*) introduced for quite different reasons by Brüning was retained[85] – resulted in a relative decline in the number of emigrants. After the introduction of the Nuremberg Laws, which despite their discriminatory provisions were seen by many German Jews as providing a definitive statement of their legal position, Jewish emigration declined significantly.[86] Even more significant were the steps that undermined the economic position of the Jewish community. A series of measures was enacted to exclude them from professions in the public service, to withdraw legal protection from them, to discriminate against them economically, and to confiscate Jewish businesses by means of 'Aryanization' (a process that began long before November 1938). Such campaigns ensured that those Jews who remained, who were often older members of the community, frequently did not have enough money to leave; the emigration rate was correspondingly reduced.[87] The reluctance of the potential host countries to accept large numbers of Jews, so fateful in the light of later developments, also made emigration more difficult.[88]

The expropriation, proletarianization and ostracization of the Jewish minority cut their social contacts with the majority of the population and forced them to seek refuge in the anonymity of the cities. The well-intended efforts of Bernhard Lösener, the official responsible for racial affairs in the Reich Ministry of the Interior, to exempt half-Jews and Jews living in so-called 'privileged mixed marriages',[89] actually heightened the isolation of the Jews. The segregation and extreme social isolation of the Jewish community were vital in ensuring that the majority of Germans – with the exception of genuine opposition groups – remained indifferent to their fate.[90] Gestapo terror helped to complete the social ostracization of the Jews.

The intensified persecution of the Jews after 1938 was unquestionably connected with the foreign policy successes of the regime, which made caution in its dealings with foreign powers appear less necessary and also led to a more robust style in other areas of National Socialist politics. The *Anschluss* with Austria resulted in a marked radicalization, especially as regards 'Aryanization'. This policy had long been demanded by groups within the party but it had been postponed, not least owing to the influence of Schacht, because of its negative effects on the economy and particularly on armaments production.[91] Subsequently, the important phases of radicalization were first tried out in the 'colonial territories' and then transferred to the Old Reich. The annexation of Austria, and by analogy all subsequent territorial extension of German rule, ensured that the size of the emigration problem grew constantly. Eichmann's successes in establishing the Office for Jewish Emigration in Vienna, and subsequently the Reich Central Office for Jewish Emigration within the RSHA in 1939, were thus cancelled out.

The creation of Jewish ghettos, first mentioned during the conference at the Reich Air Ministry on 12 November 1938, and the transformation of the 'Jewish question' into a Police problem, resulted in a transfer of authority for the Jewish question to the RSHA, despite Goering's official responsibility for it. Both Himmler and Heydrich had, for different reasons, disapproved of the orchestration of the *Kristallnacht* pogrom by Goebbels; characteristically, the participants then reached agreement on the most radical line imaginable. All sides were thus saved from any loss of prestige by this approach, which was possible because no established interests stood in its way.[92]

The RSHA remained committed to the emigration programme even after the outbreak of the Second World War had drastically curtailed the opportunities for Jews to emigrate. Because of their powerful position in the occupied Polish territories, and also Himmler's personal position as Reich Commissar for the Strengthening of Germandom (*Reichskommissar für die Festigung Deutschen Volkstums*), the SS were able to take almost complete control of initiatives in the 'Jewish question'. It was crucially significant that the fate of the vastly increased numbers of Jews in German hands became inextricably linked with Himmler's scheme for the resettlement of ethnic Germans in the East, which culminated in the *Generalplan Ost* (resettlement programme for Eastern Europe). As Reich Commissar for the Strengthening of Germandom, Himmler ordered on 30 October 1939 that the Jewish population of those Polish territories that had been annexed by the Reich should be deported to the *Generalgouvernement*, a policy that was to be implemented side by side with the creation of Jewish ghettos.[93] A preliminary decree by Heydrich on 21 September had already distinguished between a long-term 'ultimate objective', which was to be kept top secret, and the intermediate stage of 'forced explusion'.[94] The primary motive was revealed in the executory provisions of Himmler's decree for the *Reichsgau* Wartheland: 'The purging and protection of the new German areas' was designed to provide housing and employment prospects for the ethnic German settlers (*Volksdeutsche*).[95] There is no doubt that the resettlement programme agreed to in the Nazi–Soviet Non-Aggression Pact, whereby ethnic Germans living in the Soviet Union were to be settled mainly in the Wartheland, provided the impetus for the large-scale deportation programme, which affected Poles as well as Jews.[96]

Although there was as yet no thought of systematic mass annihilation, a qualitatively new situation was created by ghettoization and the system of enforced labour for Jews, which was ordered at the same time.[97] These measures were crucially significant, although they were hampered by the opposition of the *Generalgouverneur*, Hans Frank, by the preparation and waging of war in the West, and by sheer organizational chaos. Methods that were later extended to the Old Reich were first tested in the *Generalgouvernement*; moreover, the deportation programme encouraged the *Gauleiter* of the Reich to send 'their' Jews to the *Generalgouvernement*. Hans Frank staunchly resisted further mass deportations of Jews, as demanded by *Gauleiter* Greiser in particular; he argued that the Lodz ghetto had become a transit camp for deported Jews and that intolerable conditions prevailed there.[98] This brought the deportation programme to a temporary halt.[99]

The debates of late 1939 and early 1940 reveal that there was as yet no single, comprehensive programme of persecution. In March 1940 Frank stressed that the deportation of Jews from the Old Reich could be achieved only after the war.[100] One new feature was the fact that emigration, including forced emigration, was no longer regarded as the only 'solution', because there were now more than 3 million Jews under German rule.[101] The various departments concerned therefore produced schemes for the creation of a 'Jewish reservation'. The *Ostministerium* (Ministry for the Occupied Eastern Territories) suggested that such a 'reservation' should be created along the German–Soviet demarcation line.[102] This potential solution, which was supported by Hitler, was taken up eagerly by Eichmann, who was responsible for the deportation programme. The Nisco Project and similar attempts failed not so much because of the objections of Frank but because of catastrophically inept organization. On 24 March 1940, Goering responded by prohibiting further deportations from the Old Reich.[103]

It is certain that the reservation plans were not intended for implementation until after the war. On 25 June 1940, the representative of the Reich Association of Jews in Germany was informed of a plan to settle vast numbers of Jews in some as yet undesignated colonial reservation area; at this stage Eichmann still favoured an extensive programme of emigration to Palestine.[104] The scheme was to involve the Jewish communities of the Old Reich, Austria, the Protectorate (Bohemia and Moravia), the *Generalgouvernement*, Scandinavia and Western Europe, including Britain. However, the scheme was developed more rapidly than had been anticipated, especially after the defeat of France made the end of the war seem very near. On 12 June 1940 *Legationsrat* (legation councillor) Karl Rademacher of the German Foreign Ministry submitted the Madagascar Plan.[105] Even if Britain had agreed to it – which was most unlikely – the Madagascar project was actually completely unsuitable as a 'European solution to the Jewish question', quite apart from the fact that a rapid reduction of the population was anticipated due to the harshness of the climate and to the effects of severe overcrowding. Nevertheless, the project was taken up by Eichmann and the RSHA. Subsequently, Eichmann distinguished between a 'short-term plan' – i.e. an intermediate solution in the form of concentrating the Jewish population in certain parts of the *Generalgouvernement* – and a 'long-term plan' of deportation to Madagascar. Once the Russian campaign had begun these considerations receded into the background; however, not until 10 February 1941 did Rademacher report that the war against the Soviet Union had offered the possibility of using other territories for the Final Solution and that, on the instruction of the Führer, the Madagascar Plan could be dropped. There is no basis for the argument that the Madagascar project had the subjective function of concealing the regime's intention to annihilate the Jews.[106]

The resumption of deportations to the *Generalgouvernement* and the deportation of 7,500 Jews from Baden and the Saarpfalz to France[107] were carried out as temporary measures and following pressure from the local *Gauleiter*. Heydrich's 'third short-term plan' of 8 February restricted to 250,000 the numbers to be deported from the annexed Polish territories; however, this total was not achieved and deportations were halted once more.[108] These facts indicate that the 'territorial final solution', a programme demanded by Heydrich as early as June 1940 and that gradually replaced the now unworkable emigration scheme, was to be achieved only after the war.

Considerable efforts were made to exploit Jewish forced labour in the Reich instead, something that had hitherto been imperilled by bureaucratic friction.[109] Hitler intervened in this issue to reject any repatriation of Jewish labour from the East to the Reich for such purposes, a decision that was connected with his reluctance to revoke decisions once they had been made.[110]

The attack on the Soviet Union on 22 June 1941, and the dazzling early successes of the German armies, influenced the planning process in the RSHA. The Commissar Order, and the deliberate use of the *Einsatzgruppen* to liquidate Jewish population groups in the occupied areas, signalled the start of a new phase.[111] Initially, however, the belief that a 'solution' of the 'Jewish question' could be implemented only after the war was retained. In summer 1941 the Nazi leadership expected the Soviet Union to be defeated in a matter of weeks, and at latest by autumn of that year, although they accepted that skirmishes might continue in the Asiatic regions of the Soviet Union.[112] It was taken for granted that Britain would have been forced to yield by this time.[113]

Only against this background is a correct interpretation possible of the authorization given by Goering to Heydrich on 31 July 1941 in which Heydrich was instructed 'to present for my early consideration an overall draft plan describing the organizational, technical and material requirements for carrying out the Final Solution which we seek'.[114] The authorization, drafted by Eichmann and submitted to Goering for his signature,[115] is not connected with any preceding order from Hitler, although the existence of such an order has often been suspected. Its context is clearly that of the strategy pursued until that point, which was not yet directed towards systematic extermination. Its aim was a 'solution' that would no longer be implemented under the cover of war in the East.

At the same time, the *Einsatzgruppen* were carrying out their massacres. These were based on the Commissar Order, unlike the systematic policy of the Final Solution that followed. There can be no doubt that Hitler approved and supported these measures, although it is a matter for conjecture how far he took notice of actual events.[116] Approximately 1.4 million Jews were murdered in these extensive operations, which were carried out on the pretext of securing the rear area of the battle zone; Hitler had from the outset declared the campaign against the Soviet Union to be a war of annihilation. Nevertheless, it is almost inexplicable that the leaders and members of the *Einsatzgruppen* lent themselves to this unimaginably barbarous slaughter and that the Army – with few exceptions – either stood by, weapons at the ready, or in many cases gave active support to the *Einsatzgruppen*.[117] In the framework of National Socialist propaganda against 'subhumanity', the Russian Jews, like the Polish Jews before them, were classed as the lowest of the low. The massacres also provided an opportunity to rid the German-occupied territories of a part of the Jewish population, which had by then increased beyond any 'manageable' size. The fact that the killings were carried out on oral orders only, and that the *Einsatz-gruppen* were careful to avoid giving only racial reasons for them in their reports,[118] indicates that the decision to liquidate the entire Jewish population had not yet fully matured.

A decisive turning-point was necessary before leading officials would adopt a course of action that had been unthinkable only a short time before. Certainly, everything was propelling events towards a violent 'solution' of the 'Jewish problem' which the Nazis had created for themselves. The logistic prerequisites for the mass movement of populations were completely lacking. Conditions in the improvised ghettos were appalling, and appeared completely unacceptable to the German sense of order. In summer 1940 Greiser had already described conditions in the Lodz ghetto as untenable from the 'point of view of nutrition and the control of epidemics'.[119] On 16 July 1941, SS-*Sturmbannführer* Höppner drew attention to the catastrophic conditions in the ghetto which, as a transit camp for the Jews transported from the Old Reich, was permanently over-crowded. Besides, it was the only ghetto within the Reich and was regarded by Greiser as an intolerable burden. Höppner added in his letter to Eichmann that 'it should be seriously considered whether it might not be the most humane solution to dispose of those Jews who are unfit for work by some quick-acting means. At any rate this would be more agreeable than letting them starve'.[120]

Martin Broszat has emphasized the symptomatic significance of this reaction.[121] It is not an isolated one. The idea that it would ultimately be more 'humane' to finish off the victims quickly had already emerged in 1940; it was frequently prompted by the sight of countless trains standing at stations in the biting cold, with their captive Jewish passengers deprived even of drinking water during the dreadful journey to the *Generalgouvernement*. The war in the East provided even more reasons for such arguments. The indescribably cruel treatment of the civilian population caused few protests and produced instead a fatal blunting of moral feeling among the Germans. The partial liquidation of transports of Jews from the Old Reich and the annexed territories was a desperate new step. It could not be justified as part of the destruction of Bolshevik resistance cells. A pseudo-moral justification was needed as a precondition for the systematic implementation of the Final Solution. Inhumanity had first to be declared as 'humanity' before it could be put into technocratic practice,[122] with moral inhibitions thereafter reduced to a minimum. Then, once the necessary bureaucratic apparatus had been created, a programme could be set in motion that was applicable to all deportees, including women and children.

The operations of the *Einsatzgruppen* served as the link that enabled the exception – premeditated liquidation – to become the general rule. The immediate liquidation of groups of German Jews deported to the *Reichskommissariat* Ostland, to Riga, Kovno and Minsk, did not proceed smoothly. Moreover, like the killings begun with the assistance of the 'euthanasia' experts in Chelmno in December 1941, they also encountered opposition, which led to the suspension of further transports.[123] Even if only for this reason, the change in the Jewish policy of the RSHA was by no means abrupt. One indication of such a change was that Jewish emigration from German-occupied areas of continental Europe was halted, although it had previously been explicitly supported. The head of the *Gestapo*, Müller, announced the prohibition of further Jewish emigration on 23 October 1941. Only ten days previously, Heydrich had actually approved a proposal by the Under-Secretary of State, Martin Luther, that Spanish Jews resident in France should be included in the Spanish Cabinet's plan to send 'their' Jews to Spanish Morocco. A few days later his decision was revoked on the grounds that these Jews would then be too far outside the German sphere of influence to be included in the Final Solution to be implemented after the war.[124]

The reference to a 'post-war solution' reveals that at this point the decision for systematic genocide had not yet been reached. On 16 December 1941, Frank stated that 3.5 million Jews in the *Generalgouvernement* could not be liquidated, but that 'action will have to be taken that will lead to successful destruction, in connection with the major measures which are to be discussed at Reich level'.[125] This was a reference to the impending Wannsee Conference, which is usually equated with the immediate launch of the genocide campaign throughout Europe. However, the 'operations' mentioned by Heydrich in connection with the 'evacuation of the Jews to the East' were presented simply as opportunities to gain practical experience 'in view of the coming Final Solution of the Jewish question'. The liquidation of those Jews who were deemed unfit for work was implied, and the subsequent destruction of the 'remaining stock' explicitly disclosed.[126] The psychological bridge between the emigration and reservation 'solutions' and the Holocaust itself was created by the fiction of *Arbeitseinsatz* ('labour mobilization'); reference was also still made to the chimerical 'territorial final solution', which was now to be achieved east of the Urals. On the other hand, the formulation that 'certain preparatory work for the Final Solution' should be carried out 'in the areas concerned', i.e. the *Generalgouvernement*, signified the beginning of selective liquidations. These started early in 1942 and from spring onwards acquired the character of a planned and systematic programme. Even then, however, it was implemented with varying degrees of intensity; initially the measures were mainly improvised and some operations had to be countermanded.[127] It is important to note that the programme of annihilation thus retained its character as a temporary measure taken during the wartime state of emergency. The inclusion in the programme of the Jews in the occupied countries and satellite states[128] originally occurred within the framework of a long-term 'labour mobilization' programme; however, even the most elementary requirements for the fulfilment of such a scheme were lacking.[129]

One further development was important for the implementation of the Final Solution. Since autumn 1941, Auschwitz–Birkenau had been expanded into an enormous 'prisoner and munitions centre', mainly for the 'utilization' of Soviet prisoners of war.[130] The selection of Soviet prisoners, and the brutal treatment inflicted upon them, reflected Himmler's own belief that there were unlimited human reserves in the East.[131] However, the turn of the tide in the war, and the appalling death-rate among the prisoners, meant that fewer human reserves than anticipated were available and that they were urgently needed to fill gaps in the labour market in the Reich itself.[132] Scarcely a week after the Wannsee Conference, Himmler issued his instruction to 'equip' the SS concentration camps primarily with German Jews.[133] Birkenau camp, where the technology of gassing had been developed with Soviet prisoners of war as the victims,[134] was now to be part of a comprehensive programme for genocide. The *Generalplan Ost* stood in the background, preventing any attempt to fall back on interim territorial 'solutions' to the 'Jewish question' in the occupied territory of the Soviet Union. The programme of annihilation was now implemented with astonishing speed and in several waves. This operation (later named 'Reinhard' after Reinhard Heydrich, assassinated in Prague in May 1942) formed the direct link between the *Einsatzgruppen* and the factory techniques of the Final Solution. The systematic destruction of the ghettos was followed by the withdrawal of Jewish labour from war industries; Jewish workers were also removed from the SS enterprises in the Lublin region, which then collapsed.[135]

The use of gas vans as a transitional stage in the development of factory methods to destroy human life had begun because of a desire to prevent undesirable side-effects on the SS men caused by the semi-public shootings at Vilna and elsewhere.[136] The fiction that only those Jews who were unfit for work were to be killed remained psychologically important. The selection process on the ramp at Birkenau helped Himmler's thugs to preserve this fiction. It was only a short step from this way of thinking to 'orderly' destruction, which could be justified on the grounds that organized killing was more practical and 'humane' than death from starvation or epidemics in the ghettos and camps.[137] The horrific conditions produced by the brutal and inhumane treatment of the deported Jews were actually exploited by Goebbels to justify the deadly theory of 'subhumanity'.[138] More importantly, people who under normal circumstances would have been roused to anger by the treatment of the Jews became indifferent, and their feelings of compassion were dulled. How many had the personal courage to see the whole truth behind the chain of cruelties, rather than putting the blame on occasional abuses?

After all, work camps of all kinds – voluntary Labour service, compulsory labour and ultimately the practice of working people to death – were the civilian counterpart of military service, which sent millions to the slaughter. Everywhere in occupied Europe, even in the Reich itself, the labour camp became part of ordinary life. The atomization of the family, the destruction of traditional social structures, the sending of all age groups and professions to labour camps, training camps, education camps – these were everyday features of the Third Reich. The network of concentration camps and prisoner-of-war camps appeared to be part of this second civilization, offering an extreme example of the exercise of power over human beings.[139]

The transfer of people within this labyrinthine network of camps was nothing unusual. However, the concentration of Jewish citizens in labour camps became an increasingly important transitional stage on the path to the Final Solution. The circumstances in which deportations occurred sometimes excited public criticism, but in general people chose to believe the fiction of the 'mobilization of labour'; moreover, the removal of Jews to transit camps ensured that their fate was decided out of sight of their fellow citizens. Even in the occupied areas, resistance to the 'mobilization' of Jewish labour occurred only rarely. Within the concentration camps, it had long been the practice to work people literally to death. The concept that arose as a result – that of 'destruction by labour' – was one of the most effective pieces of cynicism in National Socialist ideology. The inscription on the gates of Auschwitz – '*Arbeit macht frei*' ('freedom through work') – reveals that cynicism; it illuminates the entire master-race mentality, which degraded human beings into mere numbers and had no respect even for the dead. This attitude first manifested itself in the 'euthanasia' programme.[140]

The fiction of mobilizing Jewish labour was used by the perpetrators of the Final Solution as a psychological justification for their actions. It is symptomatic that fanatical anti-semites such as Hans Frank and Wilhelm Kube began to protest against the systematic implementation of the extermination programme when it was turned against the reserves of indispensable Jewish labour in the Eastern regions.[141] When the liquidations were not justified by the pretence that they were measures to combat partisans and to weaken 'Jewish–Bolshevik' potential, as was the case with the *Einsatzgruppen*, then they were frequently accounted for by the need to make space for fresh transports. There were phases during which the pace of the extermination programme was slowed, to permit the temporary exploitation of the prisoners by means of forced labour. Many Jews saw this as their only chance of survival.[142]

The use of bureaucratic and technocratic methods to destroy human life also served to suppress quasi-moral inhibitions.[143] The original motive behind the development of technical methods of killing such as carbon monoxide and *Zyklon B* had been to avoid unrest among the general public. However, it was rapidly transformed into a problem of killing-capacity. The decisive preliminary stages of the systematic policy of the Final Solution were thus accompanied by the efforts of the RSHA to learn about these technical possibilities; the instructions given to Eichmann and Höss in autumn 1941 were of this nature.[144]

The Holocaust was not based upon a programme that had been developed over a long period. It was founded upon improvised measures that were rooted in earlier stages of planning and also escalated them. Once it had been set in motion, the extermination of those people who were deemed unfit for work developed a dynamic of its own. The bureaucratic machinery created by Eichmann and Heydrich functioned more or less automatically; it was thus symptomatic that Eichmann consciously circumvented Himmler's order, at the end of 1944, to stop the Final Solution.[145] There was no need for external ideological impulses to keep the process of extermination going. Protests from those parties interested in saving the

Jewish workforce – the *Wehrmacht*, the armaments industry, SS-owned factories in the concentration camps, and the administration of the *Generalgouvernement* – proved largely ineffective.[146]

The widespread assumption that the systematic policy of genocide rested on a clear directive from Hitler[147] is based on a misunderstanding of the decision-making process in the *Führer's* headquarters. If such an order had been given, even if only orally, then those in high office around Hitler must have known about it; they had no motive to deny the existence of such a directive in their personal records and testimonies after 1945.[148] Gerald Fleming has made a comprehensive search for traces of such an order from the *Führer*. All he can prove is that at the middle level of command there was talk of it in one form or another; however, Hitler's express approval of criminal orders and his intensification of the fight against partisans seem to be the only concrete basis for these opinions.[149]

In fact, the idea that Hitler set the genocide policy in motion by means of a direct instruction can be completely rejected. Such an order would have compromised the fiction of the 'mobilization of labour', which included the theory of 'destruction by labour'. This could not have been in the *Führer's* interests, especially as he would then have had to choose between the destruction of human lives and the mobilization of labour demanded by the war economy. Hitler consistently avoided making such a choice.[150] This situation made it particularly difficult for the parties opposed to the extermination process to marshal their arguments: first, there was no one to whom they could appeal, and secondly, even if there were, they would have had to break through the taboo that surrounded the Final Solution. Thus it was that *Generalgouverneur* Hans Frank saw no possibility of appealing to Hitler over the withdrawal of urgently needed Jewish workers.[151]

The absence of any direct order for extermination also explains how almost all those in an influential position were able to suppress their awareness of the fact of genocide. Albert Speer provides the most striking example of this tendency.[152] Hitler's dominant position at the centre of all the National Socialist elites reinforced such behaviour, because his conduct was exactly the same as theirs: he took care not to allow conversation to turn to events in the concentration camps. This gave rise to the widespread impression that Heinrich Himmler was the driving force. In terms of ideological motivation this was not the case, for Hitler was always the advocate of radicalization.[153]

The utopian dream of exterminating the Jews could become

reality only in the half-light of unclear orders and ideological fanaticism. Then, despite all opposing interests, the process developed its own internal dynamic. It is therefore impossible to assign sole responsibility for events to Hitler, Himmler, Heydrich, Bormann, the SS and the activists in the German Foreign Ministry. Many leading National Socialists tended to stay out of events as much as possible, although they had actively supported the deportation programme. The willingness with which the Ministries of Justice and the Interior gave up to the Security Service (SD) and the *Gestapo* their jurisdiction over the deportations, which they had initially defended strenuously, is a striking example of a general endeavour among officials to divest themselves of any responsibility whilst accepting that the events themselves were inevitable.[154]

Adolf Eichmann offers a spectacular example of the mechanism of compartmentalized responsibility, which in his case was combined with bureaucratic perfectionism and submissiveness to the demands of the authoritarian state. As he testified in Jerusalem, his authority extended only as far as the gates of Auschwitz-Birkenau; he was just responsible for carrying out the deportations.[155] This fragmenting of responsibilities was a typical feature of the regime. It had its roots in the organization of the NSDAP, which had been imposed by Hitler and his followers during the 1920s.[156] The relative efficiency of the National Socialist system was based precisely upon Hitler's principle of conferring unlimited powers for specific tasks and allowing political co-ordination between institutions only where it was unavoidable. Any institutionalized communication between the lower levels of government was systematically prevented. Responsibilities were thus segmented. In the various war crimes trials, the former satraps of the regime always pleaded that they had merely followed orders and been cogs in the machine. No one was prepared to accept overall responsibility or to consider the political consequences of the individual decisions that they made. Non-communication and collective suppression of knowledge complemented each other and, when these mechanisms failed, they were replaced by a vague awareness that involvement in the escalation of crime had gone too far for any opposition to be possible.[157]

If these psychological mechanisms prevented the National Socialist elite from facing up to the escalation of criminality and drawing the necessary conclusions, then we can more easily accept that most ordinary Germans were reluctant to believe rumours and incomplete information. It is significant, in this respect, that the truth about the Holocaust was accepted only with hesitation and reluctance even by Western public opinion and Allied governments.[158] In so far as German civilians must bear a share of moral responsibility, this does not lie in the fact that they did not protest against the Holocaust, particularly in view of its all-pervasive activity; instead, it is to be found in the passive acceptance of the exclusion of the Jewish population, which prepared the way for the Final Solution. An awareness of increasing injustice definitely did exist, as can be seen in the reaction of public opinion to the revelations about the Katyn massacre.[159]

Ideological factors – the effects of anti-semitic propaganda and the authoritarian element in traditional German political culture – are not sufficient in themselves to explain how the Holocaust became reality. The political and bureaucratic mechanisms that permitted the idea of mass extermination to be realized could also have occurred under different social conditions. The ultimately atavistic structure of the National Socialist regime, coupled with the effective power of newly established bureaucracies, proved to be the decisive factor in the selection of negative 'elements of *Weltanschauung*'[160] and in the overwhelming loss of reality that was epitomized by Hitler's mentality.[161] The genesis of the Holocaust offers a deterrent example of the way in which otherwise normal individuals can be led astray when they live in a permanent state of emergency, when legal and institutional structures collapse, and when criminal deeds are publicly justified as national achievements. The Holocaust is a warning against racial phobias and social resentment of minority groups; but it is also a reminder that the manipulation and deformation of public and private morality are a constant threat even in advanced industrial societies.

NOTES

An abridged version of this chapter was first published as 'Die Realisierung des Utopischen: die "Endlösung der Judenfrage" im "Dritten Reich"'; in *Geschichte und Gesellschaft*, 9 (1983), pp. 381–420.

1 Gerald Reitlinger, *The Final Solution. The Attempt to Exterminate the Jews of Europe*, 2nd edn (London, 1956); his work was preceded by Leon Poliakov, *Brévriare de la Haine* (Paris, 1951).
2 Konrad Kwiet provides a survey of the vast specialized literature on the subject in 'Zur historiographischen Behandlung der Judenverfolgung im Dritten Reich', *Militärgeschichtliche Mitteilungen*, 27 (1980/81), pp. 149–92. West German historians have so far addressed this subject

only hesitantly. Apart from Wolfgang Scheffler's creditable survey, *Judenverfolgung im Dritten Reich 1933–1945* (Berlin, 1960; 2nd edn, 1979), Helmut Genschel, *Die Verdrängung der Juden aus der Wirtschaft im Dritten Reich* (Göttingen, 1966) and Uwe Dietrich Adam, *Judenpolitik im Dritten Reich* (Düsseldorf, 1972), no comprehensive monograph has been published on the Holocaust and its origins. Among West German writers, Helmut Krausnick, 'Judenverfolgung', in Hans Buchheim *et al.*, *Anatomie des SS-Staates*, vol. 2 (Olten/Freiburg i.Br., 1965), pp. 283–448, still provides the best overall analysis. See also M. Broszat, '"Holocaust" und die deutsche Geschichtswissenschaft', *Vierteljahrshefte für Zeitgeschichte*, 27 (1979), pp. 285–98.

3   The literature of the extreme right must therefore be disregarded. See Wolfgang Benz, 'Die Opfer und die Täter. Rechtsextremisten in der Bundesrepublik', *Aus Politik und Zeitgeschichte*, supplement to *Parlament*, B 27/80, pp. 29–45; Wolfgang Benz, 'Judenvernichtung aus Notwehr', *Vierteljahrshefte für Zeitgeschichte*, 29 (1981), pp. 615–17.

4   The Institut für Zeitgeschichte, Munich, is preparing a study: Wolfgang Benz (ed.), *Die Zahl der jüdischen Opfer des Nationalsozialismus* (forthcoming).

5   On the number of Jews murdered, see Raul Hilberg, *The Destruction of the European Jews*, new edition (New York, 1983), p. 767. The figure of 5.1 million victims can only be an approximation.

6   See Alexander and Margaret Mitscherlich, *Die Unfähigkeit zu trauern. Grundlagen kollektiven Verhaltens*, 2nd edn (Munich, 1968), pp. 28–9, 205–6; Pierre Aycoberry, *The Nazi Question. An Essay on the Interpretation of National Socialism* (New York, 1981), pp. 182–3. Of survivors' portrayals, one that seems to me exemplary is Hermann Langbein, *Menschen in Auschwitz* (Vienna, 1972).

7   See Martin Broszat, 'Nationalsozialistische Konzentrationslager 1933–1945', in Hans Buchheim *et al.*, *Anatomie des SS-Staates* vol. 2, 2nd edn (Munich, 1967) pp. 77–8; Hilberg, *Destruction of European Jews* (as in n. 5), pp. 572–5.

8   Raul Hilberg investigates this question methodically in *Sonderzüge nach Auschwitz* (Mainz, 1981); see Lawrence D. Stokes, 'The German People and the Destruction of the European Jews', *Central European History*, 6 (1973), pp. 167–91 and particularly pp. 187–9; Marlis G. Steinert, *Hitler's War and the Germans. Public Mood and Attitudes during the Second World War* (Athens, Ohio, 1977) pp. 140–2; Christopher Browning, *The Final Solution and the German Foreign Office* (New York, 1978); Christian Streit, *Keine Kameraden. Die Wehrmacht und die sowjetischen Kriegsgefangenen 1941–1945* (Stuttgart, 1978), pp. 109–11; Ian Kershaw, 'Antisemitismus und Volksmeinung. Reaktionen auf die Judenverfolgung', in M. Broszat and Elke Fröhlich (eds), *Bayern in der NS-Zeit. Herrschaft und Gesellschaft im Konflikt*, vol. 2 (Munich, 1979), pp. 340–2.

9   Hannah Arendt, *Eichmann in Jerusalem. Ein Bericht von der Banalität des Bösen* (Munich, 1964), pp. 188–90, 300. F. A. Krummacher (ed.), *Die*

Kontroverse. Hannah Arendt, Eichmann und die Juden (Munich, 1964) documents the spirit in which Arendt's interpretation was received. The older view is found in Robert M. W. Kempner, *Eichmann und Komplizen* (Zurich, 1961).

10 See the introduction to Martin Broszat (ed.), *Kommandant in Auschwitz. Autobiographische Aufzeichnungen von Rudolf Höss* (Stuttgart, 1958), pp. 16–18.

11 See Reinhard Höhne, *Der Orden unter dem Totenkopf. Die Geschichte der SS* (Hamburg, 1966), pp. 149–50, 351–3.

12 Heinrich Himmler on 6 October 1943:

> Perhaps at a much later date one will be able to consider telling the German people more about it [the destruction of the Jews]. I believe it is better that *all of us together* have borne this for our people, have taken the responsibility on ourselves (the responsibility for a deed, *not only for an idea*) and then take the secret with us to the grave.

Quoted in Bradley F. Smith and Agnes Peterson (eds), *Heinrich Himmler. Geheimreden 1933 bis 1945 und andere Ansprachen*, Frankfurt/M., 1974, pp. 170–1; emphasis added.

13 On attempts to destroy the evidence see Hilberg, *Destruction of European Jews* (as in n. 5), pp. 628–9; Adalbert Rückerl (ed.), *Nationalsozialistische Vernichtungslager im Spiegel deutscher Strafprozesse* (Munich, 1977), pp. 273–4 and passim.

14 The speech of 6 October is quoted in Smith and Peterson, *Heinrich Himmler. Geheimreden* (as in n. 12), pp. 162–3; that of 16 December 1943 (extract), ibid., p. 201; that of 26 January 1944, ibid., pp. 201–3; that of 24 May 1944, ibid., p. 203; that of 21 June 1944, ibid., pp. 203–5. Himmler's use of the word 'we' constantly involves the entire SS apparatus in what happened. His statement that 'we' are not justified 'in putting off anything hard or difficult that can be done today' is typical. It is made in connection with his advice that the problem should not be postponed until after Hitler's death (ibid., pp. 202, 204). Himmler's increasing degree of psychological strain was partly responsible for his disclosure of the crime to the higher functionaries and generals (see Höhne, *Orden unter dem Totenkopf*, as in n. 11, pp. 335–6). It was also related to the fact that he had begun to distance himself from Hitler inwardly. At the very least, he was aware of the state of Hitler's health and knew that he could not expect the support he normally received from Hitler to last much longer.

15 On Hans Frank's contradictory behaviour during the trial see Bradley F. Smith, *Der Jahrhundertprozess. Die Motive der Richter von Nürnberg* (Frankfurt, 1977), pp. 214–16; Goering denied however that in signing Heydrich's authorization of 31 July 1941 he had been giving notice of any intention to liquidate the Jews. See *Der Prozess gegen die Hauptkriegsverbrecher vor dem Internationalen Militärgerichtshof. Nürnberg, 14 Oktober 1945 – 1 Oktober 1946* [IMG], vol. 9, pp. 574–6. See

also the survey in Hilberg, *Destruction of European Jews* (as in n. 5), pp. 684–6. On the problem of Speer, see Erich Goldhagen, 'Albert Speer, Himmler and the Secrecy of the Final Solution', *Midstream* (October, 1971), pp. 43–50; Speer's responses to this, and to W. Malanowsky's position, stated in *Der Spiegel*, 29, no. 46 (October 1975) have not yet been refuted. See my review of the 'Spandau Diaries' in *Politische Vierteljahrsschrift*, 17 (1976), pp. 108–10; the proof adduced by Matthias Schmidt in *Albert Speer: Das Ende eines Mythos* (Bern, 1972), pp. 232–3, does not refute his defence. Whatever one's doubts about this, it is a fact that the genocide was suppressed. Speer's later justification in *Der Sklavenstaat* (Stuttgart, 1981), pp. 376–8, tends to detract from his credibility.

16 This is the traditional view. It is put most consistently by Eberhard Jäckel, *Hitlers Weltanschauung*, new edn (Stuttgart, 1981), p. 68 in particular. Jäckel's thesis that Hitler's attitude became more radical as his *Weltanschauung* developed (pp. 66–7) is not convincing in view of earlier statements by Hitler in a similar tone: see E. Jäckel (ed.), *Hitler. Sämtliche Aufzeichnungen 1905–1923* (Stuttgart, 1980): the connection between anti-semitism and anti-Bolshevism is clear from the start. Gerald Fleming, *Hitler and the Final Solution* (London, 1985) and Lucy Dawidowicz, *The War against the Jews: 1933–1945* (New York, 1975), p. 494, follow Jäckel. Fleming's reference to Albrecht Tyrell in Guido Knopp (ed.), *Hitler heute. Gespräche über ein deutsches Trauma* (Aschaffenburg, 1979) does not apply here. With Martin Broszat, 'Soziale Motivation und Führerbindung des Nationalsozialismus', *Vierteljahrshefte für Zeitgeschichte*, 18 (1970), pp. 400–2, I emphasize that the propagandist nature of Hitler's statements is inconsistent with any firm intention to translate the metaphor of extermination into reality, despite the fact that he undoubtedly used them as a stylistic device to demonstrate tactical 'moderation', and that he had no psychological inhibitions preventing him from pursuing a policy of annihilation. See Broszat's objections to Jäckel's over-emphasis on Hitler's *Weltanschauung* (ibid., pp. 399–401).

17 See Helmut Auerbach, 'Hitlers politische Lehrjahre und die Münchener Gesellschaft 1919–1923', *Vierteljahrshefte für Zeitgeschichte*, 25 (1977), pp. 8–10, and the literature cited in his n. 33. Further, Margaret Plewina, *Auf dem Weg zu Hitler. Der 'völkische' Publizist Dietrich Eckart* (Bremen, 1970); George L. Mosse, *Rassismus. Ein Krankheitssymptom der europäischen Geistesgeschichte des 19. und 20. Jahrhunderts* (Königstein, 1978); also the literature cited by Kwiet, 'Judenverfolgung' (as in n. 2), p. 186; see also Broszat, 'Soziale Motivation' (as in n. 16), p. 400. The total identification of NS propaganda with Hitler's *Weltanschauung*, frequently found in the literature, overlooks the correspondence between the anti-semitism of the party and that of the *völkisch* (racial-nationalist) right, and indeed that of much of the conservative nationalist right as well. This minimizes the extent of racial anti-semitism; see also Werner E. Mosse (ed.), *Entscheidungsjahr*

1932. Zur Judenfrage in der Endphase der Weimarer Republik (Tübingen, 1966).

18 Hilberg, *Destruction of European Jews* (as in n. 5), pp. 293–4.

19 See Hans Mommsen, 'Hitlers Stellung im nationalsozialistischen Herrschaftssystem', in Gerhard Hirschfeld and Lothar Kettenacker (eds), *The Führer-State: Myth and Reality. Studies in the Structure and Politics of the Third Reich* (Stuttgart, 1981), particularly pp. 66–8; Karl A. Schleunes, *The Twisted Road to Auschwitz. Nazi Policy towards German Jews 1933–1939* (Chicago, 1970), pp. 73, 258–60; Adam, *Judenpolitik* (as in n. 2), pp. 163–5, 217.

20 On this issue see Adam, *Judenpolitik* (as in n. 2), pp. 125–9; the Lösener files, Institut für Zeitgeschichte [IfZ] F 71/2; B. Lösener, 'Als Rassenreferent im Reichsministerium des Innern', *Vierteljahrshefte für Zeitgeschichte*, 9 (1961), pp. 264–6.

21 On Hitler's evasions in settling the issues of '*Mischlinge*' and racially mixed marriages, see Adam, *Judenpolitik* (as in n. 2), pp. 329–30, and David Irving, *Hitler's War* (London, 1977), p. 391. His position did not mean that Hitler was definitely yielding; it is in fact characteristic of a way of thinking that waits for the development of situations in which individual decisions of this sort are rendered unnecessary.

22 See Klaus Hildebrand, *Deutsche Aussenpolitik 1933–1945. Kalkül oder Dogma?* (Stuttgart, 1971), pp. 26–8; Klaus Hildebrand, 'Innenpolitische Antriebskräfte der nationalsozialistischen Aussenpolitik', in Manfred Funke (ed.), *Hitler, Deutschland und die Mächte* (Düsseldorf, 1976), pp. 237–9 and passim; Hans-Adolf Jacobsen, 'Zur Struktur der NS-Aussenpolitik 1933–1945', ibid., pp. 172–4; A. Kuhn, *Hitlers aussenpolitisches Programm* (Stuttgart, 1970).

23 See Joachim C. Fest, *Hitler. Eine Biographie* (Frankfurt/M., 1973), p. 927; Broszat, 'Soziale Motivation' (as in n. 16), pp. 401–2.

24 On the April boycott see Genschel, *Verdrängung der Juden* (as in n. 2), pp. 43–5. The boycott was announced before Hitler and Goebbels made their decision on 26 March. See Hitler's typical justification of the boycott, ibid., p. 47. Also Karl Dietrich Bracher *et al.*, *Die nationalsozialistische Machtergreifung*, 2nd edn (Cologne, 1962), pp. 277–8. The *Münchener Neueste Nachrichten* of 15 September commented on the Nuremberg Laws: 'Jews within the borders of the German Reich have been offered the opportunity to become a national minority.' The laws actually sanctioned measures that had already been implemented in many cases; this, together with the language used in Nazi propaganda at this time, implying that there would be no further encroachments, created the impression that a definitive solution had been found.

25 See Hermann Graml, *Der 9. November 1938 – 'Reichskristallnacht'*, 2nd edn (Bonn, 1958), and Adam, *Judenpolitik* (as in n. 2), pp. 206–7. It is by no means certain that Hitler approved in advance the extensive pogrom organized by Goebbels. See Wolfgang Scheffler, 'Ausgewählte Dokumente zur Geschichte des Novemberpogroms 1938', *Aus Politik und Zeitgeschichte*, B 4/78, 4 November 1978, pp. 3–30; IMG, vol. 20,

p. 320; *IMG*, vol. 32, p. 28; *IMG*, vol. 14, pp. 465–6; Klaus Moritz in Klaus Moritz and Ernst Noam (eds), *Justiz und Judenverfolgung*, vol. 2: *NS-Verbrechen vor Gericht* (Wiesbaden, 1978), p. 213. According to Schallermeier's affidavit (*IMG*, vol. 42, pp. 510–12), when Himmler called on Hitler during the night, he received the impression that Hitler 'knew nothing about the course of events', i.e. knew nothing about an extensively organized pogrom as opposed to 'spontaneous' actions.

26 Adam, *Judenpolitik* (as in n. 2), comments that 'the Chancellor of the Reich in the last analysis determined the course of Jewish policy' (p. 19), while Schleunes, *The Twisted Road* (as in n. 19), p. 131, emphasizes that 'Hitler's hand appeared occasionally at crucial moments, but it was usually a vacillating and indecisive one. He did not delegate responsibility for Jewish policy, nor did he keep a close check on it'. On 'Aryanization' see Adam, *Judenpolitik* (as in n. 2), pp. 208–10; Genschel, *Verdrängung der Juden* (as in n. 2), pp. 180–2.

27 See Schleunes, *The Twisted Road* (as in n. 19), pp. 90–1, 97–9.

28 See Mommsen, 'Hitlers Stellung' (as in n. 19), pp. 55–6.

29 See Genschel, *Verdrängung der Juden* (as in n. 2), pp. 46–8.

30 See Otto D. Kulka, *The Jewish Question in the Third Reich. Its Significance in National Socialist Ideology and Politics*, 2 vols (Jerusalem, 1975), pp. 200–2.

31 Jäckel, *Hitlers Weltanschauung* (as in n. 16), pp. 72–4; Krausnick, 'Judenverfolgung' (as in n. 2), pp. 38–40; Adam, *Judenpolitik* (as in n. 2), pp. 25–6. The fact that such expressions were paraphrased in Nazi propaganda after 1933 enabled the public not to take the threat seriously.

32 See, for example, Irving, *Hitler's War* (as in n. 21), pp. 311–12.

33 ibid., p. 576. On this issue see M. Broszat, 'Genesis der "Endlösung"', *Vierteljahrshefte für Zeitgeschichte*, 25 (1977), pp. 759–61 and Fleming, *Hitler and the Final Solution* (as in n. 16), pp. 17–20 and passim.

34 Vertrauliche Informationen der Parteikanzlei, Institut für Zeitgeschichte, Db 15.06; see Broszat, 'Genesis der "Endlösung"' (as in n. 33), pp. 763–5. Any consideration of a 'future total solution' was to be avoided in public discussion. In view of Hitler's deliberate restraint in referring to the mass exterminations, Fleming agrees with Broszat (see pp. 61–3).

35 See Fleming, *Hitler and the Final Solution* (as in n. 16), pp. 135–9. There is an obvious inconsistency here. On the one hand, the expression 'special treatment of the Jews' was to be avoided, on Himmler's instructions (ibid., pp. 136–7); on the other, according to Eichmann's statement (ibid., pp. 138–9), Hitler himself broke the prescriptions governing language.

36 'Here we are going to destroy the Jews. The Jews did not cause the ninth of November for nothing. This day will be avenged.' Note by Hewel, 21 January 1939, *Akten zur deutschen auswärtigen Politik*, Series D, vol. IV, p. 170. This remark should be seen in the context of the *Reichstag* speech shortly afterwards, on 30 January 1939; it is difficult to interpret it as a declaration of intent to liquidate the Jews (see Adam,

Judenpolitik (as in n. 2), p. 235), especially since the term '*Vernichtung*' (destruction) was generally used as a metaphor for economic elimination.

37 W. Jochmann (ed.), *Adolf Hitler. Monologe im Führerhauptquartier 1941–1944* (Hamburg, 1980), p. 44. See Broszat, 'Genesis der "Endlösung"' (as in n. 33), p. 757.

38 See the basic study by Helmut Krausnick and Hans-Heinrich Wilhelm, *Die Truppe des Weltanschauungskrieges. Die Einsatzgruppen der Sicherheitspolizei und des SD 1938–1942* (Stuttgart, 1981).

39 Louis P. Lochner (ed.), *The Goebbels Diaries* (London, 1948), p. 48 and Broszat, 'Genesis der "Endlösung"' (as in n. 33), p. 758.

40 Andreas Hillgruber, *Staatsmänner und Diplomaten bei Hitler*, vol. 2 (Frankfurt, 1970), pp. 232–3, 245, 256–7; talks with Antonescu on 13 April 1943 and with Horthy on 16/17 April 1943.

41 Broszat, 'Genesis der "Endlösung"' (as in n. 33), pp. 773–4.

42 See Hilberg, *Destruction of European Jews* (as in n. 5), p. 652, note 39, and Henriette von Schirach, *Der Preis der Herrlichkeit* (Wiesbaden, 1956), pp. 187–8.

43 See Helmut Stierlin, *Adolf Hitler. Familienperspektiven* (Frankfurt, 1975), p. 118.

44 Pers. Stab RFSS, IfZ: MA 316, p. 4994 ff.

45 See Eberhard Jäckel, *Hitlers Weltanschauung* (as in n. 16), pp. 77–8 and, following him, Klaus Hildebrand, 'Hitlers "Programm" und seine Realisierung 1939–1942', in Manfred Funke (ed.), *Hitler, Deutschland und die Mächte* (Düsseldorf, 1976), pp. 78–80.

46 Fleming, *Hitler and the Final Solution* (as in n. 16), pp. 63–5; Irving, *Hitler's War* (as in n. 21), pp. 391–2. Why should Hitler have broken the normal codes governing language when speaking to Globocnik? See Broszat, 'Genesis der "Endlösung"' (as in n. 33), p. 760.

47 Fleming, *Hitler and the Final Solution* (as in n. 16), p. 20; also Broszat, 'Genesis der "Endlösung"' (as in n. 33), pp. 763–4; Krausnick and Wilhelm, *Truppe des Weltanschauungskrieges* (as in n. 38), p. 633; William Carr, *Hitler. A Study in Personality and Politics* (London, 1978), pp. 72, 76.

48 Smith and Peterson, *Heinrich Himmler. Geheimreden* (as in n. 12), p. 202; in the later speeches, Himmler talks of an 'order' (*Befehl*) or 'instruction' (*Auftrag*), which suggests a connection with the Commissar Order.

49 Fleming, *Hitler and the Final Solution* (as in n. 16), p. 44, quotes from the record of the interrogation of the *Höherer SS- und Polizeiführer* Jeckeln on 14 December 1945, for the period November 1941, that the liquidation of the Riga ghetto had been 'the *Führer*'s wish'. The testimony of Rudolf-Christoph Freiherr von Gersdorf, quoted by Fleming on p. 53, stands alone; none of the other statements refer to the *European* 'Programme for the Final Solution'. In this they accord with Heydrich's position of May 1942, as testified by Otto Wagner.

50 On the indisputable oral propagation of the Commissar Order see

Krausnick and Wilhelm, *Truppe des Weltanschauungskrieges* (as in n. 38), pp. 150–1, 348. On Hitler's role, ibid., pp. 114–15.

51 Krausnick, 'Judenverfolgung' (as in n. 2), p. 361.

52 Henry Picker (ed.), *Hitlers Tischgespräche im Führerhauptquartier*, 2nd edn (Stuttgart, 1977), p. 189: record of 24 July 1942. See Browning, *Final Solution* (as in n. 8), pp. 35–7. The sources presented by Browning make it difficult to sustain Leni Yahil's interpretation that, from the start, the Madagascar Plan was merely a cover for the Final Solution, although the plan would itself have meant mass physical destruction; Leni Yahil, 'Madagascar, Phantom of a Solution for the Jewish Question', in Bela Vago and George Mosse (eds), *Jews and Non-Jews in Eastern Europe* (New York, 1974).

53 See Fest, *Hitler* (as in n. 23), pp. 925, 927, 931; Broszat, 'Soziale Motivation' (as in n. 16), pp. 402–3, 407; J. P. Stern, *Hitler. The Führer and the People* (Glasgow, 1975), esp. pp. 83–4.

54 Max Domarus (ed.), *Hitler. Reden und Proklamationen 1932– 1945*, vol. II, Part 1 (Munich, 1965), pp. 1057–8.

55 ibid., vol. 4, pp. 1663, 1828, 1920, 1937; see Karl Dietrich Bracher, *Die Deutsche Diktatur* (Cologne, 1969), pp. 399–400.

56 IMG, vol. 27, pp. 499–500; see Adam, *Judenpolitik* (as in n. 2), pp. 209–11.

57 See Andreas Hillgruber, 'Die "Endlösung" und das deutsche Ostimperium als Kernstück des rassenideologischen Programms des Nationalsozialismus', in Manfred Funke (ed.), *Hitler, Deutschland und die Mächte* (Düsseldorf, 1976), pp. 94–114.

58 *Hitlers Politisches Testament* (Frankfurt, 1981). Incidentally, the self-protective method of expression is maintained even here: 'I have not kept anyone in the dark about the fact that this time millions of European children of the Aryan peoples will not starve, millions of grown men will not die, and hundreds of thousands of women and children will not be burned and bombed to death in the cities, without the real guilty party being made to atone for his guilt, *though by more humane methods*' (emphasis added).

59 On this issue see Krausnick and Wilhelm, *Truppe des Weltanschauungskrieges* (as in n. 38), pp. 165–7. Krausnick concludes that there was a corresponding regulation of language. Hilberg, *Destruction of European Jews* (as in n. 5), p. 217, by contrast, convincingly points out 'that psychological justifications were an essential part of the killing operations. If a proposed action could not be justified, it did not take place'.

60 Stern, *Hitler* (as in n. 53), pp. 23–5.

61 See Fest, *Hitler* (as in n. 23), pp. 772–4; Carr, *Hitler* (as in n. 47), pp. 135–7.

62 See Tim Mason, 'The Legacy of 1918 for National Socialism', in Anthony Nicholls and Erich Matthias (eds), *German Democracy and the Triumph of Hitler* (London, 1971), pp. 215–39.

63 See Wilhelm in Krausnick and Wilhelm, *Truppe des Weltanschauungskrieges* (as in n. 38), pp. 585–7. Irving, *Hitler's War* (as in n. 21),

pp. 330–1, concludes from this that Hitler forbade the liquidation, once and for all. Irving's reasoning is faulty, because this solution presupposes a detailed knowledge of plans that Himmler had not yet fully developed, and that Irving denies existed until October 1943. See the explanation in Broszat, 'Genesis der "Endlösung"' (as in n. 33), pp. 760–1. Broszat suspects that Hitler was not involved at all; Himmler would have anticipated Hitler's antipathy towards campaigns that provoked public protests.

64 See Broszat, 'Soziale Motivation' (as in n. 16), p. 408.

65 Most of the specialist literature casts doubt on the existence of a comprehensive plan by Hitler; see Hilberg, *Destruction of European Jews* (as in n. 5), p. 31; he nevertheless sees a consistent structure in the process of destruction. For my part, I argue that this is an inevitable result of the cumulative radicalization of the system; see Hans Mommsen, 'Hitlers Stellung' (as in n. 19), pp. 61–3; see Adam, *Judenpolitik* (as in n. 2), p. 357; Schleunes, *The Twisted Road* (as in n. 19), p. 2; Yehuda Bauer, *The Holocaust in Historical Perspective* (Canberra, 1978); Yehuda Bauer, 'Genocide: Was it the Nazi Original Plan?', *Annals of the American Academy of Political and Social Science* (July 1980), pp. 34–45.

66 Irving's interpretation (see *Hitler's War*, as in n. 21, introduction, pp. xiii–xv) that, while Hitler explicitly supported and approved the deportation of the Jews 'to the East', he forbade liquidations and postponed a definitive solution until after the war, rests on an inaccurate assessment of Hitler's comments concerning genocide. These were all made in a 'futuristic' context, and present the aim of eliminating the European Jews, and indeed Jews all over the world, as a vision of the future. Unlike Himmler (see n. 11) or Goebbels (see Hans-Heinrich Wilhelm, 'Wie geheim war die Endlösung?' in *Miscellanea. Festschrift für Helmut Krausnick*, Stuttgart, 1980, pp. 137–9), Hitler never refers to it as a programme directly implemented and in its final stages. This is not inconsistent with greater radicality after Stalingrad as established by Broszat ('Genesis der "Endlösung"', as in n. 33, p. 772) and connected with Hitler's attitude, which became increasingly visionary and unrealistic as he confined himself more and more to his bunker. Hitler was intoxicated with the 'idea' of annihilation, but he endeavoured to ignore the reality; here, at least, we must agree with Irving. It is typical that Hitler, who normally had statistical details at his fingertips, used pre-war figures for the proportion of Jews in the population in his conversation with Horthy (see n. 40).

67 Schleunes, *The Twisted Road* (as in n. 19), p. 258.

68 See Genschel, *Verdrängung der Juden* (as in n. 2), pp. 240–2, on the 'Aryanization' in Franconia; Peter Hüttenberger's creditable study, *Die Gauleiter* (Stuttgart, 1969), does not include this aspect.

69 See Helmut Heiber, *Joseph Goebbels* (Berlin, 1962), pp. 280–1; Adam, *Judenpolitik* (as in n. 2), pp. 206–7.

70 See Gerhard Botz, *Wien vom 'Anschluss' zum Krieg. Nationalsozialistische*

Machtübernahme und politisch-soziale Umgestaltung am Beispiel der Stadt Wien (Vienna, 1978), pp. 93–5; Genschel, *Verdrängung der Juden* (as in n. 2), pp. 160–2.

71 See Enno Georg, *Die wirtschaftliche Unternehmungen der SS* (Stuttgart, 1963); see also Speer's polemical, but factually accurate, *Sklavenstaat* (as in n. 15), pp. 346–8 and 381–3.

72 See Hilberg, *Destruction of European Jews* (as in n. 5), pp. 166–8, 334–6, 341–2, 586–600. The role of individual banks in the 'Aryanization process' requires more detailed investigation.

73 The basic study is Heinrich Uhlig, *Die Warenhäuser im Dritten Reich* (Cologne, 1965); Genschel, *Verdrängung der Juden* (as in n. 2), pp. 67–9.

74 The boundless corruption of the functionaries of the regime, especially over the expropriation of the Jews, contributed to the fact that criticism of the deportation and liquidation was limited to a few individual cases.

75 See Schmidt, *Speer* (as in n. 15), pp. 216–18.

76 See the survey in Bruno Blau, *Das Ausnahmerecht für die Juden in den europäischen Ländern*, Part 1: *Deutschland*, 3rd edn (Düsseldorf, 1965).

77 Impressive examples in Paul Sauer (ed.), *Dokumente über die Verfolgung der jüdischen Bürger in Baden-Württemberg durch das nationalsozialistische Regime 1933–1945*, 2 vols (Stuttgart, 1966); *Dokumente zur Geschichte der Frankfurter Juden* (Frankfurt, 1963); Maria Zelzer, *Weg und Schicksal der Stuttgarter Juden* (Stuttgart, 1964).

78 H. Robinson, *Justiz als politische Verfolgung. Die Rechtsprechung in 'Rassenschandefällen' beim Landgericht Hamburg 1936–1943* (Stuttgart, 1977); also Ernst Noam and Wolf-Arno Kropat (eds), *Juden vor Gericht 1933–1945* (Wiesbaden, 1975); Bernd Rüthers, *Die unbegrenzte Auslegung. Zum Wandel der Privatrechtsordnung im Nationalsozialismus* (Frankfurt, 1973), pp. 15–77; Ilse Haff, *Justiz im Dritten Reich* (Frankfurt, 1978).

79 See the indications in Hitler's speech of 15 September 1935 (Domarus, *Hitler* (as in n. 54), vol. I, Part 2, p. 537). See also Abraham Margaliot, 'The Reaction of the Jewish Public in Germany to the Nuremberg Laws', *Yad Vashem Studies*, XII (1977), esp. pp. 85–6. Von Freytag-Loringhoven, a *Reichstag* member, expressed similar sentiments.

80 See William Sheridan Allen, 'Die deutsche Öffentlichkeit und die "Reichskristallnacht" – Konflikte zwischen Werthierarchie und Propaganda im Dritten Reich', in D. Peukert and J. Reulecke (eds), *Alltag im Nationalsozialismus* (Wuppertal, 1981), pp. 397–411. See Botz, *Wien* (as in n. 70), pp. 403–4, on the different response to March 1938.

81 See Ian Kershaw, 'The Persecution of the Jews and German Popular Opinion in the Third Reich', *Leo Baeck Year Book*, 26 (1981), pp. 261–89.

82 Schleunes, *The Twisted Road* (as in n. 19), pp. 97, 100–2; Krausnick, 'Judenverfolgung' (as in n. 2), pp. 315–17. See also Hans Mommsen, 'Der nationalsozialistische Polizeistaat und die Judenverfolgung vor 1938' *Vierteljahrshefte für Zeitgeschichte*, 10 (1962), pp. 68–70.

83 See the interpretation given by Schleunes, *The Twisted Road* (as in

n. 19), pp. 71–3; the opposing view is given by Adam, *Judenpolitik* (as in n. 2), p. 46, following Sauer in K. D. Bracher, W. Sauer and W. Schulz, *Die nationalsozialistische Machtergreifung* (Cologne, 1962), pp. 870–1, and Bracher, in ibid., p. 54.

84 Schleunes, *The Twisted Road* (as in n. 19), pp. 253–5; Krausnick, 'Judenverfolgung' (as in n. 2), pp. 341–3.

85 Schleunes, *The Twisted Road* (as in n. 19), pp. 212–13.

86 See Werner Rosenstock, 'Exodus 1933–1939. Ein Überblick über die jüdische Auswanderung aus Deutschland', in *Deutsches Judentum. Aufstieg und Krise* (Stuttgart, 1963), p. 386; Paul Sauer, *Die Schicksale der jüdischen Bürger Baden-Württembergs während der nationalistische Verfolgungzeit 1933–1945* (Stuttgart, 1969), p. 123; Herbert A. Strauss, 'Jewish Emigration from Germany. Nazi Policies and Jewish Responses', *Leo Baeck Year Book*, 25 (1980), pp. 317–39; Hans Lamm, 'Die innere und äussere Entwicklung des deutschen Judentums', Ph.D. dissertation, University of Erlangen, 1951, p. 46.

87 Schleunes, *The Twisted Road* (as in n. 19), pp. 212–13.

88 Strauss, 'Jewish Emigration' (as in n. 86), pp. 351–3; see Bernard Wasserstein, *Britain and the Jews of Europe 1939–1945* (Oxford, 1979), pp. 6–8, 43–5.

89 See Lösener, 'Als Rassenreferent im Reichsministerium des Innern' (as in n. 20), pp. 264–6; Sauer, *Schicksale* (as in n. 86), p. 103. The number of '*Mischlinge* of the first and second grades' was declining demographically, standing at 84,000 in 1938.

90 Kershaw, 'Persecution' (as in n. 81), pp. 283–4; Stokes, 'German People' (as in n. 8), pp. 180–2.

91 Genschel, *Verdrängung der Juden* (as in n. 2), pp. 121–2. The flyleaf of Globke's commentary on the Nuremberg Laws (W. Stuckart and H. Globke, *Reichsbürgergesetz, Blutschutzgesetz und Ehegesundheitsgesetz*, Munich, 1936) announces a forthcoming commentary by Globke on the economic laws concerning the Jews. When Genschel asked Dr Hans Globke about this, Globke replied that he never intended to write such a commentary. Obviously a law was not passed because it would have resulted in undesirable restrictions of the kind opposed by Schacht. See Schleunes, *The Twisted Road* (as in n. 19), p. 156.

92 See Genschel, *Verdrängung der Juden* (as in n. 2), pp. 213–15.

93 See Kurt Pätzold, 'Von der Vertreibung zum Genocid. Zu den Ursachen, Triebkräften und Bedingungen der antijüdischen Politik des faschistischen deutschen Imperialismus', in Dietrich Eichholtz and Kurt Gossweiler (eds), *Faschismusforschung. Positionen, Probleme, Polemik* (East Berlin, 1980), p. 194; W. Präg and W. Jacobmeyer (eds), *Das Diensttagebuch des deutschen Generalgouverneurs in Polen 1939–1945* (Stuttgart, 1975), pp. 52–3.

94 Pätzold, 'Von der Vertreibung zum Genocid' (as in n. 93), p. 193.

95 ibid., pp. 194–5; Martin Broszat, *Nationalsozialistische Polenpolitik* (Stuttgart, 1961), pp. 86–8.

96 See Robert L. Koehl, '*RKFVD*'. *German Settlement and Population*

Policy, 1939–1945 (Cambridge, Mass., 1957), pp. 49–51, 95–7; Helmut Heiber, 'Der Generalplan Ost', *Vierteljahrshefte für Zeitgeschichte*, 6 (1958), pp. 281–3.

97 Pätzold, 'Von der Vertreibung zum Genocid' (as in n. 93), pp. 196–97; Adam, *Judenpolitik* (as in n. 2), pp. 248–50. As Pätzold rightly emphasizes, forced labour was a dominant motive.

98 Pätzold, 'Von der Vertreibung zum Genocid' (as in n. 93), p. 917; Broszat, 'Genesis der "Endlösung" ' (as in n. 33), pp. 748–50.

99 See Höhne, *Orden unter dem Totenkopf* (as in n. 11), pp. 280–2. Blaskowitz's intervention with Hitler effected a delay only; the planned measures were eventually frustrated by the opposition of Goering (Broszat, *Polenpolitik* (as in n. 95), p. 48).

100 Pätzold, 'Von der Vertreibung zum Genocid' (as in n. 93), p. 198. Nevertheless, Frank expected to receive between 400,000 and 600,000 Jews into the *Generalgouvernement* (Präg and Jacobmeyer, *Diensttagebuch* (as in n. 93), p. 131); on 12 July, Frank reported the *Führer's* decision, made at his request, 'that no more Jewish transports to the *Generalgouvernement* were to take place' (ibid., p. 252).

101 See Heydrich to Ribbentrop on 24 June 1940 (quoted by Pätzold, 'Von der Vertreibung zum Genocid', as in n. 93, p. 201): 'The problem *as a whole* – it is already a matter of around 3½ million Jews in the areas under German jurisdiction *today* – can no longer be solved by emigration. A territorial Final Solution has therefore become necessary.'

102 Adam, *Judenpolitik* (as in n. 2), pp. 294–5. Frank too had originally been prepared for such plans, which appeared feasible when the USSR handed over the district of Lublin.

103 Seev Goshen, 'Eichmann und die Nisco-Aktion im Oktober 1939', *Vierteljahrshefte für Zeitgeschichte*, 29 (1981), pp. 94–5.

104 See Kulka, *The Jewish Question* (as in n. 30), vol. 1, Document 51, pp. 501–3; notes by Dr Eppstein on 25 June 1940 and 3 July 1940 concerning discussions in the RSHA.

105 See Andreas Hillgruber, *Hitlers Strategie. Politik und Kriegsführung 1940–1941* (Frankfurt, 1965), pp. 148–9.

106 See n. 52; also Pätzold, 'Von der Vertreibung zum Genocid' (as in n. 93), pp. 201–3.

107 Krausnick, 'Judenverfolgung' (as in n. 2), pp. 357–8. These deportations – inconsistent with all medium-term planning – were, symptomatically, done with Hitler's approval.

108 See Adam, *Judenpolitik* (as in n. 2), pp. 257–8, 289.

109 ibid., pp. 185–7.

110 ibid., p. 290; this decision was to be repeated when it came to the question of using Russian prisoners of war in the Reich; see Christian Streit, *Keine Kameraden* (as in n. 8), pp. 192–4.

111 It is of fundamental importance that the generals now offered almost no resistance to Hitler's ideas and, in particular, accepted the equation of Bolshevism and Jewishness. See H. Krausnick, 'Kommissarbefehl

und "Gerichtsbarkeitserlass Barbarossa" in neuer Sicht', *Viertel-jahrshefte für Zeitgeschichte*, 25 (1977), pp. 716–18; Streit, *Keine Kameraden* (as in n. 8), pp. 51–3.

112 An official cessation of hostilities had not been thought of; see Hillgruber, *Hitlers Strategie* (as in n. 105), pp. 541–2, 555.

113 This does not, of course, exclude wide-ranging strategic planning; see Hillgruber, *Hitlers Strategie* (as in n. 105), pp. 377–9; moreover, Hitler revealed considerable personal uncertainty over the question of England.

114 *IMG*, vol. 26, p. 266; Document 710-PS. Adam's suggestion (*Judenpolitik* (as in n. 2), p. 308) – made with reference to Kempner (*Eichmann* (as in n. 9), p. 227) – that the authorization was given on Hitler's instructions, is not conclusive.

115 Hilberg, *Destruction of European Jews* (as in n. 5), p. 262. Hilberg refers to Eichmann, (see *Ich, Adolf Eichmann*, Leoni, 1980, p. 479), but this procedure is completely plausible, particularly in view of the long-term tendency to give the RSHA full responsibility for the 'Jewish question'.

116 In contrast, Fleming, *Hitler and the Final Solution* (as in n. 16), p. 110, points out that instructions were issued that Hitler was to receive 'continual updating on the progress of the *Einsatzgruppen*'. See Krausnick and Wilhelm, *Die Truppe des Weltanschauungskrieges* (as in n. 38), pp. 165–6, 335–6.

117 On the latter, see ibid., pp. 223–5, 232–4.

118 This changed after the systematic Final Solution had been set in motion; see ibid., p. 166.

119 Pätzold, 'Von der Vertreibung zum Genocid' (as in n. 93), p. 197.

120 Quoted in Hilberg, *Destruction of European Jews* (as in n. 5), p. 261.

121 Broszat, 'Genesis der "Endlösung" ' (as in n. 33), p. 749.

122 Himmler's memorandum of May 1940 about the treatment of '*Fremdvölkische*' in the East (ed. Helmut Krausnick, *Vierteljahrshefte für Zeitgeschichte*, 5 (1957), pp. 1944–6) still rejects 'the Bolshevik method of exterminating a people from inner conviction that it is ungermanic and impossible', but this occurs in the context of a consideration whether 'harshness' would not, in some circumstances, be less cruel.

123 See Broszat, 'Genesis der "Endlösung" ' (as in n. 33), pp. 751–2.

124 Krausnick, 'Judenverfolgung' (as in n. 2), p. 373; Browning, *Final Solution* (as in n. 8), pp. 66–7, 69.

125 Präg and Jacobmeyer, *Diensttagebuch* (as in n. 93), pp. 457–8.

126 Wannsee *Protocol* of 20 January 1942, quoted here from W. Jochmann and H. A. Jacobsen, *Ausgewählte Dokumente zur Geschichte des Nationalsozialismus* (Bielefeld, 1966), pp. 2, 3–5. According to Eichmann's testimony, liquidation techniques themselves were discussed at the conference. In view of the reaction of *Ministerialdirektor* Kritzinger, who was present (see *Gutachten des Instituts für Zeitgeschichte*, vol. 2, Stuttgart, 1966, p. 381 n. 38), this seems to me unlikely: Eichmann is

more likely to be referring to a discussion between the experts involved on the same occasion.

127 See Broszat, 'Genesis der "Endlösung" ' (as in n. 33), pp. 755–6.
128 On the part played by the Foreign Ministry see Browning, *The Final Solution* (as in n. 8), pp. 92–4.
129 See Broszat, 'Genesis der "Endlösung" ' (as in n. 33), and Hilberg, *Destruction of European Jews* (as in n. 5), pp. 586–600; also Rückerl, *Vernichtungslager* (as in n. 13), pp. 13–15.
130 Streit, *Keine Kameraden* (as in n. 8), pp. 219–21.
131 See Pätzold, 'Von der Vertreibung zum Genocid' (as in n. 93), p. 207.
132 Streit, *Keine Kameraden* (as in n. 8), pp. 222–3.
133 Broszat, 'Nationalsozialistische Konzentrationslager' (as in n. 7), pp. 108–9.
134 Streit, *Keine Kameraden* (as in n. 8), p. 223.
135 See Speer's description in *Sklavenstaat* (as in n. 15), pp. 381–3, and Höhne, *Orden unter dem Totenkopf* (as in n. 11), p. 403.
136 On *Aktion T4*'s recruitment of personnel and its methods, see Ino Arndt and Wolfgang Sheffler, 'Organisierter Massenmord an Juden in nationalsozialistischen Vernichtungslagern', *Vierteljahrshefte für Zeitgeschichte*, 24 (1976), pp. 114–16.
137 See Arendt, *Eichmann* (as in n. 9), pp. 135–7, 143–5.
138 See Broszat, 'Genesis der "Endlösung" ' (as in n. 33), p. 755, n. 39.
139 See *Studien zur Geschichte der Konzentrationslager* (Stuttgart, 1970); Broszat, 'Nationalsozialistische Konzentrationslager' (as in n. 7), pp. 41–3.
140 See Frank Trommler, 'Die "Nationalisierung" der Arbeit', in Reinhold Grün and Jost Hermand, *Arbeit als Thema in der deutschen Literatur vom Mittelalter bis zur Gegenwart* (Königstein, 1979), pp. 102–25.
141 See Fleming, *Hitler and the Final Solution* (as in n. 16), pp. 116–19; Hilberg, *Destruction of European Jews* (as in n. 5), pp. 253–4; Präg and Jacobmeyer, *Diensttagebuch* (as in n. 93), entry for 9 December 1942, p. 588.
142 See Hilberg, *Destruction of European Jews* (as in n. 5), p. 343.
143 See Rainer C. Baum's attempt to find a solution, *The Holocaust and the German Elite. Genocide and National Suicide in Germany 1871–1945* (London, 1981), pp. 294–6; cf. pp. 265–7. In addition to the problem of moral indifference, there is also that of the suppression of moral inhibitions, for instance in the deportation of Jewish children.
144 Fleming, *Hitler and the Final Solution* (as in n. 16), pp. 93–4, puts forward the view that the Wannsee Conference was postponed because SS-*Sturmbannführer* Lange was unable to attend on 9 December. What seems to have happened is that Heydrich asked Eichmann for information about technical possibilities for mass killings in the late autumn of 1941 (see ibid., p. 73 and Jochen von Lang, *Das Eichmann-Protokoll. Tonbandaufzeichnungen der israelischen Verhöre* (Berlin, 1982), pp. 69–71).

145 Kempner, *Eichmann* (as in n.9), pp. 424–6; Andreas Biss, *Der Stopp der Endlösung* (Stuttgart, 1966), pp. 227–8.

146 Survey in Hilberg, *Destruction of European Jews* (as in n.5), pp. 334–6, 344–5.

147 Adam, *Judenpolitik* (as in n.2), dates the destruction order from Hitler to the period between September and November 1941 (pp. 311–12). Hilberg, *Destruction of European Jews* (as in n.5), p. 263, surmises that Hitler's decision was made in September, on the basis of information given by Eichmann and Höss, as well as a diary entry by Himmler on 17 November – 'extermination [*Beiseitigung*] of the Jews'. Fleming, *Hitler and the Final Solution* (as in n.16), pp. 66–7 and passim, suspects that there was a secret order. Wilhelm (*Die Truppe des Weltanschauungskrieges* (as in n.38), pp. 630–2) argues that Himmler and Heydrich could not have begun an extensive extermination campaign without Hitler's approval. I, however, concur with Broszat ('Genesis der "Endlösung"', as in n.33) in seeing a mixture of improvisation and planning as characteristic of the process (see Krausnick and Wilhelm, *Die Truppe des Weltanschauungskrieges*, as in n.38, p. 635).

148 Christopher Browning's criticism ('Zur Genesis der "Endlösung". Eine Antwort an Martin Broszat', *Vierteljahrshefte für Zeitgeschichte*, 29, 1981, pp. 97–9) rests on the assumption that Hitler instructed Goering, Himmler and Heydrich, in the summer of 1941, 'to prepare a practicable programme for the destruction of the Jews'. He suggests that Goebbels was not necessarily informed, and that Hermann Goering, the only surviving witness, lied at Nuremberg (see *IMG*, vol. 9, pp. 574–6). The testimonies of Höss and Eichmann referring to late summer 1941, on which he relies, are not very specific and also relate to the period before the definitive destruction order which he assumes was given in October/November.

149 Fleming, *Hitler and the Final Solution* (as in n.16), passim. It is indisputable that at no time has there been any doubt that Hitler supported the genocide measures; however, there are different views about the factors that led to the implementation of the policy. For the *Führer* directive on fighting the partisans, see Walter Hubatsch (ed.), *Hitlers Weisungen für die Kriegsführung 1939–1945* (Frankfurt, 1962), pp. 201–3.

150 On Hitler's equivocation about the deployment of labour, see Speer, *Sklavenstaat* (as in n.15), pp. 367–9.

151 See Präg and Jacobmeyer, *Diensttagebuch* (as in n.93), p. 583; Speer, *Sklavenstaat* (as in n.15), pp. 372–4. Obviously, Frank did not dare to broach this issue in his conversation with Hitler on 9 May 1943.

152 See n.12.

153 See Broszat, 'Genesis der "Endlösung"' (as in n.33), pp. 758–9 and passim. He justifiably points to the contradictions in Irving's position. However, the systematic transformation of the idea of genocide was the work of the SS bureaucracy.

154 On this see Adam, *Judenpolitik* (as in n.2), pp. 349–51; Hans

Mommsen, 'Aufgabenkreis und Verantwortlichkeit des Staatssekretärs der Reichskanzlei', in *Gutachten des Instituts für Zeitgeschichte*, vol. 2 (Stuttgart, 1966), pp. 369–71.

155 See von Lang, *Eichmann-Protokoll* (as in n.144), p. 88: '. . . with the delivery of the transports to their destination according to the timetable, my responsibilities ended.' On this, see Arendt, *Eichmann* (as in n.9), pp. 258–9.

156 See Albrecht Tyrell, *Vom Trommler zum Führer. Der Wandel von Hitlers Selbstverständnis zwischen 1919 und 1924 und die Entwicklung der NSDAP* (Munich, 1975).

157 Mommsen, 'Hitlers Stellung' (as in n.19), pp. 58–9.

158 See Walter Laqueur, *The Terrible Secret. An Investigation into the Suppression of Information about Hitler's Final Solution* (London, 1980); Wasserstein, *Jews of Europe* (as in n.88); Helen Fein, *Accounting for Genocide. National Responses and Jewish Victimization during the Holocaust* (New York, 1979), esp. pp. 169–71.

159 See Steinert, *Hitler's War* (as in n.8), pp. 143–4; Kershaw, 'Antisemitismus und Volksmeinung' (as in n.8), pp. 339–40; Otto D. Kulka, '"Public Opinion" in Nazi Germany: The Final Solution', *The Jerusalem Quarterly*, 26 (1983), pp. 149–51.

160 Broszat, 'Soziale Motivation' (as in n.16), pp. 403–5.

161 See Fest, *Hitler* (as in n.23), pp. 925, 927; also Carr, *Hitler* (as in n.47), pp. 6–7.

Chronology of Destruction

GERHARD HIRSCHFELD

This chronology does not claim to present a comprehensive list of all anti-Jewish measures and actions against Jews and Soviet prisoners of war (PoWs) between 1933 and 1945. The sheer number of laws, decrees, orders and instructions – several thousand – that preceded, accompanied and concluded the Holocaust of European Jews and the extent of the destruction process limit all efforts to document this chapter of German and European history as it deserves. What should become clear, however, is how the destruction process developed step by step within the relatively short time the Nazis had at their disposal: from legal definition and exclusion to social and human isolation, from economic expropriation to total exploitation, from individual attacks to organized pogroms, from expulsion and deportation to mass murder on an unprecedented scale. For millions of East European Jews and Soviet PoWs there was only one step: from their concentration in ghettos and camps to extermination and starvation to death.

1933

30 January	Hitler is appointed Reich-Chancellor
March	Setting-up of first concentration camps (Dachau, Oranienburg)
1–3 April	Official boycott of Jewish businesses and numerous acts of violence against individuals
7 April	'Law for the Restoration of the Professional Civil Service': first dismissals of Jews from positions in government and public life
25 April	'Law against Overcrowding of German Schools': no admittance for more than 1.5 per cent non-Aryans in public schools and universities
10 May	Public burning of books

14 July	'Law on the Revocation of Naturalization and Annulment of German Citizenship': withdrawal of citizenship granted since 1918 from 'undesirables', in particular all East European Jews.
25 August	Decree about the denaturalization of emigrants: publication of the first *Ausbürgerungsliste* (expulsion list)

1935

21 May	'Aryan' descent is a prerequisite for active service in the German Army: Jews are to be dismissed from the *Wehrmacht* (armed forces)
15 September	'Reich Citizenship Law' and 'Law for the Protection of German Blood and German honour' (Nuremberg Laws): definition of the term 'Jew'; Jews are legally, politically and socially separated from other Germans
14 November	'First Ordinance to the Reich Citizenship Law': Jews cannot be Reich-citizens any more, Jewish civil servants are to retire, definition of mixed marriages (*Mischlinge*) (Followed by twelve further supplementary decrees until 1 July 1943)

1936

12 July	Erection of the concentration camp in Sachsenhausen (near Berlin)
15 October	Jewish teachers are banned from private education of 'Aryan' children
December	Number of refugees from Nazi Germany exceeds 100,000

1937

12 June	Secret directive by head of the Security Police (SiPo), Heydrich, that Jewish 'race-violators' should be put into 'protective custody' after serving their sentences
24 July	According to the Reich and the Prussian Ministeries of the Interior, Jews are to be separated from other guests in German public baths and health resorts

146

1938

13 March	Annexation of Austria (*Anschluss*)
26 April	Registration of all Jews with assets exceeding 5,000 *Reichsmark*
9 June	Destruction of the synagogue in Munich
14 June	Definition of Jewish enterprises; all Jewish firms have to be listed with the Ministry of Economics; no credit to Jews and Jewish firms by public savings banks (*Sparkhassen*)
15 June	Approx. 1,500 Jews in a so-called 'June Action' are sent to concentration camps
6 July	Decree provides for the termination (by 31 December) of Jewish business activities involved in guard services, credit information bureaus, estate agencies, broking agencies, tourist offices, marriage agencies (for non-Jews) and peddling
23 July	Decree providing for special identification cards for Jews (1 January 1939)
25 July	'Fourth Ordinance to the Reich Citizenship Law' revoking the general medical licences of Jewish doctors (30 September 1938) and restricting them to the treatment of Jews only
10 August	Destruction of the Nuremberg synagogue
27 September	'Fifth Ordinance to the Reich Citizenship Law' removing Jewish lawyers from the bar and reducing them to 'consultants'
5 October	German passports held by Jews are to be stamped with a large red 'J' whenever the document is presented to the authorities
26 October	17,000 Polish Jews living inside Germany are made 'stateless' and forced to cross the border to Poland, often in appalling conditions
7 November	A minor German diplomat, *Legationssekretär* (legation secretary) E. vom Rath, is assassinated in Paris by a 17-year-old Polish Jew, Herschel Grynszpan, whose family had previously been expelled from Germany
9–10 November	*Reichskristallnacht* ('night of broken glass'): using the vom Rath murder as an excuse, the Minister of Propaganda, Goebbels, launches an anti-Jewish campaign; violence all over Germany and Austria (burning of synagogues, looting of Jewish shops, beating of Jews); as a result of these organized pogroms 91 Jews are killed, 26,000 male Jews are sent to concentration camps

12 November	Jews are 'fined' 1 billion *Reichsmark* to 'make good' the murder of vom Rath. Jewish property owners are ordered to repair the damage 'to restore the street appearance'
	Jewish firms are made subject to liquidation and compulsory transfer (enforced 'Aryanization'). German firms are asked to dismiss all Jewish managers by the end of the year. Jews are forbidden to visit theatres, cinemas, concerts, exhibitions, etc.
15 November	Jewish children are excluded from German schools
21 November	Implementaion of 'fine' on all Jews owning more than 5,000 *Reichsmark*: each liable Jew has to pay 20 per cent of his registered assets, due in four instalments
28 November	Movements of Jews are restricted
2–3 December	Decrees authorize local authorities to bar Jews from the street on certain days (Nazi holidays) and from public places (pools, entertainment areas, etc.); driving licences and permits held by Jews are withdrawn
3 December	Decree provides for the compulsory 'Aryanization' of Jewish firms within a specified time; a 'trustee' can be appointed to effect the sale or liquidation; Jews are ordered to deposit their stocks, bonds and other securities with local tax offices
8 December	Final exclusion of all Jews from teaching or research at universities or other institutions of higher eduction (including libraries)
14 December	Decree replaces the Jewish owner or director of a firm with an 'Aryan' general manager (*Betriebsführer*)
28 December	Secret directive by Goering provides for the confinement of Jews in their homes; Jews are forbidden to use dining and sleeping compartments on railways
December	The number of refugees from Germany and Austria exceeds 250,000

1939

1 January	All Jews have to carry the middle name Israel or Sara
17 January	'Eighth Ordinance to the Reich Citizenship Law' revokes licences for Jewish dentists, veterinary surgeons and pharmacists
30 January	Hitler prophesies to the German *Reichstag* 'the annihilation of the Jewish race in Europe' in the event of war
15 March	German troops invade Czechoslovakia: Bohemia and

	Moravia become a German protectorate, Slovakia a mere puppet state
30 April	An official decree provides that German tenancy laws do not apply to Jews: Jews can be evicted by a German landlord; homeless Jews have to be accepted as tenants by other Jews still in possession of their apartments or houses
4 July	'Tenth Ordinance to the Reich Citizenship Law' establishing the *Reichsvereinigung* (Reich Association) of Jews in Germany as the sole and compulsory representative of persons classified as Jews by the definition decree
1 September	German attack on Poland: beginning of Second World War
	Introduction of curfew laws for Jews to remain inside houses (summer after 9 p.m., winter after 8 p.m.)
9 September	All male Jews of Gelsenkirchen in the Ruhr are sent to the concentration camp of Sachsenhausen
19–20 September	Confiscation of all radios owned by Jews
21 September	Heydrich instructs leaders of SS *Einsatzgruppen* (Special Forces) in Poland about 'planned ultimate objective' (concentration of Jews, ghettoization); numerous pogroms organized by SS and certain Army units
6–7 October	Himmler is appointed 'Reich Commissioner for the Strengthening of Germandom' and given charge of all resettlement plans
17 October	Hitler orders that SS and Police are to be exempt from military and ordinary jurisdiction
20–21 October	First deportation of Jews from Vienna, Hamburg and Prague to Poland (Lublin)
30 October	Himmler orders the expulsion of all Jews from the rural areas of western Poland within three months
23 November	Introduction of a yellow star for all Jews in the *Generalgouvernement* Poland
1 December	Regional Food Offices are instructed by the Ministry of Food and Agriculture that Jews are to be deprived of special food allocations in the next ration period; further reductions in food supply for Jews are ordered in 1941 and 1942
December	Expulsion of approx. 90,000 Poles and Jews from the new German province Warthegau to the *Generalgouvernement* Poland, which now becomes the human 'dumping ground' of the Third Reich

1940

Early January	First experimental gassing of mental patients, Jewish and others, in German hospitals; the order for the *Aktion T4* ('euthanasia programme') was given by Hitler in October 1939 and dated back to 1 September
12–13 February	Deportation of Jews from Stettin to Poland (Lublin)
9 April	Germany invades Denmark and Norway
27 April	Himmler issues a directive ordering the establishment of a concentration camp at Auschwitz
10 May	Germany invades the Netherlands and Belgium
22 June	France surrenders: the country is placed under military rule, except for the southern zone under Marshall Pétain (Vichy-France)
4 July	Jews in Berlin are allowed to buy food only in the afternoon between 4 and 5 p.m.
19–29 July	Jews are excluded from using private telephones
October	Jews of Warsaw are confined to a newly established ghetto area, the largest of all ghettos erected by the Nazi authorities in Poland since October 1939
22 October	7,500 German Jews from the Saar, Baden and Alsace Lorraine are deported to internment camps in France near the Pyrenees (Gurs)

1941

22–23 January	First massacre of Jews in Rumania by members of the fascist Iron Guard
27 February	Nearly 400 Jews are deported from Amsterdam to the concentration camps at Buchenwald and Mauthausen (near Linz) following raids on the Jewish quarter (22 February)
February–April	Deportation of 72,000 Jews to the Warsaw ghetto
1 March	Himmler orders the erection of a prisoner-of-war camp at Auschwitz-Birkenau for 100,000 (Soviet) PoWs; the concentration camp at Auschwitz had then approx. 8,000, mostly Polish, inmates
30 March	Hitler reveals to his Army and Airforce commanders that the forthcoming war against Russia will be a 'war of extermination'
6 April	German troops invade Yugoslavia and Greece
28 April	Army High Command (OKH) agrees to the operation of SS

	Sonderkommandos and *Einsatzkommandos* in the rear Army areas
13 May	Barbarossa Directive provides that German soldiers who commit 'ideologically motivated offences' against the Soviet civilian population are to remain exempt from any prosecution
May	Final arrangements for the formation of three (later four) SS *Einsatzgruppen* (with 2–3,000 men): their task is the total elimination of Jews, Communists and other 'undesirable elements' in all Army-occupied areas
6 June	*Wehrmacht* High Command issues Commissar Order stipulating that Red Army political commissars should be segregated from other prisoners and handed over to the SS for liquidation; those 'captured in battle or when offering resistance are to be summarily executed on the spot'
17 June	Heydrich gives further details to the leaders of SS *Einsatzgruppen* and *-kommandos* in Berlin about their forthcoming operations in Russia.
22 June	The invasion of the Soviet Union by German troops is followed by countless pogroms against Russian Jews and mass killings by SS *Einsatzgruppen* in the occupied areas during the following months
28 June	*Wehrmacht* and SS agree about the selection and execution of certain PoWs by SS *Einsatzkommandos*: between now and May 1944 approx. 500,000 – 600,000 Soviet PoWs will be handed over to the SS by Army units
31 July	Goering issues the first written order for the liquidation of European Jews (*Endlösung*): Heydrich should make all necessary preparations for an 'overall solution to the Jewish question in Germany's sphere of influence in Europe'
24 August	After denouncement of the 'euthanasia'-actions by bishops and other church leaders, Hitler orders the 'official' end to *Aktion T4*; so far over 70,000 mental patients have been killed (gassed)
3 September	First experimental gassing with *Zyklon B* of Jewish prisoners in Auschwitz
15 September	All German Jews over the age of 6 have to wear the yellow star in public; Jews are not allowed to leave their place of residence
29–30 September	Mass killings of Jews (33,771) in Kiev (Babi Yar)

September–October	The first 10,000 Soviet PoWs arrive at Auschwitz; at least 900 of them are killed during further experiments with *Zyklon B*
3–31 October	Introduction of a separate labour status for Jews: they are not entitled to payment other than for the work they have actually done; Jews have to accept every job assigned to them by labour offices; Jewish youth, between the ages of 14 and 18, can be employed at all hours; invalids also have to accept all assignments
14 October	First deportation order for Jews from the Reich
23 October	Emigration of Jews from Germany is prohibited
24 October	Friendly relations between Germans and Jews are forbidden and will be prosecuted
October–November	Mass killings of Jews by SS *Einsatzgruppen* in southern Russia
	Experimental gassing of Soviet PoWs in Sachsenhausen
3 November	Units of the *Einsatzgruppe* A kill 10,000 Jews at Riga, among them the first Jewish transports from Germany
End November–March 1942	Start of operation 'Reinhard' (later named after Reinhard Heydrich, who was assassinated in Prague in May 1942): special extermination camps in Chelmno (near Lodz) and Belzec (near Lublin) are prepared for mass killings (gassing) of Jews

1942

Mid-January	5,000 gypsies are deported from Lodz ghetto to Chelmno and gassed on arrival
20 January	An interdepartmental conference at Wannsee/Berlin outlines practical measures for the mass extermination of European Jews
February–March	'Evacuation' of Polish ghettos and deportation of Jews to extermination camps
2 March	164 Soviet PoWs are gassed in Mauthausen/Gusen
13 March	German Jews are ordered by the Reich Security Head Office to mark their apartments with a black star
24 March	First deportation of Jews from southern Germany (Würzburg) to the extermination camp in Belzec
26–27 March	First transport from occupied Western Europe (Drancy/France) with foreign-born Jews arrives in Auschwitz
April	*Einsatzgruppen* report to Himmler that they have so far executed 461,500 Soviet Jews

End of April	Extermination camp at Sobibor is 'ready for use'
May–June	Introduction of the yellow star to mark all Jews in occupied countries of Netherlands, France and Belgium
4 May	Start of mass gassing of Jews in Auschwitz-Birkenau, where four gas chambers and crematoria are built during 1942 and early 1943
7 July	Jewish schools in Germany are closed
15–16 July	First deportation of Dutch Jews from Westerbork to Auschwitz
16–18 July	French police arrest almost 13,000 'stateless' Jews in Paris; 9,000 of them, among them 4,000 children, are deported via Drancy to Auschwitz
19 July	Himmler orders the extermination of all Jews inside Poland with few exceptions by the end of 1942
22 July	Start of deportation of Jews from the Warsaw ghetto to Treblinka, where in one month alone 66,701 Jews are gassed on arrival
July–September	First phase of mass deportation of Jews from Western Europe (Netherlands, Belgium, France) to Auschwitz
August– September	First round-up and deportation of 7,000 Jews from unoccupied Vichy-France; by December 1942 about 42,500 Jews have been sent via Drancy to Auschwitz
Last two weeks in August	More than 200,000 Jews are murdered in the extermination camps of Chelmno, Treblinka and Belzec
September– October	Start of mass gassing in the former concentration camp of Majdanek (near Lublin)
September	193 Soviet PoWs are gassed in the concentration camp of Neuengamme (near Hamburg)
9 October	It is forbidden for German Jews to buy books
Beginning of November	According to Himmler's order, all concentration camps inside Germany are to be made '*judenfrei*' (free of Jews): Jews are to be deported to Auschwitz and Lublin
November	251 Soviet PoWs are gassed in the concentration camp of Neuengamme
25–26 November	Start of the deportation of Norwegian Jews to Auschwitz
16 December	Reich Security Head Office orders the deportation of all German gypsies to Auschwitz: by 1945 more than 220,000 of Europe's 700,000 gypsies have been murdered

1943

18 January	First organized Jewish resistance inside the Warsaw ghetto against deportations
2 February	Surrender of the 6th German Army at Stalingrad
27 February	Jewish armament workers in Berlin are deported to Auschwitz
Early March– end of July	Dutch Jews are deported from Westerbork to Sobibor: most of the 34,000 are gassed on arrival
15 March	Start of the deportation of Greek Jews from Salonica: by August 1943 more than 43,000 of Salonica's 56,000 Jews have been deported to Auschwitz
7 April	End of mass killings in Chelmno and destruction of gas chambers by SS: approx. 152,000 have been murdered there
19 April	Warsaw ghetto rising: German military enters the Warsaw ghetto to resume the interrupted deportations from the ghetto and crush organized Jewish resistance (Commander Mordechai Anielewicz); several thousand Jews die in street-to-street fighting
End of April	Setting-up of a concentration camp at Bergen-Belsen for 'special' categories of Jews (neutral countries, wealthy Jews, etc.)
16 May	'The Jewish Quarter of Warsaw is no more' (SS *Obergruppenführer* Stroop): of the remaining 56,000 Jews (from approx. 350,000) 7,000 are shot immediately, the rest are sent to the killing centre of Treblinka and the extermination and concentration camps of Lublin
8 June	Transport with 3,000 children and their mothers leaves the Netherlands for Sobibor; all are gassed on arrival
11 June	Himmler orders the liquidation of all Polish ghettos
19 June	Goebbels declares Berlin to be '*judenfrei*'
21 June	Order for the liquidation of Russian ghettos
1 July	'Thirteenth Ordinance to the Reich Citizenship Law' provides for the property of a Jew to be confiscated after his death
2 August	Revolt by prisoners in Treblinka: destruction of gas chambers
August– December	'Evacuation' of all Russian ghettos and deportation of the remaining Soviet Jews to extermination camps
16–23 August	The deportation of 8,000 Jews from the Bialystok ghetto to Treblinka leads to major resistance actions against SS-guards; liquidation of the ghetto

September	More than 7,500 Danish Jews are rescued from deportation and ferried to safety in Sweden
14 October	Revolt by inmates of Sobibor: end of gassings
19 October	End of Operation 'Reinhard': approx. 1½ million Jews were killed between November 1941 and October 1943 in the extermination camps of Belzec, Sobibor and Treblinka alone
October–November	After the German occupation of Northern Italy (16 September) 8,360 Italian Jews are deported to Auschwitz
3 November	Liquidation of Riga ghetto and killing of the remaining Jews in Majdanek (17,000)
18 December	German Jews from mixed marriages and other 'privileged' Jews are sent to the ghetto of Theresienstadt in the German protectorate of Bohemia

1944 23

March–April	Deportation of over 6,000 Greek Jews from Athens and mainland Greece to Auschwitz, followed by further round-up of Jews on all the major islands; 1,500 manage to escape to Turkey by boat
April–May	After the German take-over of government control in Hungary (19 March), Hungarian Jews are moved into special ghetto areas and (from 15 May) rapidly deported: by 7 July over 437,000 Jews have been deported to Auschwitz
May–August	Resumption of mass gassings in Chelmno
6 June	VE-Day: Allied landings in Normandy
13–29 June	First major 'evacuation' transport from Auschwitz to Mauthausen and Stutthof. The liquidation of other extermination camps began – in the face of the advancing Soviet army – as early as autumn 1943 (Treblinka, Sobibor, Belzec); after August 1944 Auschwitz remained the only killing centre still operating at full capacity
20 July	Assassination attempt on Hitler fails
24 July	Soviet troops enter the extermination camp of Majdanek
July–December	Further transports and death marches of prisoners from Auschwitz and other camps to the West
1 August	The special gypsy camp in Auschwitz-Birkenau is liquidated: nearly 3,000 gypsies are killed
14 September	American troops cross the German border at Aachen
28 September	First of 'evacuation' transports from Theresienstadt reaches Auschwitz; only 2,000 of more than 18,000 deported 'special' Jews survive

7 October	Revolt by a Jewish *Sonderkommando* in Auschwitz
27 November	Himmler orders an end to the gassings in Auschwitz and the destruction of all gas chambers and crematoria

1945

24

1 January	The last transport with five (!) Jews from Berlin reaches Auschwitz
18 January	SS orders the total 'evacuation' of Auschwitz
27 January	Soviet troops liberate Auschwitz: they find 5,000 mostly sick prisoners who were unable to be marched away by SS guards
15 April	British troops enter the concentration camp of Bergen-Belsen, where over 18,000 inmates had died in March alone owing to the appalling conditions created by the camp authorities; even after liberation 500 people die each day from typhoid and starvation
21–28 April	Last gassings of (mostly sick) concentration camp inmates in Ravensbrück and Mauthausen
29 April	American forces enter Dachau, the first concentration camp of the Reich, where 40,000 prisoners have died since the establishment of the camp in March 1933
30 April	Adolf Hitler commits suicide in Berlin
6 May	The last remaining concentration camp Mauthausen, in Austria, is liberated by American troops; there, in the previous four months, more than 30,000 people had been murdered or had died from starvation and disease, among them Jews, gypsies, homosexuals, Jehovah's Witnesses, Soviet PoWs and tens of thousands of Spanish Republicans
7–9 May	The Allies accept the unconditional surrender of Nazi Germany

Appendix 1: Concentration and Extermination Camps

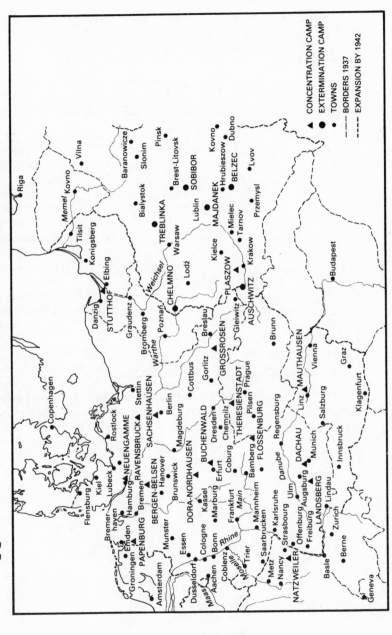

CONCENTRATION CAMP ▲
EXTERMINATION CAMP ●
TOWNS •
BORDERS 1937 — —
EXPANSION BY 1942 - - - -

Source: Der gelbe Stern. Die Judenverfolgung in Europa 1933 bis 1945 (Munich, 1978), p. 214

Appendix 2: The German Invasion of Russia, and Mass Murder Plans, 22 June 1941

Source: Martin Gilbert, *Atlas of the Holocaust* (London, 1982), p. 65, map 71.

Appendix 3: Main Deportation Railways to Auschwitz, March 1942 – November 1944

Source: Martin Gilbert, *Atlas of the Holocaust* (London, 1982) p. 4, map 1.

Appendix 4: Jews Murdered between 1 September 1939 and 8 May 1945: an estimate

Source: Martin Gilbert, *Atlas of the Holocaust* (London, 1982), p. 244, map, 316.

Appendix 5: Survivors, and those who returned, 1945

NORWAY
1,000

FINLAND
2,000

SWEDEN

BALTIC STATES
25,000

DENMARK
5,500

Memel

WESTERN SOVIET UNION
300,000

NETHERLANDS
20,000

DANZIG
8,000

GERMANY
330,000

POLAND
225,000

BELGIUM
40,000

CZECHOSLOVAKIA
44,000

LUXEMBURG
1,000

AUSTRIA
7,000

HUNGARY
300,000

RUMANIA
430,000

SWITZERLAND

FRANCE
200,000

YUGOSLAVIA
12,000

BULGARIA
50,000

ITALY
35,000

ALBANIA
200

GREECE
12,000

RHODES
161

CRETE
7

0   400
kilometres

—·—·— Frontiers of 1937

Source: Martin Gilbert, *Atlas of the Holocaust* (London, 1982), p. 242, map 315.

Appendix 6

COMPARATIVE OFFICER RANKS

SS	German Army	British Army
SS-Untersturmführer	Leutnant	Second Lieutenant
SS-Obersturmführer	Oberleutnant	Lieutenant
SS-Hauptsturmführer	Hauptmann	Captain
SS-Sturmbannführer	Major	Major
SS-Obersturmbannführer	Oberstleutnant	Lieutenant Colonel
SS-Standartenführer \}	Oberst	Colonel
SS-Oberführer		
SS-Brigadeführer	Generalmajor	Brigadier
SS-Gruppenführer	Generalleutnant	Major General
SS-Obergruppenführer	General	Lieutenant General
SS-Obergruppenführer	Generaloberst	General
Reichsführer-SS	Generalfeldmarschall	Field Marshal

MOBILE EXECUTION UNITS IN EASTERN EUROPE

Einsatzgruppe A (Baltic countries)
Einsatzkommandos 2, 3
Sonderkommandos 1a, 1b

Einsatzgruppe B (White Russia)
Einsatzkommandos 8, 9
Sonderkommandos 7a, 7b
'*Vorkommando Moskau*' (November 1941)
('Advance Party Moscow')

Einsatzgruppe C (Northern and Middle Ukraine)
Einsatzkommandos 5, 6
Sonderkommandos 4a, 4b

Einsatzgruppe D (Bessarabia, Caucasia, Southern Ukraine)
Einsatzkommandos 11a, 11b, 12
Sonderkommandos 10a, 10b

Glossary and List of Abbreviations

Aktion T4	Extermination of the so-called 'incurables' (mentally and physically handicapped people) (*T4*: after address of central office in Berlin – Tiergartenstrasse 4)
Alter Kämpfer	(*lit.* 'Old Fighter') Party member who joined the NSDAP before 30 January 1933
Anschluss	Annexation of Austria in March 1938
Arbeitseinsatz	(*lit.* 'mobilization of labour') Nazi term for the deployment of labour, occasionally used as a euphemism for deportation and extermination
Blitzkrieg	(*lit.* 'lightning campaign') Germany's strategy during first years of Second World War
Blut und Boden	(*lit.* 'blood and soil') Nazi agrarian romanticism
Einsatzgruppe	Special Force: mobile SS and Police unit for the mass murder of Jews, Communists and partisans in Eastern Europe
Einsatzkommando	Special Unit, which was an individual detachment of an *Einsatzgruppe*
Endlösung	Final Solution: cover name for the planned extermination of European Jews
Führer	The Leader (Adolf Hitler)
Funktionshäftlinge	Concentration camp inmates with special duties
Gau	regional party district
Gauleiter	regional party leader
Generalgouvernement	General Government: main part of German-occupied Poland
Generalgouverneur	Governor General
Generalplan Ost	Resettlement programme for Eastern Europe
Gestapo	*Geheime Staatspolizei* (Secret State Police)

163

Gleichschaltung	(*lit.* 'bringing into line') Nazification of state and society after 1933
GPU	(Russian abbrev.) Soviet State Political Administration
Kapo	(Italian *capo* = head) Concentration camp inmate in charge of work detachment
Kommissarbefehl	Commissar Order
Kristallnacht	(*lit.* 'night of broken glass') November Pogrom 1938
Lebensraum	(*lit.* 'living space') Nazi metaphor for the desire to expand into Central and Eastern Europe
Legationsrat/-sekretär	Legation councillor/secretary (respectively, Second & Third Secretary of an Embassy or at the Foreign Ministry)
Mischlinge	Persons of partly Jewish descent
NSDAP	*Nationalsozialistische Deutsche Arbeiterpartei* – National Socialist German Workers Party (Nazi Party)
OKH	*Oberkommando des Heeres* (Army High Command)
OKW	*Oberkommando der Wehrmacht* (Armed Forces High Command)
Ostministerium	Reich Ministry for the occupied Eastern Territories under Alfred Rosenberg
Rassenschande	(*lit.* 'racial shame') sexual intercourse between Aryans and non-Aryans
Reichsbürgerbrief	Deed of Reich citizenship
Reichsgaue	Newly incorporated territorial units under direct German rule combining features of a province (*Land*) and a party district (Wartheland, Danzig–West-preussen)
Reichskommissariat	Reich Commissariat
Reichstag	German parliament
RKFDV	*Reichskommissar für die Festigung Deutschen Volkstums* (Reich Commissar for the Strengthening of Germandom)
RSHA	*Reichssicherheitshauptamt* (Reich Security Head Office), formed in 1939 under Reinhard Heydrich. Its departments included the *Gestapo*, the Criminal Police and the SD
SA	*Sturmabteilung* (storm troopers)
SD	*Sicherheitsdienst* (Security Service) of the SS

Glossary

SiPo	*Sicherheitspolizei* (Security Police) of the SS
Sonderbehandlung	(*lit.* 'special treatment') SS term for immediate execution of prisoners
Sonderkommando	Special squad: individual detachment of an *Einsatzkommando*
SS	*Schutzstaffel* (*lit.* 'defence echelon') Police and security organization run by Heinrich Himmler: the most powerful institution in the Third Reich
völkisch	Racial-nationalist
Volksdeutsche	Ethnic Germans
Volksgemeinschaft	National Folk Community: Nazi slogan for the allegedly classless German society
Wehrmacht	Armed forces (Army, Airforce and Navy)
Wehrmachtsführungsstab	Operation staff of the Armed Forces High Command

Suggestions for Further Reading

This selective list consists entirely of books and articles in English published in the last few years and still easily accessible.

Adam, Uwe Dietrich, 'Persecution, Bureaucracy and Authority in the Totalitarian State', *Yearbook of the Leo Baeck Institute*, 23 (1978), pp. 139–48

Ainsztein, Reuben, *Jewish Resistance in Nazi-occupied Eastern Europe* (London, 1974)

Barany, George, 'Jewish Prisoners of War in the Soviet Union during World War II', *Jahrbücher für die Geschichte Osteuropas N.F.*, vol. 31, 2 (1983), pp. 161–209

Bauer, Yehuda, *The Holocaust in Historical Perspective* (Canberra, 1978)

Bauer, Yehuda, *A History of the Holocaust* (New York, 1982)

Bauer, Yehuda, and Nathan Rotenstreich (eds), *The Holocaust as Historical Experience* (New York/London, 1981)

Braham, Randolph, L., *The Politics of Genocide: The Holocaust in Hungary*, 2 vols (New York, 1981)

Broszat, Martin, 'Hitler and the Genesis of the "Final Solution": an assessment of David Irving's theses', *Yad Vashem Studies*, 13 (1979), pp. 61–98

Browning, Christopher R., *The Final Solution and the German Foreign Office* (New York, 1978)

Dallin, Alexander, *German Rule in Russia 1941–1945. A Study in Occupation Policies*, 2nd edn (London/Basingstoke, 1981)

Dawidowicz, Lucy S., *The War against the Jews 1933–45* (Harmondsworth, repr. 1979)

Dobroszycki, Lucjan (ed.), *The Chronicle of the Lodz Ghetto, 1941–1944* (New Haven/London, 1984)

Feig, Konnilyn G., *Hitler's Death Camps. The Sanity of Madness* (New York/London, 1981)

Fein, Helen, *Accounting for Genocide: National Responses and Jewish Victimization during the Holocaust* (New York/London, 1979)

Fleming, Gerald, *Hitler and the Final Solution* (London, 1985)

Friedlander, Henry, 'The Deportation of the German Jews. Post-War German Trials of Nazi Criminals', *Yearbook of the Leo Baeck Institute*, 29 (1984), pp. 201–28

Friedlander, Henry, and Sybil Milton (eds), *The Holocaust: Ideology, Bureaucracy and Genocide* (Milwood, NY, 1980)

Friedmann, Philip, *Roads to Extinction. Essays on the Holocaust*, ed. by A. J. Friedman (Philadelphia, 1980)

Gilbert, Martin, *Atlas of the Holocaust* (London, 1982)

Gilbert, Martin, *Auschwitz and the Allies* (London, 1981)

Gilbert, Martin, *The Holocaust. The Jewish Tragedy* (London, 1986)

Grobman, Alex, Daniel Landes and Sybil Milton (eds), *Genocide: The Critical Issues of the Holocaust* (New York/Los Angeles, 1983)

Gutman, Yisrael, *The Jews of Warsaw, 1939–1943: Ghetto, Underground, Revolt* (Brighton, 1982)

Hilberg, Raul, *The Destruction of the European Jews* (New York, repr. 1983).

Jäckel, Eberhard, 'Hitler orders the Holocaust', *Hitler in History* (Hanover/London, 1984)

Jong, Louis de, 'Sobibor', *Encounter*, vol. 51, 6 (1978), pp. 20–8

Kershaw, Ian, 'The Persecution of the Jews and German Popular Opinion in the Third Reich', *Yearbook of the Leo Baeck Institute*, 26 (1981), pp. 261–89

Kershaw, Ian, 'Hitler and the Holocaust', *The Nazi Dictatorship. Problems and Perspectives of Interpretation* (London, 1985), pp. 82–105.

Kwiet, Konrad, 'Problems of Jewish Resistance Historiography', *Yearbook of the Leo Baeck Institute*, 24 (1979), pp. 37–57

Kwiet, Konrad, 'The Ultimate Refuge. Suicide in the Jewish Community under the Nazis', *Yearbook of the Leo Baeck Institute*, 29 (1984), pp. 135–67

Laqueur, Walter, *The Terrible Secret: An Investigation into the Suppression of Information about Hitler's 'Final Solution'* (London, 1980)

Marrus, Michael R. and Robert O. Paxton, *Vichy France and the Jews* (New York, 1981)

Marrus, Michael R. and Robert O. Paxton, 'The Nazis and the Jews in Occupied Western Europe 1940–1944', *Journal of Modern History*, 54 (1982), pp. 687–714

Milton, Sybil, 'The Expulsion of Polish Jews from Germany: October 1938 to July 1939. A Documentation', *Yearbook of the Leo Baeck Institute*, 29 (1984), pp. 169–200.

Morley, John F., *Vatican Diplomacy and the Jews during the Holocaust, 1939–1943* (New York, 1980)

The Nazi Concentration Camps. Proceedings of the Fourth Yad Vashem International Historical Conference (Jerusalem, 1984)

Penkower, Monty Noam, *The Jews were Expendable. Free World Diplomacy and the Holocaust* (Chicago, 1983)

Ryan, Michael D. (ed.), *Human Responses to the Holocaust: Perpetrators and Victims, Bystanders and Resisters* (New York/Toronto, 1981)

Schleunes, Karl A., *The Twisted Road to Auschwitz. Nazi Policies toward German Jews 1933–1939* (Chicago, 1970)

Sereny, Gitta, *Into that Darkness. From Mercy Killing to Mass Murder* (London, 1974)

Strauss, Herbert A., 'Jewish Emigration from Germany. Nazi Policies and Jewish Responses', *Yearbook of the Leo Baeck Institute*, 25 (1980), pp. 313–61

The Stroop-Report. The Jewish Quarter of Warsaw is no more, translated from the German and annotated by Sybil Milton (London, 1979)

Trunk, Isaiah, *Judenrat: The Jewish Councils in Eastern Europe under Nazi Occupation* (London, 1977)

Index